P9-CAL-473

The Universally Designed Classroom

The Universally Designed Classroom

Accessible Curriculum and Digital Technologies

Edited by

DAVID H. ROSE, ANNE MEYER, *and* CHUCK HITCHCOCK

Center for Applied Special Technology (CAST)

HARVARD EDUCATION PRESS
Cambridge, Massachusetts

Second Printing, 2006

Copyright © 2005 by the President and Fellows of Harvard College

All rights reserved. No part of this publication may be reproduced or transmitted in any form or by any means, electronic or mechanical, including photocopy, recording, or any information storage and retrieval systems, without permission in writing from the publisher.

Library of Congress Control Number 2005931438

Paperback ISBN 1-891792-63-6
Library Edition ISBN 1-891792-64-4

Published by Harvard Education Press,
an imprint of the Harvard Education Publishing Group

Harvard Education Press
8 Story Street
Cambridge, MA 02138

Cover Design: Anne Carter
Typography: Sheila Walsh

The typefaces used in this book are Sabon for text and Gill Sans for display.

Contents

Acknowledgments

The National Center on Accessing the General Curriculum (NCAC) was established at the Center for Applied Special Technology (CAST) on December 1, 1999. One activity of NCAC was to locate evidence of policies and practices that could be employed to support learners with disabilities who were struggling to make progress within the general education curriculum. Another was to explore the relationship between No Child Left Behind (NCLB) and the Individuals with Disabilities Education Improvement Act (IDEA 2004). This work stimulated the development of a number of reports and papers designed to support educators and help bring research to practice. Further, ten years of groundbreaking work on Universal Design for Learning (UDL) at CAST provided the framework necessary to provide cohesion to various educational principles and practices.

Special recognition is due David Gordon of CAST for encouraging us to collect these documents into a single volume and for many helpful editorial suggestions. Thanks also to research assistant Jennifer Jude for her diligent help in checking facts and references.

Joanne Karger has been wonderful to work with and helped clarify and document the essential intersections of two key statutes impacting schools today: NCLB and IDEA.

Tracey Hall and Nicole Strangman developed a thoughtful and productive approach to exploring and documenting effective classroom practices and curriculum enhancements and then effectively described key relationships with our UDL framework. In that process, they have also provided a valuable trail of citations of the important work of notable education researchers.

Richard Jackson, Kelly Harper, and Jenna Jackson were instrumental in examining the importance of teacher planning and effective practice for supporting learner differences within a variety of educational environments. Their insights into classroom applications of UDL are pragmatic and inspiring.

Special recognition is also owed to CAST's staff members for their contributions to shaping and applying UDL. Their work offers a new vision for improving learning opportunities and outcomes for all learners.

Finally, it is important to recognize the guidance provided by the recognize the guidance provided by Bonnie Jones, the NCAC Project Officer at the Office of Special Education Programs, U.S. Department of Education. Dr. Jones consistently supported our efforts to document our thinking about current research and practice as reflected in the lens of UDL, and as a result our products are unique and ready to be applied. We hope that this book will contribute to the development of new and more effective approaches to serving all learners.

*   *   *   *   *

CAST established NCAC through a cooperative agreement with the U.S. Department of Education's Office of Special Education Programs as part of a national initiative that emerged from the reauthorization in 1997 of the Individuals with Disabilities Education Act.

NCAC drew on the talents of five partners who were already established leaders in their fields to provide leadership in using the UDL framework to increase access to the general education curriculum for all learners. NCAC's research and recommendations covered four major areas: policy and legal issues, curriculum design, teacher preparation and training, and building consensus among varied stakeholders.

Agreement Number H324H990004, December 1, 1999–November 30, 2004
Bonnie D. Jones, Project Officer, U.S. Department of Education
David H. Rose, Principal Investigator, CAST
Chuck Hitchcock, Project Director, CAST

Introduction

DAVID H. ROSE, ANNE MEYER, AND
CHUCK HITCHCOCK

Since the late 1990s, federal laws have sparked dramatic changes in academic expectations for students with disabilities. The 1997 reauthorization of the Individuals with Disabilities Education Act (IDEA) broke new ground by articulating the right of special education students to participate and progress in the general education curriculum and requiring states to evaluate such students within the same accountability systems as their peers. Four years later, the No Child Left Behind Act of 2001 (NCLB) realigned separate general and special education standards, curricula, and accountability, supporting the idea that students with disabilities, given the means, are able to interact with the general education curriculum, benefit from it, and achieve measurably improved performance. The 2004 IDEA reauthorization emphasized the same concept and called for greater efforts to provide universally designed curriculum to support the learning of students with disabilities.

As a result of these laws and a general trend toward more inclusive education policies, students with disabilities are included in standards-based reform systems in ways that few anticipated a decade earlier. For example, by 2003 the average participation by such students in achievement testing had risen to 85 percent, up from just 10 percent in the early 1990s (Quenemoen & Marion, 2003). In addition, the movement in most states toward standards-based educational reform has resulted in an increased emphasis on learning outcomes for students with disabilities (Jorgensen, 1997). While there have been numerous successful efforts to reduce the barriers to access, participation, and progress within the general education curriculum, students with disabilities still experience significant difficulty obtaining accessible and usable educational resources in a timely manner. As a result, students with disabilities are chronically at high risk for school failure and underperformance (Blackorby & Wagner, 2004; Frieden, 2004).

Of course, facilitating genuine access, participation, and progress in the general education curriculum requires much more than physical inclusion in classrooms. Many students remain at risk because classroom learning is still dominated by inaccessible printed textbooks: Students who are blind or visually impaired cannot see the words or images on a page, those with physical disabilities cannot hold a book or turn its pages, those with learning or cognitive disabilities cannot decode the text. For all of these students, the printed book presents a common barrier. As a result, they lack basic access to the content and activities that would support them in reaching high standards. Educators routinely scan and digitize books for students in order to level the playing field. When the cost in time and lost opportunity is totaled, many millions of dollars and valuable instructional time are wasted by the duplication of such efforts across the country.

These concerns became particularly pressing with the passage of IDEA '97. In response, the National Center on Accessing the General Curriculum (NCAC) was created through a collaborative agreement between the Center for Applied Special Technology (CAST) and the U.S. Department of Education Office of Special Education Programs (OSEP). NCAC set out to provide a practical vision of how to shape curricula, teaching practices, and policies to improve access to the general curriculum by students with disabilities. NCAC would accomplish this by synthesizing existing knowledge and research about curriculum access and by conducting national leadership and dissemination activities to raise awareness.

CAST brought to its leadership of NCAC 15 years of experience in improving education for children with disabilities not only through innovative uses of computer technologies but by rethinking fundamental assumptions of special education. As the developer of nationally known learning and accessibility tools such as WiggleWorks (Scholastic), CAST eReader, Bobby (Watchfire), and Thinking Reader (Tom Snyder Productions/Scholastic), CAST had established itself as a key contributor to ongoing efforts to improve life and learning for students with disabilities.

While CAST is often thought of as a technology group, it is in fact an educational research and development organization with a staff composed primarily of lifelong educators, curriculum specialists, and special education experts. Its experiments with technology in education reflect a desire to find the most powerful and practical means of solving pressing issues in K–12 classrooms. Each year, CAST conducts extensive classroom research and provides training for classroom teachers and school administrators, keeping a close tab on the pulse of today's classrooms and the special challenges teachers face.

CAST's unique framework for reshaping education—called Universal Design for Learning, or UDL—offered NCAC a powerful means by which to assess barriers and promising designs in current curricula; best teaching practices and successful educational reform efforts; and existing and promising policies at state and national levels. UDL provides a blueprint for creating flexible goals, methods, materials, and assessments that meet the needs of diverse learners. It draws on the principles of the universal design movement in architecture and product development, which call for designs that from the outset accommodate the greatest variety of individuals, making the need for costly and unattractive after-the-fact retrofitting unnecessary. Speaker phones, curb cuts, and close-captioned television are all examples of universally designed products that are made to accommodate a variety of users, including but not limited to those with disabilities. TV captions, for example, enable those in a busy, noisy restaurant or airport lobby to understand and learn from what is being shown on the screen. The same innovations that provide disabled individuals with everyday access to information or places also enhance the experiences of those who do not have disabilities per se but may have unrecognized situational needs, challenges, or preferences that enable them to benefit from universally designed solutions.

In the same way, UDL leverages technology's power to make education more inclusive and effective. UDL helps educators customize for individual differences by offering 1) multiple means of representation, to give learners various ways of acquiring information and knowledge; 2) multiple means of expression, to offer learners alternatives for demonstrating what they know; and 3) multiple means of engagement, to tap into learners' interests, challenge them appropriately, and motivate them to learn (Rose & Meyer, 2002).

In addition to providing technological know-how and an educational framework, CAST brought to its leadership of NCAC extensive experience in developing and sustaining productive partnerships with leading publishers, research organizations, and universities. This was important because NCAC's mission required collaboration among experts in universal curriculum design, advanced teaching practices, educational policy, and consensus building.

To establish a base of interdisciplinary expertise, CAST enlisted four organizations—all established as national leaders in their fields—as NCAC partners:

- Boston College School of Education, Department of Teacher Education/Special Education, Curriculum, & Instruction, to provide leadership in integrating best practices in regular and special education;
- Harvard University Children's Initiative/Harvard Law School, to provide leadership in policy analysis and development, as well as program evaluation;
- The Council for Exceptional Children, to advise on appropriate governmental policies and professional standards and to contribute to consensus-building with professionals, educational organizations, parents, and individuals with disabilities;
- Parent Advocacy Coalition for Educational Rights, to support dissemination efforts and provide expertise from parent perspectives.

THE DEVELOPMENT OF NIMAS

During NCAC's five-year term (1999–2004), its partners accomplished much in identifying both the need and potential solutions for increasing access to the general education curriculum for all students. NCAC's most significant outcome—and the work that continues today through two new federal centers led by CAST—was the development of the first National Instructional Materials Accessibility Standard, or NIMAS, to guide the creation and distribution of digital accessible instructional materials.

Driving the development of the standard was the realization that the mandates of IDEA and NCLB cannot be implemented successfully by merely adapting existing curriculum and methods. Although curriculum adaptation may be effective in individual instances and can serve as a necessary stopgap, this approach is costly and inefficient and does not contribute to the kind of global, or universal, solution that is needed to help the greatest number of learners. Digital text is not available for the vast majority of students with disabilities, partly because its benefits are not widely known, and partly because acquiring these materials can be a challenge, even among those who realize its potential. In schools throughout the country, highly motivated teachers are making Herculean efforts to adapt individual books by scanning them into an electronic format to accommodate their students. Some schools and districts are even digitizing their entire curriculum. While beneficial for individual students, these local efforts are often costly, redundant, and lacking a research basis (Espin, 2001).

Fortunately, technologies for designing flexible and customizable instructional materials hold great promise for improving access and learning for students with disabilities—a subject discussed in more detail throughout this collection. With a digital version of a textbook, a student who is blind can have text read aloud through text-to-speech technologies or transformed into braille. Students with physical disabilities can turn the pages of the book with a click of a single switch. Those with learning disabilities can hear an unfamiliar word read aloud or link to a definition or related background knowledge. Students who are deaf can view an embedded sign-language video of the text.

Some states and nonprofit organizations are building systemic strategies for providing flexible, alternate-format materials. For example, nonprofits such as Recordings for the Blind & Dyslexic, the American Printing House for the Blind, and the American Foundation for the Blind have been supporting schools over the years by producing alternate-format materials, including audio books and braille. While very important, these solutions are each designed for students with specific disabilities and therefore are not usually sufficiently flexible to reach all students.

There is no systematic research-based approach for creating and disseminating digital curriculum materials in the United States—or anywhere else, for that matter. The barriers to developing such an approach are numerous and include technical, economic, commercial, and legislative factors. The leading cause—the inconsistency of file formats used by publishers and others creating digital material—impedes the creation of flexible digital formats that can be adapted to each individual learner. Educational publishers face challenges in both production and distribution: A conflict between copyright law and federal disability statutes creates problems around permissions and intellectual property protections. And the novelty of the market for digital materials makes it difficult to create a robust business solution to these challenges.

Aware of these issues, NCAC received special funding from OSEP in 2002 to convene the National File Format Technical Panel to develop a single standard for accessible curricular materials. The panel brought together key stakeholders, including disability advocacy groups, publishers, technology experts, and production and distribution experts. The result: version 1.0 of NIMAS (pronounced "NYE-mas").

NIMAS represents a consensus of disability advocates, curriculum publishers, educators, and technology and policy experts that established a unified foundation for the development of accessible materials, improvements in their quality and consistency, and timely distribution to qualified students with special needs. It is a file format that is sufficiently flexible to create multiple output transformations (contracted braille, digital talking book, etc.) from the same source file, eliminating the need for repetitious and ineffective transformations.

In July 2004, the U.S. Department of Education endorsed NIMAS 1.0. Later that year, the U.S. Congress did so too, through its reauthorization of IDEA, which passed with overwhelming bipartisan support. IDEA 2004, which established Universal Design for Learning as a national educational priority, mandated the adoption of NIMAS (or a NIMAS equivalent) by states, local education agencies, and curriculum publishers. However, until NIMAS is actually implemented, educators will continue to struggle to acquire alternate-format materials, and students with print disabilities will continue to receive a lesser educational experience than students without such disabilities.

NIMAS details the baseline technological specifications for the creation of valid digital source files of preK–12 textbooks and related instructional materials. NIMAS is sufficiently flexible to guide the creation of multiple student-ready versions that meet the needs of a variety of users from the same publisher-provided source-file package, eliminating the need for repetitious and inefficient transformations. NIMAS codifies the minimum requirements for a subset of students with disabilities, particularly those with blindness/low vision and other print disabilities. NIMAS will help to ensure that the ubiquitous textbook will be within reach of many students with disabilities at the critical point of instruction in an accessible and usable form.

In order to fully participate in standards-based reform and accountability systems, students with disabilities must have opportunities to learn (Elmore & Fuhrman, 1995; Guiton & Oakes, 1995).

NIMAS will help states and districts provide those opportunities, serving as an essential first step that provides the foundation for the subsequent creation of a variety of alternate-format versions designed to meet the needs of students with varied disabilities.

The environment is ripe for the large-scale implementation of NIMAS. At the present time, 31 states have alternate-format requirements specifically relating to the provision of files for the creation of braille versions of print textbooks (American Foundation for the Blind, n.d.). In addition, a smaller but expanding number of states (Arizona, California, Georgia, New Mexico, and New York) either require publishers to provide accessible versions of textbooks, require publishers to provide digital versions, or give preference to publishers who provide accessible versions.

While there are many barriers to accessibility, the problems caused by multiple formats are particularly frustrating and easily remedied. The adoption of a common, or standard, format is a simplifying step that has been crucial to progress in many other fields—from railroads (adopting a common track gauge) to video technology (adopting a common format for DVD and HDTV). Similarly, progress in accessibility will be greatly aided by defining a common national file format. With that single change, a number of barriers at many points in the educational system can be addressed.

The next challenge is to extend the standard to address the needs of a wider range of students with disabilities and to develop a free-market model for providing evidenced-based, accessible curriculum materials while simultaneously compensating the publishers who create them. In answer to this challenge, CAST and OSEP have entered into two more cooperative agreements to provide national leadership in maintaining and extending NIMAS. With its establishment and leadership of the NIMAS Development and Technical Assistance Centers, CAST will engage a wide variety of stakeholders in a consensus-building process to develop and extend the standard and address production and dissemination issues. As with NCAC, the work of the new centers will be informed by curriculum publishers, disability advocates and researchers, textbook adoption organizations, alternate-format repositories, assistive technology developers, states, educators, and parents. The centers will recommend updates to NIMAS to take advantage of advances in technology, gather knowledge of accessible educational practices that are shown to support student learning, and explore ways to facilitate efficient production and distribution of digital materials.

Without basic access to the textbooks that are a part of the general education curriculum, students with disabilities are put at an immediate disadvantage in relation to the rest of the student population. The provision of accessible materials increases the likelihood that teacher expectations and the quality of instruction and learning activities for these students will be raised. Families will also benefit when students are able to participate more independently in homework activities based on core educational materials.

The benefit of NIMAS will extend to a significant number of students with disabilities. For students with visual impairments, we anticipate timely delivery following a rapid conversion from NIMAS source files to embossed and refreshable braille, along with digital talking books. Students with physical disabilities will benefit from having access to electronic books that can be easily navigated with a switch, and students with learning disabilities will have access to text-to-speech supports and the capacity to organize the content in ways that support individual executive functions. Students who are deaf or hard of hearing will, for the first time, have digital content that can be transformed to exact signed English using a digital avatar. Furthermore, the adoption of NIMAS source files will provide the necessary foundation for the subsequent creation of learning resources that contain both ASL and text versions of the same instructional content. For students with mental retardation, text to speech can support reading, and the material can be marked and chunked to support improved comprehension.

It is our hope that the work NCAC has accomplished—especially the development of NIMAS—will make the widespread adoption of universally designed curriculum achievable. Universal Design for Learning sets high standards for all students, but it also provides flexibility in the means of representing information, expressing ideas, and engaging students. Such a flexible curriculum will not only serve the needs of students with physical, sensory, or learning disabilities, but will also be more effective and efficient for all students, whose learning needs and styles are wonderfully diverse (Rose & Meyer, 2002). If we truly want to "leave no child behind," we need better, fairer, and more effective ways of delivering curriculum and assessing student performance.

THE CONTENTS OF THIS BOOK

The articles in this collection—written during the past four years at NCAC and updated for this volume—are divided into two parts. The first part covers broad conceptual topics and findings, including Universal Design for Learning, an evolving understanding of curriculum and curriculum access, and legislative/policy changes affecting special and general education. In "The Future Is in the Margins: The Role of Technology and Disability in Educational Reform" (chapter 1), Meyer and Rose discuss UDL in greater depth, laying out its pedagogical and neurobiological underpinnings. Brain-imaging technologies have helped to demonstrate that learning styles and needs can be as unique as fingerprints or DNA. The authors describe ways the coming digital curriculum promises to improve our capacity to align content standards and curriculum more precisely to students' individual strengths and needs along a wide spectrum of abilities.

How can we customize instruction so that students of diverse abilities, skills, and interests can learn the same standards-based classroom material and be assessed fairly on what they know? As research at CAST demonstrates, digital technologies make it possible to individualize instruction and engage many kinds of learners. The result of new technologies will be a recentering of the core agenda of schools on learning instead of on content. Students with disabilities, for whom such transformations and multiple representations (e.g., talking books, descriptive video, ASL captioning) will vastly increase access and learning opportunities, will be the first among many beneficiaries of the new media. Incidental beneficiaries will include the teachers of subject matters like math, music, geography, physics, and other subjects that have never easily yielded their magic through linear text. But the ultimate beneficiaries will be learners of all kinds, because everyone experiences, in one way or another, barriers to motivation and comprehension from the prevailing overreliance on text and other fixed media.

In "Equal Access, Participation, and Progress in the General Education Curriculum" (chapter 2), Hitchcock et al. survey the new challenges and accountability requirements posed by recent federal laws (IDEA, NCLB). They demonstrate ways that current practice falls short of the IDEA imperative. The reasons are multiple and complex, but the primary problem is the nature of the curriculum. Therefore, the primary solution will be found in the curriculum as well. To explain why, the authors explore how our changing understanding and implementation of the general education curriculum has affected diverse students' ability to truly access, participate, and progress within it.

Lawyer and educator Joanne Karger explains "What IDEA and NCLB Suggest about Curriculum Access for Students with Disabilities" (chapter 3). In examining the concept of "access to the general curriculum" as presented in recent federal law, Karger clarifies what IDEA and NCLB require of states and school districts, providing a better understanding of the challenges educators and policymakers face in adopting high-quality content standards, performance standards, and curriculum for students with disabilities. The inclusion of students with disabilities in standards-based reform efforts raises issues not only about curriculum but also about statewide or districtwide assessments: What accommodations are appropriate for students with various disabilities? What impact do such accommodations have on how we measure student learning? Finally, what implication does the relatively new emphasis on "highly qualified" teachers have for the involvement of students with disabilities in the general education curriculum?

The second half of the collection turns to addressing specific applications of Universal Design for Learning and digital media to support students in accessing and succeeding in the general education curriculum. These chapters are certainly informative for practitioners, but they will also provide policymakers with a vision of how flexible digital media can help educators customize educational content and its delivery in the most practical ways to more precisely match individual strengths and needs. Without a digital curriculum, the transformations and adaptations classroom materials and activities must undergo to permit participation in the general curriculum are onerous. But digital media and related technologies open up the curriculum to all learners with efficiency and effectiveness.

In "Teacher Planning for Accessibility: The Universal Design of Learning Environments" (chapter 4), researchers from CAST and Boston College's School of Education first consider what it means to plan curriculum and instruction in the UDL framework. What does UDL look like in action? Richard Jackson and Kelly Harper provide a concrete demonstration of how to apply UDL to classroom activities. Using a fifth-grade model unit, they describe ways that educators can develop instructional units, identify resources, and design activities to reach all learners in the classroom. In "Teaching for Accessibility: Effective Practices, Classroom Barriers" (chapter 5), Jackson et al. review the literature on barriers to access and on promising teaching practices that create new opportunities to learn. Topics include the use of digital curricular materials, flexible grouping, peer support, teacher collaboration, and more.

In the final chapter, "UDL Implementation: Examples Using Best Practices and Curriculum Enhancements," Tracey Hall and colleagues offer detailed discussions of curriculum enhancements and classroom practices that can contribute to universally designed learning environments. These include text transformations (such as text-to-speech technology), curriculum modifications, differentiated instruction, graphic organizers, computer simulations/virtual reality, and background knowledge instruction. Alone these enhancements and practices do not constitute Universal Design for Learning—that is, UDL does not simply mean using differentiated instruction, graphic organizers, or enhanced background knowledge. But these strategies and tools can be powerful contributors to a UDL learning environment that seeks to provide multiple means of representation, expression, and engagement in order to serve all kinds of learners.

As powerful digital technologies reshape the work of schools, special education is also undergoing a significant shift in emphasis—away from meeting disability-specific needs and toward providing access to the general education curriculum. At a time when federal law guarantees every student the right to a high-quality education, it is essential to translate scientifically validated instructional interventions and teaching approaches into useful classroom practices. Using new technologies within the inclusive framework of Universal Design for Learning provides a way to do so—and thereby to increase educational opportunities for students of all abilities.

REFERENCES

American Foundation for the Blind. (n.d). *State-by-state chart of braille laws.* Retrieved July 18, 2005, from http://www.afb.org/section.asp?SectionID=44&TopicID=192& DocumentID=360

Blackorby, J., & Wagner, M. (2004). *Overview of findings from wave 1 of the Special Education Elementary Longitudinal Study (SEELS).* Menlo Park, CA: SRI. Retrieved May 1, 2005, from http://www.seels.net/designdocs/seels_wave1_9-23-04.pdf

Elmore, R. F., & Fuhrman, S. H. (1995). Opportunity-to-learn standards and the state role in education. *Teachers College Record, 96,* 433–458.

Espin, C. A. (2001). Curriculum-based measurement in the content areas: Validity of vocabulary-matching as an indicator of performance in social studies. *Learning Disabilities Research and Practices, 16*(3), 142–151.

Frieden, L. (2004). *Improving educational outcomes for students with disabilities.* Washington, DC: National Council on Disability. Retrieved May 1, 2005, from http://www.ncd.gov/newsroom/publications/2004/educationoutcomes.htm#execsummary

Guiton, G., & Oakes, J. (1995). Opportunity to learn and conceptions of educational equality. *Educational Evaluation and Policy Analysis, 17,* 323–336.

Jorgensen, C. M. (1997). Curriculum and its impact on inclusion and achievement of students with disabilities. *Consortium on Inclusive Schooling Practices Issue Brief, 2*(2), 19.

Quenemoen, R., & Marion, S. (2003). *Rethinking basic assumptions of test development: Assessment frameworks for inclusive accountability tests* (Policy Directions No. 17). Minneapolis: University of Minnesota, National Center on Educational Outcomes. Retrieved May 1, 2005, from http://education.umn.edu/NCEO/OnlinePubs/Policy17.htm

Rose, D. H., & Meyer, A. (2002). *Teaching every student in the digital age: Universal Design for Learning.* Alexandria, VA: ASCD.

CHAPTER ONE

The Future Is in the Margins: The Role of Technology and Disability in Educational Reform

ANNE MEYER AND DAVID H. ROSE

New technologies are often heralded with great fanfare and elaborate claims for their transformative power. Educational technologies, notably the personal computer, are a case in point. Scattered examples can be found across education of productive uses of new technologies: the use of the World Wide Web to connect students from around the globe in international learning communities; online learning projects that give rural, homeschooled, or night school students access to courses at distant schools or at odd hours; the use of handhelds for data collection on field trips. Yet some 25 years after the first computers found their way into schools, their anticipated role in expanding opportunities for teachers and students alike remains largely elusive. Despite their promise, these technologies still are used largely to support old goals, methods, and assessments that shut out students with disabilities from the general education curriculum.

In this chapter we examine some reasons for the slow progress toward educational innovation and change that continues to seem just around the corner, even as the power of computers and networks increases exponentially. We posit that students "on the margins," for whom current curricula are patently ineffective, can actually lead the way to true reform because they help us understand weaknesses in our educational system and curricula that impede teaching and learning for all. Through the framework of Universal Design for Learning (UDL), we articulate a new view of the nature of learner diversity and show that designing digital tools and content to respond to that diversity yields a viable blueprint for change.

IMPEDIMENTS TO CHANGE

One reason that computers have not yet fulfilled their transformative promise in education is, paradoxically, their incredible power and versatility. When technologies with radically new capacities are introduced, it takes people a long time to realize how to use those capacities creatively and productively. Indeed, the capacities themselves often change the very enterprise for which they are designed, requiring a shift of viewpoint that can only happen when users have had time to experiment with the new tools.

The early days of film offer a good example. The first moviemakers simply transferred stage productions such as plays and stand-up entertainment onto film by setting the camera in one place in front of a stage. It took nearly 20 years for filmmakers—notably, D. W. Griffith in 1913—to start experimenting with multiple camera angles, zooming, panning, and many other techniques made possible by film and video media (Stephens, 1998). The technology to do these things was in place early, but people needed time to discover the new capacities of movie cameras and to shift their mindset away from the old, more limited methodologies of the stage.

Looking back even farther, Ruth Cowan (1983), in her remarkable work of social history called *More Work for Mother: The Ironies of Household Technology from the Open Hearth to the Microwave,* examines the effects of new technologies in the kitchen. When stoves were invented in the 18th century, they were embraced very slowly. Two things slowed their acceptance. On the one hand there were widespread fears about their deleterious effects on health and family life (similar in fact to early fears about computers in the home or classroom). On the other hand, stoves seemed to provide only a marginal improvement over the open hearth—especially since they were initially used only to cook in the same old way: mixing and heating food in a large pot hung over the fire. However, the great flexibility of stoves eventually became apparent, and they ultimately transformed our culture's concept of what constituted a meal, what was meant by cooking, and even what a kitchen was for. Most important, Cowan writes, the new technologies of the kitchen democratized cuisine, bringing meals that were more nutritious, more differentiated (multiple dishes, multiple courses), and more attractive to a large number of households where such meals previously had been unavailable.

Although it seems that computers have been in the classroom for a long time now, as a technology they are still relatively young. Like most technologies in the early stages of application, classroom computers are mostly being used in traditional ways—new tools to do old things. Word processors, calculators, and learning games have been assimilated into conventional curricula to support and augment traditional instructional activities (Reinking, Labbo, & McKenna, 2000).

These tools provide improvements in efficiency over print-based technologies (pencils and paper), but the ways in which they are predominantly being used do not fundamentally change the nature of the educational enterprise. The core components of the curriculum—its goals, media and materials, teaching methods, and assessments—remain essentially as they always have been; in particular, they still rest on a print-based set of assumptions (Pailliotet, Semali, Rodenberg, Giles, & Macaul, 2000; Smagorinsky, 1995). Computers are widely used to help students become more proficient at comprehending, interpreting and analyzing, and expressing themselves with printed text.

The second reason that computers have been slow to bring about change is, again ironically, the incredible power of the technology of printed text. The advent of printed text revolutionized communication by enabling permanent recording, mass production, portability, and, at least by the 20th century, affordability. Print made possible the very idea of education for everyone and became its cornerstone. Learning to read and write text, to interpret, organize, and apply information encoded in text have been the keys to learning and to citizenship, and have therefore been at the core of the educational system. These assumptions are of such long standing that they are almost invisible, and they are so entrenched that to consider dislodging them seems radical and possibly dangerous. Why should we dislodge the print-centric curriculum, and what would bring this about?

FIRST PRECIPITANT TO CHANGE: THE NEEDS OF STUDENTS "IN THE MARGINS"

The urgency for change stems in part from schools' inability to meet the needs of increasing numbers of students "in the margins," those for whom the mastery of printed text is difficult or impossible. A significant minority of people can be considered "print disabled," because of visual impairments, learning and other cognitive disabilities, sensory or motor disabilities, and many other reasons. The medium of printed text can be partially or totally inaccessible, or simply not the optimal medium for learning and expression. One urgent reason for change derives from the rapidly increasing diversity of learners in our classrooms and the limited capacity of printed media to respond to that diversity.

Printed text is inaccessible for students who cannot see; for those who have difficulty recognizing phonemes, letters, letter to sound correspondences, words, or sentences; or for those who have trouble distinguishing different print formats and their associated reading conventions (Adams, 1990; Anderson, Hiebert, Scott, & Wilkinson, 1985). In addition, because reading is not only an act of recognition but also one of strategy (Anderson et al., 1985; Graves & Levin, 1989; Richek, List, & Lerner, 1989), printed text can also be a challenge for students who have strategic difficulties (Rayner, 1986). Difficulties in setting a reading goal, interpreting structural cues and meaning within text, making connections to background knowledge, and self-monitoring all exemplify strategic weaknesses that can make printed text a barrier. Moreover, learners who cannot readily decode the words must recruit strategic resources for the task, limiting the availability of these resources for the construction of meaning. Printed text can also inhibit those who do not have disabilities per se but could be considered to have print disabilities. For example, English-language learners in the United States often lack the vocabulary or background knowledge they need to succeed in a learning environment dominated by printed text (Proctor, Carlo, August, & Snow, 2005).

Beyond issues of skill and access, emotional and motivational issues can inhibit progress. Students whose failures with printed text have built negative associations with the medium can be discouraged and lack the confidence that further efforts will yield progress. Finding the will to persist with an unforgiving and unsupportive medium can be daunting (Richek & McTague, 1988). And students for whom printed text is just not an optimal medium can also become disaffected in a print-centric classroom. These students may flourish when provided with other presentational and expressive options, such as multimedia or the arts. For example, filmmaker George Lucas, creator of *Star Wars* and *Indiana Jones*, admits he was not very engaged in school, in "memorizing isolated names and facts." But his obvious gifts in the medium of film made him realize that other avenues for success are highly legitimate. These insights motivated him to establish an educational foundation to explore new ways of teaching and learning using multimedia (Lucas, 2002).

All such learners may share the same classroom; all may struggle to learn the same material. Yet the heterogeneity of their learning needs contrasts with the monolithic label of "struggling learner." The students struggling with text may actually have little in common and be inappropriately grouped under any kind of label. The common barrier they face is a curriculum based in printed text. The fundamental quality of printed text that renders it inaccessible and unforgiving is its fixed nature. Printed materials cannot be modified from their original format (unless an enterprising teacher takes out scissors and tape!), nor can printed content be enhanced or modified to make it supportive in diverse ways for diverse learners. Until the advent of computers and digital media, there was really no workable alternative to a print- and text-centric curriculum.

Disenfranchised students in the margins of our educational system provide the needed challenge for curriculum designers, administrators, policymakers, and teachers. They help us to see and understand the opportunities offered by computers and digital media. With the federal mandate of the Individuals with Disabilities Education Act and No Child Left Behind Act to provide access, participation, and progress in the general education curriculum to all students (Hitchcock, Meyer, Rose, & Jackson, 2002; Karger, 2005), schools face intense pressure to succeed with diverse learners, yet many of these learners cannot thrive in a print-based classroom. This pressure drives us to examine the qualities and capacities of new media in light of the needs of diverse learners, and to forge a path to significant change that ultimately helps all learners.

SECOND PRECIPITANT TO CHANGE: THE CAPACITIES OF COMPUTERS AND DIGITAL MEDIA

Of profound significance for education is the unequaled flexibility of digital media. Unlike fixed printed media, digital media (if so designed) are malleable: they can be transformed, marked, linked, networked, and customized for each individual learner. New media (digital text, digital images, digital audio, digital video, digital multimedia, hypertext, and hypermedia) are notable for this malleability. While, like print, they can provide a permanent representation, they do not have print's fixed quality—they are more like raw clay than fired pottery. The malleability of digital media (when the materials are designed well) translates to enormous flexibility for teachers and learners: as we have noted previously, "Teaching is all about responsiveness, adaptability, and multiple strategies and resources, so the computer's flexibility—rather than any one particular feature—is what gives it so much potential as a teaching tool" (Meyer & Rose, 1998, p. 83).

Digital text separates the content from the display, which can then be flexible in several key ways. Content can be displayed in a variety of media (onscreen or printed text, speech, still images, video, animation, simulations, or combinations of these; Heimann, Nelson, Tjus, & Gillberg, 1995; Mayer, 2003). Transformations can occur both within and between these media (e.g., text-to-speech, speech-to-text, text to American Sign Language, text to braille; Elbro, Rasmussen, & Spelling, 1996; Hasselbring & Glaser, 2000; Loeterman, Paul, & Donahue, 2002). Within a medium, the presentation can be altered in a variety of ways to suit the individual—changes can be made to typeface, font size, font color, sound volume, presentation rate, conversational versus formal style, and difficulty of information; images can be turned on or off; main ideas can be highlighted (Edyburn, 2003; Elkind, Cohen, & Murray, 1993; Hay, 1997; Mayer, 2003). The networked nature of digital media adds further flexibility, such as inserting hyperlinks to learning supports such as multimedia explanations, maps, and encyclopedias; e-mail, which provides an opportunity to consult with peers and experts; and even weblogs, a flexible opportunity to publish.

The provision of such customized, multimedia content—or even just digital text as an entry point—can reduce barriers to learning for many students. Beyond reducing barriers, it can improve learning by allowing for multiple representations of meaning that may be used redundantly for clarity, complementarily for enhanced meaning, or even discordantly for multiple meanings (e.g., multiple soundtracks with additional commentary or narration, providing alternate points of view).

Digital media's tremendous flexibility enables teachers to differentiate their approaches in a way that is simply not feasible when restricted to traditional media such as print, speech, and images. With traditional media, teachers would have to create or assemble a huge assortment of materials. With digital media, one piece of a curriculum can be designed with built-in customization features so that it can be adapted to suit many different students (Edyburn, 2003; Erdner, Guy, & Bush, 1998; Hay, 1997; MacArthur & Haynes, 1995). The capacity to use multiple media leads to a more diversified, flexible palette for communication—a palette that takes advantage of the varied strengths and weaknesses of each medium and enables teachers to select the medium best suited to a particular student and learning task.

THE CHANGE: UNIVERSAL DESIGN FOR LEARNING

The needs of diverse learners who have until now been disenfranchised in a print-centric world can drive us to discover, develop, and apply the astonishing power of new media to expand educational opportunities. Learning is supported and facilitated by the interaction between the learner and the curriculum. When that support and facilitation is missing, "learning disabilities" arise. If the curriculum can be flexibly designed, it can meet more learners where they need to be met. It can challenge and support the vast variety of needs, skills, and interests arrayed in a diverse classroom. Using new tools to support traditional, print-based curriculum has taught us some important things. But like the use of other new technologies in the early stages, this approach has not really taken advantage of the true power of digital tools and media, nor has it provoked fundamental and significant change in education. With the early stages of educational technology adoption behind us, we are ready to take full advantage of the power and flexibility that digital tools and content offer, and to envision new ways for teachers to teach and learners to learn.

How can we make sense of these complex changes and move forward responsibly and quickly? At CAST we have been researching and developing a framework to guide this work: Universal Design for Learning. UDL is based on our two decades of research into the nature of learner differences, the capacities of new media, the most effective teaching practices, and assessments that, while based on high standards, are fair and accurate measures of student learning (Meyer & Rose, 1998; Rose & Meyer, 2000, 2002). It provides a research-based framework for applying insights about students in the margins to the design of curriculum. UDL's basic premise is that barriers to learning occur in the interaction with the curriculum—they are not inherent solely in the capacities of the learner. Thus, when education fails, the curriculum, not the learner, should take responsibility for adaptation. With the UDL framework, curriculum designers anticipate and reduce or eliminate barriers by making curricula flexible.

UDL is an educational extension of the universal design movement in architecture. Originally formulated by Ron Mace at North Carolina State University, universal design's objective is to build innately accessible structures by addressing the mobility and communication needs of individuals with disabilities at the design stage, a practice that spread to areas such as civic engineering and commercial product design. Designs that increase accessibility for individuals with disabilities—those who are typically in the margins—tend to yield benefits that make everyone's experience better.

A good example from product development is television captioning. When captioning first became available, it was intended for people with hearing impairments, who had to retrofit their televisions by purchasing expensive decoder boxes to access the captions. Later, decoder chips were built into every television, making captioning standard and available to all viewers. This universal design feature now benefits not only those with hearing impairments, but also exercisers in health clubs, travelers in airports, individuals working on their language skills, and couples who go to sleep at different times. Furthermore, as a built-in feature, access to television captioning costs a few cents rather than several hundred dollars.

The development of UDL was also driven by the needs of individuals in the margins, for whom regular curriculum often does not work, and by an appreciation for the flexibility of new digital tools. Early experiences with flexible technologies revealed that addressing the needs of special populations improved opportunities for everyone. With the help of UDL, next-stage educational technologies will go beyond providing better access to existing methods and materials; they will embody fundamentally different concepts of learning, and thus of teaching (Dalton, Pisha, Coyne, Eagleton, & Deysher, 2001; Pisha & Coyne, 2001; Rose & Meyer, 2002). Applying the increasing power of emerging technologies, including tools used in modern brain research, and guided by the needs and talents of diverse learners, UDL can help us move past the early-stage, old-use applications of new learning technologies and change the outdated, print-centric assumptions underlying educational practice.

What assumptions need to be reevaluated to reap the true benefits of digital technology and really reform education? First and foremost, our understanding of learner differences. A new understanding of these differences emerges from advances in digital technologies that are parallel to those in instruction, specifically, the improvements in current brain research fueled by digital-imaging technologies.

UDL and Learning: A New View of Learner Differences

Computer-driven technologies such as positron emission tomography (PET), functional magnetic resonance imaging (fMRI), and quantitative electroencephalography (Qeeg) are revolutionizing the study of learning as it happens in the brain. These new tools and methodologies allow us to "see" the brain as it learns by performing enormously complicated computations on subtle changes in brain activity, which are then displayed on a computer screen. Insights gleaned from these new techniques do not support traditional views of learners' abilities that are based on global measures such as IQ, or that segregate people into simple categories such as "the learning disabled."

Brain research and more recent theories of intelligence, such as those of Howard Gardner (1983, 1999), are showing that learning ability is far more diversified than was previously described. There are many different elements to learning, each one subject to individual differences. As a consequence, we can expect that students can be intelligent, or less so, in a near endless number of ways. Indeed, teachers today are beginning to discover a far more elaborate spectrum of learning ability in their classrooms.

Through new brain-imaging techniques, we can actually see the activity in three elaborate sets of nerve networks that play a primary role in learning. We refer to them as the recognition, strategic, and affective networks, to reflect their individual specializations. Briefly, the recognition networks are specialized to receive and analyze information (the "what" of learning); the strategic networks are specialized to plan and execute actions (the "how" of learning); and the affective networks are specialized to evaluate and set priorities (the "why" of learning). Collectively, these networks coordinate how we work and learn (Dolan & Hall, 2001; Rose & Meyer, 2000, 2002).

The dominant impression from computed brain images is how modular learning seems to be. To take recognition as an example, there is not one recognition center in the brain but many different areas managing different aspects of recognition. Brain-imaging techniques reveal that we learn about the motion, shape, orientation, and color of an object using different parts of our recognition networks (Tootell et al., 1995; Wallis & Bülthoff, 1999). Similarly, our brains process the word "cat" in different regions when the word is presented in print versus speech, and we use an entirely different brain area to compose the word "cat" for speaking (Kent, 1998; Petersen, Fox, Posner, Mintun, & Raichle, 1988). Brain-imaging studies also reveal that reading is the result of interplay between multiple brain areas managing different types of processing (Nichelli et al., 1995). For example, one area is required to discriminate fonts, another to process grammar, another to interpret meaning, and another to identify a story's moral.

Different aspects of learning are distributed across numerous brain regions, each module highly specialized for learning about specific aspects of the world. Each of the three learning networks has a large number of such distributed modules that work in parallel, simultaneously, to coordinate the complex task of learning. Thus, even the simplest task activates multiple modules in our learning networks. The pattern of activity across different modules depends on the task—a different set of modules is active when one listens to a speech versus a symphony, for example. In a general sense, there is a signature of brain activity that corresponds to the task being performed. The distribution of activity varies not only across tasks but also across individuals (Xiong et al., 2000). The relative size of modules and their placement can differ from person to person, and for a given task each brain exhibits a unique map of activity, distinguishable from others by the precise set of modules involved and/or the extent of their activity (Schlaug, Jancke, Huang, & Steinmetz, 1995).

Another interesting—and significant—insight gleaned from brain imaging is that the map of activity changes as a person learns. Recent research has shown that novices and experts use very different sets of modules to perform the same task. For example, when professional piano players and non-musicians perform the same finger-tapping task, the distribution of activity in their brains is quite different (Hund-Georgiadis & von Cramon, 1999). Both the intensity of brain activation and the set of modules engaged may vary according to the degree of experience with a learning task (e.g., Shaywitz, 2003).

New brain-imaging technologies allow us to actually watch the brain as learners develop expertise and see it shift from using one set of modules to another. The new technologies have also shown that the size of an individual processing module can grow (and others can shrink) with experience, even in adults (Karni et al., 1995; Merzenich & Jenkins, 1995; Petersen, van Mier, Fiez, & Raichle, 1998; Raichle et al., 1994). For example, the brain is able to generalize, expending less effort to process the demands of a task similar to one it has dealt with many times before. Because the brain is highly impressionable and plastic, repetition and practice produce changes not only at the behavioral level in the form of improved performance, but also at the neural level.

This new brain research is yielding an increasingly clear articulation of the concept of learning—revealing not one, two, or three generalized learning capacities, but many different modules and distributed processes for learning within the same brain, all of which may differ from person to person and as a function of experience. Furthermore, it is becoming clear that individual brains differ from each other not in a general ability (like IQ) but in many different kinds of specific abilities. One consequence of this fact is that students that we think of as disabled because of the deficits that we see in one area may in fact have exquisite strengths in other areas. In the same context, myriad differences emerge between learners formerly classified in the category "normal"—differences in ability to recognize patterns, concepts, and information; differences in strategic and processing abilities; and variations in engagement and motivation (Vygotsky, 1962).

The categories we have used for so long belie a far more elaborate spectrum of learning ability than is typically assumed in the classroom. Continuing the pioneering work of Gardner and others, research continues to show that there is not one typical learner with a limited number of variants but a great variety of learners—as many as the interactions among modules in our brains (Gardner, 1983, 1999; Gevins & Smith, 2000; Habib, McIntosh, & Tulving, 2000; Rypma & D'Esposito, 1999).

Against this backdrop, individuals with disabilities fall along a spectrum of difference, and the convention of the regular student disappears as a normative model:

> One of the clearest and most important revelations stemming from brain research is that there are no "regular" students. The notion of broad categories of learners—smart, not smart; disabled, not disabled; regular, not regular—is a gross oversimplification that does not reflect reality. By categorizing students in this way, we miss many subtle and important qualities and focus instead on a single characteristic (Rose & Meyer, 2002, p. 38).

In addition, the more differentiated use of media for instruction reveals that individuals who are defined as learning disabled within print-based learning environments are not the same individuals who are defined as learning disabled within video- or audio-based learning environments. Such revelations splinter the old categorical divisions between disability and ability and create new descriptors that explicitly recognize the *interaction between student and environment* in the definition of strengths and weaknesses.

Given these revelations, educators now take more notice of the strengths of individuals with disabilities—for example, the prodigious feats of visual memory in a child with autism, the strong visual/artistic or visual expressive skills in a student with dyslexia, or the extraordinary capacity to recognize facial expression in an individual with aphasia. Thanks in part to new technologies, we can appreciate more fully every student's uniqueness and the importance of considering each one's strengths and needs.

UDL and Teaching: Designing Curriculum to Reach Diverse Learners

Changing concepts of learning and individual differences compel more flexible and diversified teaching so that all learners can be appropriately challenged, supported, and engaged. UDL turns the knowledge that has been gained from brain research into a guide for differentiating instruction to accommodate many different modes of learning. The UDL framework is structured around the three sets of learning networks. Each of its three guiding principles calls for a kind of flexibility that will support individual differences relating to one of these sets of networks: differences in how students recognize essential cues and patterns, master skillful strategies for action, and engage with learning.

FIGURE I   *Principles of Universal Design for Learning*

Principle 1: To support recognition learning, provide multiple, flexible methods of presentation

Principle 2: To support strategic learning, provide multiple, flexible methods of expression and apprenticeship

Principle 3: To support affective learning, provide multiple, flexible options for engagement

Source: Rose & Meyer, 2002

These principles frame emerging research on guidelines, practices, and tools intended to provide teachers with flexible approaches and students with a flexible range of learning options rather than a monolithic fixed curriculum. UDL helps teachers meet every student's needs and preferences by guiding flexibility in the way teachers present information, offer opportunities for skill building and expression, and engage students (Rose & Meyer, 2002). (Editors' Note: For more detail and specific examples of UDL teaching methods, see chapter 6 in this book.)

In support of diversity in *recognition networks*, a UDL curriculum provides *multiple means of representation*. UDL materials reflect the knowledge that there is little value in a single canonical representation of the information in any particular task or problem. Instead, we should assume that to provide basic access for students with sensory disabilities or other challenges, and multiple routes to meaning for all students (e.g., representing a math concept both in text and graphically), it is necessary and preferable to provide multiple, redundant, and varied representations of concepts and information.

To support diversity in *strategic networks*, a UDL curriculum provides *multiple means of expression*, giving students flexible models of skilled performance to learn from, opportunities to practice skills and strategies in a supported environment, relevant and ongoing feedback, and flexible opportunities for demonstrating skill using a variety of media and styles. While many students may write (or type or dictate) essays, other alternatives may include rich mixes of writing, illustrating, speaking, animating, and video-making. With UDL, the method of evaluation suits the task and the means. Students are required to meet a higher standard of expressive literacy—knowing in what contexts (for which purposes and for which audiences) to use text, images, sound, video, or combinations of media. At the same time, these options enable students for whom one medium may be a barrier to find a more effective and engaging medium for their purpose.

In support of *affective learning*, a UDL curriculum provides *multiple means of engagement*. This recognizes the centrality of motivation in learning and the individual differences that underlie motivation and engagement. Offering a choice of content and tools, providing adjustable levels of challenge and support, offering a variety of rewards or incentives, and offering a choice of learning context are effective strategies to support affective learning. Of course, there is no single solution to the problem of engaging students because of individual differences—there are many different reasons for students' lack of engagement. Students with disabilities, as usual, highlight the issues. The same design that would likely engage a student with attention deficit hyperactivity disorder (a high degree of novelty and surprise, for example) would be absolutely terrifying (and thus disengaging) to a student with Asperger's syndrome or autism, for whom predictability is paramount.

As a fundamental component of the learning environment, instructional media can have a tremendous impact on how a student fares. Because printed text, images, and speech make unique demands on learners, different strengths and needs may surface depending upon the medium that a student encounters (Rose & Meyer, 2002). In a UDL curriculum, teachers consider the instructional media during the evaluation of ability. Rather than retrofit inflexible materials, the flexibility and interactivity inherent in digital media provide the basis for more flexible educational designs that can anticipate students' different experiences of instructional media. A UDL curriculum provides a rich enough set of options to optimize every student's learning.

Universal designs reflect a more articulated understanding of learning and contextualize presentational environments (like books and lectures) in a broader palette of truly instructional environments, where students are consistently supported in learning how to learn—mastering skills and strategies, not merely consuming information. Individualizable challenges and supports are built into every element of the curriculum and every learning experience. Skill-development materials, for example, can be designed to provide built-in models of performance, opportunities for supported practice, immediate feedback, and extended communities of practice (Dalton, Pisha, Coyne, Eagleton, & Deysher, 2001). In that respect, these new environments more closely resemble traditional models of apprentice learning than book learning (Meyer & Rose, 1998). A teacher in a large classroom will be able not only to model a process for a student but to provide the kind of customized attention necessary to maximize a student's progress, delivering personalized feedback, practice, and scaffolds.

All of these methods are facilitated and enriched by the use of digital materials and tools (Meyer & Rose, 1998; Rose & Meyer, 2002). Teachers can expand their options for presenting information, for student expression, and for engaging students by assembling a variety of different software tools, digital content, and Internet resources. Even now, new media and electronic tools are being used to construct curricula with the built-in flexibility to support differences in recognition, affect, and strategy.

UDL and Assessment: Improved Accuracy and Instructional Relevance

Print-based assumptions and practices underlie traditional assessments, making them especially inaccurate for students in the margins. A big problem with traditional assessments is that students' capabilities with the learning task are often confounded with their ability to use the medium of assessment: "Traditional assessments tend to measure things that teachers are not trying to measure (visual acuity, decoding ability, typing or writing ability, motivation), thus confounding the results and leading us to make inaccurate inferences about students' learning" (Rose & Meyer, 2002, p. 143). Because the expressive medium used for an assessment can influence performance independent of students' knowledge of the content or a skill (Russell & Haney, 1997, 2000), evaluation must be sensitive to its true purpose, and to the strengths and weaknesses of the learner that may not be germane to the learning being assessed. For example, the creative expression or knowledge gained by students with motor difficulties will not be accurately evaluated via handwritten assessments. For another, the acquisition of content knowledge in social studies or mathematics will not be measured accurately on a print-based multiple-choice test for a student with decoding difficulties. A more flexible approach is needed not only to improve the accuracy of assessments for students on the margins, but also to enhance the meaningfulness of assessments for all students:

Technology also offers the opportunity to assess skill learning in a deeper and more meaningful way. For example, science students might conduct virtual lab experiments, in which their actual manipulations of data, technologies, and substances would demonstrate their understanding of processes, methods, and outcomes more clearly than any written or verbal responses could (Rose & Meyer, 2002, p. 148).

Universally designed assessments will also gain accuracy from the capacity to evaluate performance under varying conditions—ranging from conditions where the student's performance is constrained by barriers inherent in specific modes of representation, expression, or engagement, to conditions where appropriate adaptations and supports are available to overcome those barriers. In this manner, it will be possible to identify with more specificity the source of difficulty for a student, yielding more effective measures of student performance and the learning process underlying that performance.

Another problem with traditional assessment is that the *outcomes* of learning are measured—the number of science facts recalled, the percentage of words spelled correctly—rather than the *processes* of learning. Such traditional outcome measures are poorly designed and ill-timed to inform instruction. The interactive capacity of new technologies allows us, on the other hand, to embed assessment dynamically within instruction—providing an enhanced basis for curriculum-based measurement and progress monitoring practices that have been linked to improved instructional decisionmaking and student performance (Espin & Foegen, 1996; Fuchs, Butterworth, & Fuchs, 1989; Fuchs, Fuchs, & Hamlett, 1989; Fuchs, Fuchs, & Stecker, 1989). By tracking what supports a student uses, the kinds of strategies that he or she follows, the kinds of strategies that seem to be missing, and the aspects of the task environment that bias the student toward successful or unsuccessful approaches, the teacher gains information about students as learners. Embedded UDL assessment provides timely information that can inform teaching, and do so differentially for each student. It also ensures that students have available the same supports during assessment that they have during learning.

UDL Applied: A Research-Based Learning Environment

An example of a UDL environment with built-in flexibility for instruction, learning, and assessment is that of Thinking Reader, a computer-based, networked program designed to improve reading comprehension (Dalton et al., 2001). Developed by CAST over several years in federally funded research projects, Thinking Reader combines the research-supported techniques of strategy instruction and reciprocal teaching (Palincsar, 1986, 1998; Palincsar & Brown, 1984) with versatile technologies. The Thinking Reader prototype—which has been recently developed and commercially distributed for classroom use by Tom Snyder Productions—consists of digital versions of high-quality children's literature embedded with tools and prompts that can be adjusted to respond to learner differences in decoding, comprehension strategies, vocabulary knowledge, visual acuity, and many other abilities. Features such as text-to-speech capability; age-appropriate, appealing literature; built-in logs for monitoring progress; and flexibility in visual or oral presentation of text all ensure that students are supported in ways that help them be ready to learn.

In such an environment they are ready to learn effective strategies for active reading, and individualized strategy instruction is delivered through prompts embedded within the text and through models and hints offered by animated characters. The prompts ask students to apply one of multiple, research-supported strategies: predict, question, clarify, summarize, visualize, describe your personal reaction, or reflect on your progress. These prompts are leveled so that teachers and students can select the degree of challenge that best supports progress. The results of controlled experiments show that the Thinking Reader was superior to traditional strategy instruction in elevating reading comprehension for middle school struggling readers (Dalton et al., 2001). More recent work focuses on improving results in the same way for students with cognitive disabilities, students who are English-language learners, and students who are deaf or hard of hearing.

CONCLUSION: STUDENTS IN THE MARGINS, TECHNOLOGY, AND EDUCATIONAL REFORM

Innovations in educational technologies are driven by the needs of students in the margins, those for whom present technologies are least effective—for example, students with disabilities or exceptional talents. These more conspicuous needs highlight the curriculum's failings. However, as new technologies help us to appreciate the full extent of learners' diversity and the variety of ways in which they can be unique, it will become apparent that the curriculum itself can be improved to the benefit of all students.

This will require a significant change in mindset about the possibilities of new technologies for education, and ultimately about our educational goals. There is understandable resistance to change, as entrenched approaches to curriculum design, assessment, teaching, and even the structure of schools and classroom practices are firmly rooted in the venerable and powerful traditions of printed text. While the hegemony of this medium has already disappeared in such high-impact fields as advertising, entertainment, and communication in the culture at large, the legacy of print continues in schools. While computers offer tremendous power for learning with text, their capacity reaches well beyond text to facilitate teaching and learning with varied media and to offer nearly infinite customizability. Yet by analogy with film, we are still in the era of the camera sitting on a stage and filming from one angle, basing our assumptions on one set of goals, tools, methods, and assessments that is expected to—but does not—work for all learners.

Students in the margins must be served, and the technology is here now to serve them effectively. UDL—both the framework and the tools for learning—transforms the pressures of diversity into opportunities for all learners because it does not resist diversity, as traditional curriculum centered around printed text does by insisting that all learners "fit the mold." Rather, it recognizes the fact that diversity in learning abilities and styles can be a tremendous asset if we are willing to reconsider the way curricula are designed and the way schooling is practiced from the "margins" perspective.

Of course, such a change will inevitably result in changed goals. The implicit goal of education will change from homogenization (all students pointed toward one outcome and measured by one yardstick) to diversification—identifying and fostering the inherent diversity among all learners, identifying new kinds of learning, new kinds of teaching, and new kinds of success. The ultimate educational goals will no longer be about the mastery of content (content will be available everywhere, anytime, electronically) but about the mastery of learning. At commencement, we will graduate students who are expert learners. They will know their own strengths and weaknesses, know the kinds of media, adaptations, strategies, and external technologies they can use to overcome their weaknesses and extend their strengths, and the kinds of colleagues who are likely to complement their own patterns of learning and performance. They will be prepared for a changing world, not a static one—prepared for the world in which they will actually live. As in any revolution, students in the margins are likely to lead the way, precipitating the shifts in thinking that will open vast opportunities for educational reform. They have much to offer in this enterprise; we all have much to gain.

REFERENCES

Adams, M. (1990). *Beginning to read: Thinking and learning about print* (3rd ed.). Cambridge, MA: MIT Press.

Anderson, R. C., Hiebert, E. H., Scott, J. A., & Wilkinson, I. A. G. (1985). *Becoming a nation of readers: The report of the commission on reading.* Washington, DC: National Institute of Education.

Asher, S. R. (1980). Topic interest and children's reading comprehension. In R. J. Spiro, B. C. Bruce, & W. F. Brewer (Eds.), *Theoretical issues in reading comprehension: Perspectives from cognitive psychology, linguistics, artificial intelligence, and education* (pp. 525–534). Hillsdale, NJ: Lawrence Erlbaum Associates.

Cowan, R. S. (1983). *More work for mother: The ironies of household technology from the open hearth to the microwave.* New York: Basic Books.

Dalton, B., Pisha, B., Coyne, P., Eagleton, M., & Deysher, S. (2001). *Engaging the text: Reciprocal teaching and questioning strategies in a scaffolded learning environment* (Final report to the U.S. Office of Special Education). Peabody, MA: CAST.

Davidson, J., Elcock, J., & Noyes, P. (1996). A preliminary study of the effect of computer-assisted practice on reading attainment. *Journal of Research in Reading, 19,* 102–110.

Dolan, R. P., & Hall, T. E. (2001). Universal Design for Learning: Implications for large-scale assessment. *IDA Perspectives, 27*(4), 22–25.

Edyburn, D. L. (2003). 2002 in review: A synthesis of the special education technology literature. *Journal of Special Education Technology, 18*(3), 5–28.

Elbro, C., Rasmussen, I., & Spelling, B. (1996). Teaching reading to disabled readers with language disorders: A controlled evaluation of synthetic speech feedback. *Scandivian Journal of Psychology, 37,* 140–155.

Elkind, J., Cohen, K., & Murray, C. (1993). Using computer-based readers to improve reading comprehension of students with dyslexia. *Annals of Dyslexia, 43,* 238–259.

Erdner, R. A., Guy, R. F., & Bush, A. (1998). The impact of a year of computer assisted instruction on the development of first grade learning skills. *Journal of Educational Computing Research, 18,* 369–386.

Espin, C., & Deno, S. L. (1993). Performance in reading from content area text as an indicator of achievement. *Remedial and Special Education, 14*(6), 47–59.

Espin, C. A., & Foegen, A. (1996). Validity of general outcome measures for predicting secondary students' performance on content-area tasks. *Exceptional Children, 62,* 497–514.

Estes, T. H., & Vaughan, J. L., Jr. (1973). Reading interest and comprehension: Implications. *Reading Teacher, 27,* 149–153.

Fink, R. P. (1995). Successful dyslexics: A constructivist study of passionate interest in reading. *Journal of Adolescent and Adult Literacy, 39,* 268–280.

Fuchs, L. S., Butterworth, J. R., & Fuchs, D. (1989). Effects of ongoing curriculum-based measurement on student awareness of goals and progress. *Education and Treatment of Children, 12*(1), 63–72.

Fuchs, L. S., Fuchs, D., & Hamlett, C. L. (1989). Monitoring reading growth using student recalls: Effects of two teacher feedback systems. *Journal of Educational Research, 83,* 103–110.

Fuchs, L. S., Fuchs, D., & Stecker, P. M. (1989). Effects of curriculum-based measurement on teachers' instructional planning. *Learning Disabilities Quarterly, 22*(1), 51–59.

Gardner, H. (1983). *Frames of mind: The theory of multiple intelligences.* New York: Basic Books.

Gardner, H. (1999). *The disciplined mind: What all students should understand.* New York: Simon & Schuster.

Gevins, A., & Smith, M. E. (2000). Neurophysiological measures of working memory and individual differences in cognitive ability and cognitive style. *Cerebral Cortex, 10,* 829–839.

Graves, A. W., & Levin, J. R. (1989). Comparison of monitoring and mnemonic text-processing strategies in learning disabled students. *Learning Disabilities Quarterly, 31,* 306–332.

Greenlee-Moore, M. E., & Smith, L. L. (1996). Interactive computer software: The effects on young children's reading achievement. *Reading Psychology, 17,* 43–64.

Habib, R., McIntosh, A. R., & Tulving, E. (2000). Individual differences in the functional neuroanatomy of verbal discrimination learning revealed by positron emission tomography. *Acta Psychologica, 105*(2–3), 141–157.

Hasselbring, T. S., & Glaser, C. H. W. (2000). Use of computer technology to help students with special needs. *Future of Children, 10,* 102–122.

Hay, L. (1997). Tailor-made instructional materials using computer multimedia technology. *Computers in the Schools, 13*(1–2), 61–68.

Heimann, M., Nelson, K. E., Tjus, T., & Gillberg, C. (1995). Increasing reading and communication skills in children with autism through an interactive multimedia computer program. *Journal of Autism & Development Disorders, 25,* 459–481.

Hitchcock, C., Meyer, A., Rose, D., & Jackson, R. (2002). *Access, participation, and progress in the general curriculum* (Technical Brief). Peabody, MA: National Center on Accessing the General Curriculum.

Hund-Georgiadis, M., & von Cramon, D. Y. (1999). Motor-learning-related changes in piano players and non-musicians revealed by functional magnetic-resonance signals. *Experimental Brain Research, 125,* 417–425.

Karger, J. (2005). *Access to the general curriculum for students with disabilities: A discussion of the interrelationship between IDEA and NCLB.* Wakefield, MA: National Center on Accessing the General Curriculum. Retrieved online June 15, 2005, from http:// www.cast.org/publications/ncac/ncac_discussionson2004.html

Karni, A., Meyer, G., Jezzard, P., Adams, M. M., Turner, R., & Ungerleider, L. G. (1995). Functional MRI evidence for adult motor cortex plasticity during motor skill learning. *Nature, 377,* 155–158.

Kent, R. D. (1998). Neuroimaging studies of brain activation for language, with an emphasis on functional magnetic resonance imaging: A review. *Folia Phoniatrica et Logopaedica, 50,* 291–304.

Kulik, C., & Kulik, J. A. (1991). Effectiveness of computer-based instruction: An updated analysis. *Computers in Human Behavior, 7,* 75–94.

Loeterman, M., Paul, P. V., & Donahue, S. (2002). Reading and deaf children. *Reading Online,* Retrieved June 15, 2005, from http://www.readingonline.org/articles/loeterman/

Lucas, G. (2002). Foreword. In S. Armstrong & M. Chen (Eds.), *Edutopia: Success stories for the digital age* (xiii–xvi). San Francisco: Jossey-Bass.

MacArthur, C. A., & Haynes, J. B. (1995). Student assistant for learning from text (salt): A hypermedia reading aid. *Journal of Learning Disabilities, 28*(3), 50–59.

Marston, D., Deno, S. L., Kim, D., Diment, K., & Rogers, D. (1995). Comparison of reading intervention approaches for students with mild disabilities. *Exceptional Children, 62*(1), 20–37.

Mayer, R. E. (2003). The promise of multimedia learning: Using the same instructional design methods across different media. *Learning & Instruction, 13*(2), 125.

Merzenich, M. M., & Jenkins, W. M. (1995). Cortical plasticity, learning, and learning dysfunction. In B. Julesz & I. Kovacs (Eds.), *Maturational windows and adult cortical plasticity* (pp. 247–272). Reading, MA: Addison-Wesley.

Meyer, A., & Rose, D. H. (1998). *Learning to read in the computer age.* Cambridge, MA: Brookline Books.

Nichelli, P., Grafman, J., Pietrini, P., Clark, K., Lee, K. Y., & Miletich, R. (1995). Where the brain appreciates the moral of a story. *NeuroReport, 6,* 2309–2313.

Niemec, R., Samson, G., Weinstein, T., & Walberg, J. (1987). The effects of computer-based instruction in elementary schools: A quantitative synthesis. *Journal of Research on Computing in Education, 20*(2), 85–103.

Pailliotet, A. W., Semali, L., Rodenberg, R. K., Giles, J. K., & Macaul, S. L. (2000). Intermediality: Bridge to critical media literacy. *Reading Teacher, 54,* 208.

Palincsar, A. S. (1986). Metacognitive strategy instruction. *Exceptional Children, 53,* 118–124.

Palincsar, A. S. (1998). Keeping the metaphor of scaffolding fresh: A response to C. Addison Stone's "The metaphor of scaffolding: Its utility for the field of learning disabilities." *Journal of Learning Disabilities, 31,* 370–373.

Palincsar, A. S., & Brown, A. L. (1984). Reciprocal teaching of comprehension-fostering and comprehension-monitoring activities. *Cognition & Instruction, 1,* 117–175.

Petersen, S. E., Fox, P. T., Posner, M. I., Mintun, M., & Raichle, M. E. (1988). Positron emission tomographic studies of the cortical anatomy of single-word processing. *Nature, 331,* 585–589.

Petersen, S. E., van Mier, H., Fiez, J. A., & Raichle, M. E. (1998). The effects of practice on the functional anatomy of task performance. *Proceedings of the National Academy of Sciences, USA, 95,* 853–860.

Pisha, B., & Coyne, P. (2001). Jumping off the page: Content area curriculum for the Internet age. *Reading Online, 5*(4). Available from http://www.readingonline.org/articles/pisha

Proctor, C. P., Carlo, M., August, D., & Snow, C. (2005). Native Spanish-speaking children reading in English: Toward a model of comprehension. *Journal of Educational Psychology, 97,* 246–256.

Raichle, M. E., Fiez, J. A., Videen, T. O., MacLeod, A. M., Pardo, J. V., Fox, P. T., & Peterson, S. (1994). Practice-related changes in human brain functional anatomy during nonmotor learning. *Cerebral Cortex, 4*(1), 8–26.

Rayner, K. (1986). Eye movements and the perceptual span: Evidence for dyslexic typology. In G. T. Pavlidis & D. F. Fisher (Eds.), *Dyslexia: Its neuropsychology and treatment* (pp. 111–130). Chichester, NY: Wiley.

Reinking, D., Labbo, L. D., & McKenna, M. C. (2000). From assimilation to accommodation: A developmental framework for integrating digital technologies into literacy research and instruction. *Journal of Research in Reading, 23,* 110–122.

Renninger, K. A., Hidi, S., & Krapp, A. (Eds.). (1992). *The role of interest in learning and development.* Hillsdale, NJ: Lawrence Erlbaum Associates.

Richek, M. A., List, L. K., & Lerner, J. W. (1989). *Reading problems: Assessment and teaching strategies* (2nd ed.). Englewood Cliffs, NJ: Prentice Hall.

Richek, M. A., & McTague, B. K. (1988). The "Curious George" strategy for students with reading problems. *The Reading Teacher, 43,* 220–226.

Rose, D., & Meyer, A. (2000). Universal design for individual differences. *Educational Leadership, 58*(3), 39–43.

Rose, D. H., & Meyer, A. (2002). *Teaching every student in the digital age: Universal Design for Learning.* Alexandria, VA: Association for Supervision and Curriculum Development.

Russell, M., & Haney, W. (1997). Testing writing on computers: An experiment comparing student performance on tests conducted via computer and via paper-and-pencil. *Education Policy Analysis Archives, 5*(3). Available online at http://epaa.asu.edu/epaa/v5n3.html

Russell, M., & Haney, W. (2000). Bridging the gap between testing and technology in schools. *Education Policy Analysis Archives, 8*(19). Available online at http://epaa.asu.edu/epaa/v8n19.html

Rypma, B., & D'Esposito, M. (1999). The roles of prefrontal brain regions in components of working memory: Effects of memory load and individual differences. *Proceedings of the National Academy of Sciences, USA, 96,* 6558–6563.

Schlaug, G., Jancke, L., Huang, Y., & Steinmetz, H. (1995). In vivo evidence of structural brain asymmetry in musicians. *Science, 267,* 699–701.

Serruya, M. D., Hatsoupolos, N. G., Paninski, L., Fellows, M. R., & Donoghue, J. P. (2002). Instant neural control of a movement signal. *Nature, 416,* 141–142.

Shaywitz, S. E. (2003). *Overcoming dyslexia.* New York: Knopf.

Smagorinsky, P. (1995). Constructing meaning in the disciplines: Reconceptualizing writing across the curriculum as composing across the curriculum. *American Journal of Education, 103*(2), 160–184.

Stephens, M. (1998). *Rise of the image, fall of the word.* New York: Oxford University Press.

Tootell, R. B., Reppas, J. B., Kwong, K. K., Malach, R., Born, R. T., Brady, T. J., Rosen, B. R., & Belliveau, J. W. (1995). Functional analysis of human MT and related visual cortical areas using magnetic resonance imaging. *Journal of Neuroscience, 15*(4), 3215–3230.

Vygotsky, L. S. (1962). *Thought and language.* Cambridge, MA: MIT Press.

Vygotsky, L. S. (1978). *Mind in society: The development of higher psychological processes* (M. Cole, V. John-Steiner, S. Scribner, & E. Souberman, Eds.). Cambridge, MA: Harvard University Press.

Waldman, H. (1995). *The effects of a multimedia literacy tool on first grade reading and writing achievement.* Unpublished doctoral dissertation, University of San Francisco.

Wallis, G., & Bülthoff, H. (1999). Learning to recognize objects. *Trends in Cognitive Sciences, 3*(1), 22–31.

Xiong, J., Rao, S., Jerabek, P., Zamarripa, F., Woldorff, M., & Lancaster, J. (2000). Intersubject variability in cortical activations during a complex language task. *NeuroImage, 12,* 326–339.

An early version of this chapter was prepared under contract to the American Institutes for Research on behalf of the U.S. Department of Education, Office of Educational Technology (Contract 282-98-0029). The opinions presented herein should not be construed to represent the official positions or policies of the U.S. Department of Education, and no endorsement by the department should be inferred. The article has been significantly revised and updated for this volume.

CHAPTER TWO

Equal Access, Participation, and Progress in the General Education Curriculum

CHUCK HITCHCOCK, ANNE MEYER, DAVID H. ROSE, AND RICHARD JACKSON

Federal law stipulates that students with disabilities are entitled to access, participation, and progress within the general education curriculum. This language offers students with disabilities greater potential educational opportunities than ever before. Whether these opportunities are realized will depend on how we interpret each of the key terms—"access," "participation," "progress," and the "general education curriculum"—and whether new tools, methods, and approaches are implemented.

In our view, the conception, design, and implementation of the general education curriculum and the assumptions that underlie it are the most important determinants of whether students with disabilities can access, participate, and progress within it. Consequently, changing the curriculum itself is critical. In so doing, we will create a curriculum that is not just better for students with disabilities, but better for all students.

Because the general education curriculum itself evolves, and because legislation has dramatically advanced opportunities for students with disabilities, the terms "access," "participation," and "progress" have not always meant the same thing. For example, before the landmark 1997 amendments to the Individuals with Disabilities in Education Act (IDEA), "access" referred only to legal access to an education and physical access to buildings and classrooms. As these barriers were removed (though even these persist in some settings), new ones appeared: The building may now have been accessible, but the curriculum itself was virtually unusable for many students. The good news is that educators of students with disabilities face a moving target—an indication that things are changing and that we are progressing toward true access, participation, and progress.

The term "general education curriculum" refers to the overall plan for instruction adopted by a school or school system. Its purpose is to guide instructional activities and provide consistency of expectations, content, methods, and outcomes across differing classrooms in each school or school system. Curricula usually include an assortment of content materials for student use, teachers' guides, assessments, workbooks, and ancillary media. For the purposes of this chapter, and for our work on Universal Design for Learning (UDL), we define four main components of the general education curriculum:

1) *goals and milestones* for instruction (often in the form of a scope and sequence)
2) *media and materials* to be used by students
3) specific instructional *methods* (often described in a teachers' edition)
4) means of *assessment* to measure student progress

The design and implementation of the general education curriculum is increasingly driven by external standards that are adopted from state-wide or national school reform initiatives. Developed by national, state, and local curriculum writing groups and by subject-area experts, standards aim to articulate clearly the knowledge, skills, and understanding all students should gain in a particular subject, with more specific benchmarks of achievement by grade level. Standards articulate what schools value and, therefore, what teachers teach and assess. Under IDEA, students with disabilities are to be educated in the general curriculum and aspire to the same standards and expectations as their peers. This means that all four curriculum components apply to all students.

One of the biggest obstacles to ensuring the widespread application of this principle is that the general curriculum is largely inflexible—primarily, the printed textbook remains at its core. As a medium, print has long dominated in communication and therefore also in education and curriculum design. Once material is committed to paper it cannot be adjusted and changed; the text is one size and available only to those who can handle the physical book, see and decode the text, and understand the concepts necessary to interpret it. Consequently, many students are, for varied reasons, shut out of the general curriculum.

To illustrate in greater depth how the fixed nature of the general curriculum has affected special education, we must first provide some historical context

HISTORICAL CONTEXT

Over the past quarter century, general education classrooms have served a growing number of learners with disabilities. This trend reflects growing awareness on the part of educators and parents that students with disabilities benefit from engaging with their peers in a common, challenging curriculum. As recently as the 1960s, many students with disabilities were not being educated at all, either because they were denied access to school or because they were physically in school but not being educated. For example, the Federal Office of Special Education and Rehabilitative Services (OSERS) notes that "in 1970, U.S. schools educated only one in five children with disabilities, and many states had laws excluding certain students, including children who were deaf, blind, emotionally disturbed, or mentally retarded" (OSERS, 2001).

Sustained federal leadership in support of special education has dramatically improved educational opportunities for students with disabilities. In 1975, the Education for All Handicapped Children Act (PL 94-142) entitled students with disabilities to an individually designed, free, and appropriate public education provided in the least restrictive environment. One key purpose of this law was "to assure that all children with disabilities have available to them . . . a free, appropriate public education which emphasizes special education and related services designed to meet their unique needs" (OSERS, 2001). PL 94-142 opened doors for students who had previously been excluded from public education and for students whose disabilities were not well understood or addressed.

Although the law dramatically improved education for students with disabilities, simple access to an individualized education proved an insufficient foundation for success, especially when the general education community began to seek higher standards and accountability for all students. With the focus on individualized programming, students with disabilities were often excluded from those standards and high expectations, to their detriment.

In 1990, the Education for All Handicapped Children Act was amended and renamed the Individuals with Disabilities in Education Act. In 1997, the law went further, entitling students with disabilities not only access to free and appropriate education, but also to access, participation, and progress within the general education curriculum. Under IDEA and its amendments, schools must educate students with disabilities to meet the same state standards and pass the same state-mandated assessments designed for students without disabilities. Specifically, students with disabilities are to be included in general state- and districtwide assessments, with appropriate accommodations. IDEA supports the idea of appropriate instruction for diverse learners in mainstream settings. Furthermore, IDEA brings parent involvement and participation to the forefront by offering principles for professional/parent collaboration.

IDEA has produced significant improvements in outcomes for students with disabilities. In 2000, then U.S. secretary of education Richard Riley noted, "Twenty-five years ago, IDEA opened the doors to our schoolhouses for students with disabilities. Today, millions of students with disabilities attend our public schools. We have made steady progress toward educating students with disabilities, including them in regular classrooms, graduating them with the proper diploma and sending them off to college" (USDOE, 2000).

Progress, yes. But we have a long way to go. The mandate for access, participation, and progress in the general curriculum is a recent development. It represents a new level of accountability for special education and a new set of challenges. Despite improvements, current practice continues to fall short of the IDEA imperative in districts across the country, with many of our children failing to achieve real participation and progress in the general education curriculum. The reasons are multiple and complex, but we believe that the nature of the curriculum itself is at the heart of the problem, as well as at the heart of the solution. To explain why, we must explore how our changing understanding and implementation of curriculum has affected diverse students' ability to truly access, participate, and progress within it.

THE SPECIAL EDUCATION CURRICULUM

When special education for students with disabilities was first mandated in 1975, the only existing model was the general education curriculum. But this curriculum was not designed to include or accommodate students with disabilities. It provided "one size fits all" goals, methods, materials, and assessments that targeted a hypothetical homogeneous group of students. Before PL 94-142, students who could not use this curriculum had no viable opportunity to receive an education.

The legal mandate for "a free, appropriate public education which emphasizes special education and related services designed to meet their unique needs" was a huge step forward. At last, students with disabilities were entitled to an education designed specifically for them. The law did not specify the curriculum to be used, only that it needed to meet students' individual needs. Because the existing general curriculum could not accommodate diversity effectively, the logical response of educators and curriculum designers was to create a special education curriculum in which the goals, methods, materials, and assessments were highly individualized.

When PL 94-142 was implemented well (and of course, this was not always the case), students with disabilities benefited tremendously from the change. Through the evaluations associated with developing an Individual Education Program (IEP), their learning needs were better described and understood. The curriculum—the goals, methods, materials, and assessments—that they encountered was tailored to them as individuals, and therefore was highly accessible. Specialists trained and motivated to teach students with different disabilities understood their students' learning needs and addressed them individually in appropriate ways. And because these students now had the right to an appropriate education, they and their families could challenge barriers to the general curriculum. They could initiate an IEP process and advocate for a range of individualized services, including preferential seating, individual work with specialists, adapted assignments, and placement in a separate school.

Many students benefited tremendously from these changes. Students with low-incidence disabilities (such as blindness, deafness, and severe cognitive disabilities), who had often been denied even physical access to school buildings, saw greatly increased opportunities. Their parents embraced the increased attention to their individual needs. Students with high-incidence disabilities (such as learning disabilities and attention deficit hyperactivity disorder, or ADHD), who had previously been perceived as lazy and unmotivated, were now better studied, evaluated, and understood. New instructional methods and materials suitable to their learning needs were developed.

Hindsight shows us the risks and problems inherent in the language and approach of PL 94-142, but these were not evident at its inception. Often called the "parallel curriculum," the special education curriculum was neither parallel nor a true curriculum. It was not parallel because the work that students with disabilities undertook often bore no actual relationship to the general curriculum, and it was not a true curriculum because there was no overarching approach to setting goals and developing methods, materials, and assessments. The special education curriculum was a double-edged sword: While it offered students increased access to individually appropriate learning experiences, it also perpetuated a gap between them and their peers that remained difficult to bridge.

Goals in the special education curriculum were set according to a student's IEP, which was based on individual learning needs rather than on an external set of standards and benchmarks. The goals were more likely to be attainable with individualized instruction because they could be targeted according to students' diagnosed levels of performance. Most goals had a remedial focus, such as attainment of basic literacy skills, often with the implicit purpose of improving students' ability to "catch up" and return to the general curriculum. But when goals are nested solely in the context of the individual, they do not address students' ability to progress in relation to their peers or ultimately to function in the real world. Furthermore, separate goals foster separate methods, materials, and assessments, supporting the idea that learners with identified disabilities are inherently different from other learners.

Materials and methods in the special education curriculum saw a great deal of development and innovation. Because the printed texts and lecture format of the traditional classroom did not work for these students, new materials and methods were developed. An example of an individualized tool for blind students is the Cranmer abacus. Blind children have great difficulty setting up arithmetic problems in the standard rows and columns format. The Cranmer abacus, with its felt backing, allows blind students to set and clear beads tactually for purposes of calculation. In addition to such tools, large numbers of interactive programs, both in print and on the computer, were designed to support basic skills and strategies. For example, Educators Publishing Service developed numerous language arts books, such as *Solving Language Difficulties* (Steere, Peck, & Kahn, 1988) and *Wordly Wise* (Hodkinson & Ornato, 1968) that were motivated and informed by the challenges of students with learning disabilities but useful for any student in need of more structure. Other companies developed programs drawing upon the computer's interactive capacity to reinforce basic skills and create simulations to support strategic thinking. Examples include Oregon Trail (MECC), Math Blaster (Davidson), Reader Rabbit (Learning Company), and Millie's Math House (Edmark).

These products were marketed to both the regular education and special education communities. Understanding the particular needs of students with disabilities helped designers to create products that were useful to a variety of learners. Companies such as Educators Publishing developed a significant amount of specialized print material for students with learning challenges and helped us to understand ways to teach differently. Many of these materials were used extensively in special education and in remedial programs.

The proliferation of materials and methods designed to support learning for students with various disabilities was critical both for learners' progress at that time and for future developments. Research, development, and practice informed our understanding of the particular strengths and weaknesses among students with different disabilities and how they learn, as well as what materials and methods work best for them. Further developments, like the design of software programs with built-in options for students at different levels or "half-full" of content so that teachers could enter material appropriate for individual students, supported the special education curriculum.

But the rigidity of the general curriculum engendered a primarily remedial focus for these methods and materials. The understanding that the general curriculum, as embodied then with print-based, inflexible methods and materials, could not or did not need to change prevailed. Thus the barriers inherent in the general curriculum were not identified as such and were not addressed, and students with disabilities were by and large no better suited to using the general curriculum than they had been. Furthermore, the very separateness of disability specialties made it difficult for different disciplines to cooperate and enrich each other.

Assessment in the special education curriculum consisted primarily of formal and informal individual evaluations whose purpose was to assess progress in relation to the individual goals set out in the IEP. Since the results of these assessments applied to individual students only, they were generally not a part of the school system's overall accountability. The downside of this separation was that the success (or failure) of students with disabilities was marginalized even farther from the core of the curriculum: These students really did not "count." This lack of accountability and lack of reference to standards became increasingly untenable and unethical as the nation moved steadily toward increasing attention to standards and accountability.

Access, Participation, and Progress in the Special Education Curriculum

Though the terms "access," "participation," and "progress" were not part of the language of PL 94-142, it is instructive to consider what the special education curriculum offers to students with disabilities in these domains.

Access to the special education curriculum for students with disabilities is generally very good, because it is designed specifically for them. Overcoming the basic physical and legal access barriers to an education was a significant step. In the law's best implementations, students have maximum access to the materials and methods in the special education curriculum. However, in hindsight we see that students with disabilities found little or no access to the goals, materials, methods, and accountability systems of the general curriculum.

Participation in the special education curriculum is supported by its design. Numerous factors are expected to result in increased participation, including isolation from higher-achieving students, increased teacher/student ratios, smaller groups, slower academic pace, reduced demands and frustration, and explicit attention to affect and self-esteem. Most important to special educators is the fact that instruction and activities are targeted to the level diagnosed for the student (Jackson, Harper, & Jackson, 2001). However, participation is limited to the individualized "special" curriculum in whatever form has been devised locally and may not include any participation in the general curriculum.

Progress in the special education curriculum is generally measured against the individual goals defined in the IEP and is officially documented when students are reevaluated. These goals may, but often do not, relate to goals in the general curriculum. Thus, a student could hypothetically be progressing well in the special education curriculum but falling farther and farther behind in the general curriculum. Because of the stipulation that students be placed in the "least restrictive environment" possible, progress is sometimes also measured in terms of increased time spent within general education settings. But time spent in general education classrooms does not necessarily imply participation and progress. Thus, the special education curriculum has a kind of internal accountability—progress is defined in relation to its own goals but not to the overall goals and standards of the general curriculum—increasing the perception of difference and the implementation of separateness for students with disabilities.

Conclusions Regarding the Special Education Curriculum

The special education curriculum arose in response to the mandate of PL 94-142 to provide students with disabilities with a free and appropriate public education in the least restrictive environment. This curriculum was a critical step forward in special education because it resulted in deeper understanding of the particular needs of different students and the important, innovative materials and methods that were developed and tailored to individuals.

The key problem with the special education curriculum is its separateness from the general curriculum, with its attendant implications for students. The notion that separate schooling helps students "catch up" or "be fixed" and then return to the regular setting is flawed. If students are missing essential subject-area content and skills year after year, it is unlikely they will ever truly be able to make up lost ground. Furthermore, the separation of students with disabilities from their classmates reinforces the idea among general educators that they are in some way lacking what it takes to participate in the mainstream. This idea applies most obviously to students with low incidence disabilities, such as sensory and motor disabilities, who were often in separate classes or placements, but it also applies to students with behavior difficulties, learning disabilities, and other learning challenges. In fact, research does not support the claim that a highly individualized education in a separate setting helps students with disabilities catch up to their peers or integrate and function well in regular education settings (Hocutt, 1996).

The great expense of special education programs also created various problems, including a backlash against special education. Private placements were often deemed most responsible for budget overruns, and when schools were forced to cut other programs, many perceived the culprit to be special education. Furthermore, the curriculum designers most involved with developing materials and methods to reach students with disabilities were often not involved with the development of materials and methods of the general curriculum. Two unfortunate consequences resulted from that omission. First, the existing barriers within the general curriculum persisted because the students and teachers who were aware of them were marginalized. Second, the innovations in individualizing education that were commonplace in the "special" curriculum had little salutary effect on the general curriculum, which remained inflexible and largely ineffective for many of its students. The separation of special education perpetuated the misguided assumption that the general curriculum in its inflexible form was a given.

THE GENERAL EDUCATION CURRICULUM

Over time, growing evidence amassed suggested that the special education curriculum was not bringing about the desired outcomes for students with disabilities. The general education curriculum was moving toward high expectations, high standards, and greater accountability for student progress, and students with disabilities were being left farther and farther behind.

The 1997 IDEA reauthorization mandated that students with disabilities participate in the general education curriculum. It entitled students with disabilities to access, participate, and progress in the general curriculum and specifically stated that these students be held to the same standards and methods of assessment as their nondisabled peers. Yet, the general curriculum itself still contained major barriers for many or most of these learners. The mandate for inclusion of students with disabilities in the new accountability set forth a new challenge for educators and curriculum designers: How could goals, materials, methods, and assessments be created that would appropriately serve diverse learners when the curriculum had always assumed learners were homogeneous?

The new accountability was mandated with no initial change to the curriculum itself. Consequently, teachers were challenged to meet the demands of a more diverse student population and satisfy increasingly ambitious state and federal standards, largely without new tools, media, and methods to support them. Participation in the general education curriculum also required that special and regular education teachers work more closely toward the same goals for these students—a major shift, as both groups were accustomed to their independence. Special education teachers' workload increased greatly, because they were often called on as instructional aides in the mainstream classroom while still being responsible for improving the basic skills of students with disabilities so they could function effectively in class (Hewitt, 1999). At the same time, general education teachers felt ill prepared to work with students with disabilities because of both lack of training and lack of time (Hewitt, 1999; Scruggs & Mastropieri, 1996).

The most capable general educators often found more students with disabilities placed in their classrooms, and they felt obliged to sacrifice their lunch periods and other free time to service these students' additional needs (Moody, Vaughn, Hughes, & Fischer, 2000). These efforts were perceived by some as "taking away from other children both academically and socially" (Hewitt, 1999). There is a rampant perception in the general education curriculum that the existent tensions are rooted in the presence of students with disabilities (King-Sears, 1997)—not in the curriculum (Jackson et al., 2001).

Despite all the problems resulting from the shift to the general education curriculum, significant progress essential to future reforms was made. For example, the IDEA amendments state that in some cases assessments should be administered with accommodations (e.g., allowing more time, providing information in list rather than paragraph format) so that students with disabilities can participate. Accommodations popularized the concept that the curriculum might also need to be altered to meet the needs of diverse learners. However, retrofitting inflexible materials is a flawed approach because it suggests that there is a primary curriculum for *most* students, that one size fits most, and that altering that one size is the way to reach outliers.

Goals in the general education curriculum are intended to be aligned with state and local standards for all students. Sometimes, however, learners cannot meet goals because of the wording of those goals. This happens particularly when the goal is confused with the means for attaining it. For example, consider the common goal of writing a story.

Specified in this way, the goal requires output of a written text that some students may not be able to produce. If the goal were instead to create a narrative, written text would not be the only means of attaining it. Similarly, changing the wording from "collect information from a variety of books" to "collect information from a variety of sources" could remove a barrier for some students who might have difficulty using books but who could gather information from the Internet, by interviewing people, or from video sources. Thus, a goal that restricts students to one type of content or one method of expression is not likely to be attainable by the entire class. Most general education curricula tend to lock goals into particular means of achieving them.

Materials in the general education curriculum are within a limited range of options, with a hypothetical "typical" student in mind. For example, students generally learn the concepts and facts of history by listening to the teacher and taking notes and by reading chapters in a textbook. Students who are deaf or have language-processing difficulties and those with motor disabilities or spelling, handwriting, and organizational problems find barriers instead of access when listening to a lecture. Students with dyslexia, students who are blind or have low vision, students who are physically disabled and unable to turn the pages, and students for whom English is not their first language all encounter barriers when working with a textbook.

Of course, curriculum publishers have been modifying and modernizing their materials in response to the availability of new technologies and to the mandates of IDEA. Adjunct materials in media other than print, such as audiotapes, videos, software, and even Internet-based supports, are common today. These materials, however, are rarely created for core use and are generally considered enhancements. They constitute add-ons rather than true alternative ways of presenting essential concepts. Still, the increasing prevalence of such materials paves the way for a more central purpose for nontraditional media.

Alternative versions of materials are sometimes supplied to accommodate learner differences. These include braille or large-type texts and books on tape, as well as simplified versions of content at lower reading and cognitive levels. Though these tools can provide greater access, they are often costly and not always effective. For example, a student who has trouble decoding words may be perfectly capable of appreciating Shakespeare or understanding the subtleties of a complex period in history. But because of her reading difficulties, she might be offered a simplified version of Hamlet or a history text, thus precluding participation at the appropriate cognitive level and risking disengagement from learning.

Another development that expands the materials toolbox of the general education curriculum is the design and refinement of so-called assistive technologies, tools that help bridge the gap between mainstream curricular materials and learners with a variety of disabilities. These tools often modify the interface between the student and the material so that the material becomes more accessible. For instance, a page-turning device enables students with physical disabilities to progress through a printed book; a screen reader reads aloud text on a computer screen; an augmentative communication device enables someone who cannot speak intelligibly or at all to communicate by selecting words and phrases and having them read aloud by a portable device containing a computer; a single-ability switch enables a student who cannot use a keyboard to enter text and execute commands on a computer; and a talking calculator can support a student with low vision or a student with learning disabilities who has difficulty keeping track of numbers visually.

Most assistive technologies are "attached" to students and in some way augment their capacities and help them use materials that would otherwise be inaccessible. Something as simple as eyeglasses is a kind of assistive technology, and these technologies will always be essential and important for special education. However, to rely solely, or even primarily, on assistive technologies keeps the burden of adaptation on the student and presumes that the curriculum can remain inflexible. The general education curriculum, despite progress, is still largely predicated on that assumption.

Methods in the general education curriculum, though still based on a "one size fits most" model, have undergone small but significant changes. Of course, instructional methods are constantly changing as educational theory, research, and practice contribute to the knowledge base. Many teachers' editions now contain suggestions for how to modify a lesson when working with students with disabilities and other learning differences. Some education publishers attempt to address the needs of diverse learners by explicitly offering alternative methods for teaching a particular concept, by including varied media for students to work with, and by suggesting a variety of methods to assess progress for different students.

Many teachers and school systems faced with the need to modify and adapt teaching methods to reach diverse learners find that retrofitting is the only recourse. They allow more time on existing assignments, rewrite materials with simpler vocabulary and syntax, prepare concept maps for clarification and organization, reduce classroom distractions, and provide peer tutoring and buddies to repeat and clarify tasks and assignments. A review of common commercial curricula (O'Connell & Ruzic, 2001) reveals that the suggested accommodations and modifications are haphazard and infrequently available at best, and cannot possibly be counted on to make the curriculum accessible. For the most part, teachers must rely on their own ingenuity, training, diligence, and on the cooperation of special needs teachers for suggestions and help.

Assessment in the general education curriculum presents thorny challenges because assessments are constructed without the needs of students with disabilities in mind. Typically, students are evaluated with single-format tests (such as multiple-choice or question-and-answer printed tests), often administered at the completion of a lesson unit. For students with disabilities, proficiency with the test medium is confounded with the actual skills or knowledge that are supposedly being tested: "Traditional assessments tend to measure things that teachers are not trying to measure (visual acuity, decoding ability, typing or writing ability, motivation), thus confounding the results and leading us to make inaccurate inferences about students' learning" (Rose & Meyer, 2002, p. 143).

Because IDEA requires accommodation where necessary, many educators may soon realize the importance of using assessments that measure real learning. But many of the accommodations currently provided do not actually support students appropriately. Consequently, their progress is still not accurately measured. For example, if a student with a learning disability has "read" his history text using books on tape and then is simply given extra time on a written exam, he is unlikely to be able to truly demonstrate what he knows. Adaptations in testing need to parallel the supports and scaffolds that students use in their daily schoolwork. Currently, general education assessments are still constructed in a rigid way for one type of learner, excluding many with learning differences.

Access, Participation, and Progress in the General Education Curriculum

IDEA specifies that students with disabilities should be able to access, participate, and progress in the general curriculum. The general education curriculum, as currently designed, offers students some improved ability to achieve these goals but contains many barriers, primarily the underlying assumption that there is one set of goals, methods, materials, and assessments that works for "most," and an alternative or adapted set for "special" learners.

Access to the general education curriculum is largely made possible through post hoc adaptations and assistive technologies that help students bridge the gap to a largely inflexible curriculum. Though certainly better than nothing, these approaches rarely provide true access. Adaptations can sometimes significantly change or dilute the concepts and skills of the curriculum, in effect offering access to a different, diminished curriculum. And some assistive devices are cumbersome to use in a school setting. A page turner is a large machine that cannot easily be transported from class to class; an electronic magnifier, such as a closed circuit television reader, makes text literally visible to someone with low vision, but information from the page image cannot be readily skimmed or captured for note-taking.

Participation in the general education curriculum is required by IDEA to emphasize that physical placement in a regular classroom does not guarantee that a student will be learning there. To the extent possible, the aim is to reduce dependence on separate or "special" activities as the vehicle for participation and to find ways to increase the involvement of all students in common, mainstream activities.

Because the general education curriculum has not been designed with the needs or capacities of students with disabilities in mind, participation is often achieved in a limited fashion. Equivalent participation among all students is not usually assumed. In fact, with the fixed goals, methods, materials, and assessments that they have in their toolbox, teachers have no viable way to make across-the-board participation happen. Because they must either find or create adaptations, teachers often have to resort to offering students with disabilities rote or more basic tasks, while other students are involved in higher-order tasks such as goal-setting, problem-solving, self-monitoring, or enrichment activities. Even cooperative learning, which can be a very effective way to call on students' strengths and scaffold their weaknesses, can end up reducing learning opportunities if some students are only nominally contributing or are not in fact being challenged.

Many of these practices can inadvertently replicate the problems inherent in the special education curriculum, where the goals, challenges, and experiences are substantially different, and less interesting or valuable, for students with disabilities. Participation for students with disabilities may be difficult to achieve until the inclusion setting is able to provide not only a shared classroom and curriculum but also equivalent learning opportunities.

Progress in the general education curriculum is defined in the same way and measured by the same yardstick for students with disabilities as for any other student. In theory, the same goals and benchmarks apply to all. In reality, however, goals are often defined differently for students with disabilities, in part because the curriculum itself has been watered down rather than made truly accessible. With lowered expectations, goals that are lower than might actually be possible are accepted as sufficient. Furthermore, in order to demonstrate progress in the general education curriculum, students with disabilities must first demonstrate progress in their ability to overcome the barriers in the curriculum, an extra burden not experienced by students without disabilities.

Because the general education curriculum is not built with diverse learners in mind, teachers have few resources, such as time and training, to support progress (Klingner & Vaughn, 1999). Although assistive technologies and other ancillary materials and methods can be added on to the curriculum to support progress, these efforts are often inadequate. Accommodations and modifications need to be made in the context of a specific goal, or they can actually undermine learning. A book on tape is a useful scaffold when a student's goal is to grasp science concepts, but it impedes learning and eliminates the healthy challenge when it is used during a reading lesson. Even worse, accommodations may become seen as "crutches" that succeed primarily in identifying the student as handicapped.

The rigid nature of assessment as currently practiced is one of the most significant barriers to progress for students with disabilities. Post hoc testing, usually requiring paper and pencil and offering formats like multiple choice, question and answer, or fill in the blank, simply eliminates participation for some, such as students who are blind or physically disabled, and presents extra hurdles for others, such as students with learning disabilities. Such assessments do not accurately reflect the knowledge and skills of students who have difficulty with the format and medium of the test itself.

Conclusions Regarding the General Education Curriculum

The general education curriculum arose out of IDEA's mandate to provide students with disabilities with the same educational opportunities as their peers. Because the general curriculum did not consider the diverse needs of students with disabilities in its original design, adaptations, modifications, and assistive technologies proliferated to support these learners' progress. These techniques and tools are in themselves valuable for special education because they expand student capacities and opportunities. But even more important is the conceptual shift that underlies the work of adapting and modifying the curriculum. For the first time, the idea emerged that the curriculum itself, rather than the students, might be in need of change. In the special education curriculum model, the "one size fits all" general curriculum remained essentially untouched. In the general education curriculum model, the "one size fits most" general curriculum has taken a step forward, becoming part of the formula for a better fit between the learner and the learning experience. However, the general education curriculum model is still hampered by an assumption found in the traditional print-based curriculum—that there is one predominant design for most students that must be retrofitted for "different" learners.

THE UNIVERSALLY DESIGNED CURRICULUM

It has been said many times that if a person from the 1800s were to observe our culture now, the only thing that would look the same would be the schools. In contrast, were a teacher or parent of a student with a disability from 1970 able to view the current status of special education, he or she would be amazed at how far we have come. So much more is known about these students and the approaches, tools, and contexts that help them learn. Policy changes have brought unprecedented opportunities, and innovative ideas and approaches are continually developing. Yet, there are still flaws and shortcomings in the overall approach to special education.

The general curriculum is still largely designed to serve a core group of students exclusive of students with disabilities. Even when publishers explicitly include techniques for diverse learners, those learners are considered outliers and exceptions. These exceptions include not only students with disabilities, but also students with exceptional talents, those whose native language is not English, and many others.

The assumption that there *is* a "core" group of learners that is mostly homogeneous, outside of which other learners fall, is itself flawed. Common sense, and increasingly neuroscience, tells us that learners considered to be within a group are at least as diverse along various dimensions affecting learning as are learners considered to be in different groups (Rose & Meyer, 2002). In fact, we know that myriad subtle differences make each learner unique.

The retrofitted solutions that spring from the assumption of homogeneity consume much time and money, with only modest effectiveness. These drawbacks stem from the mistaken view that students with diverse learning needs are "the problem" (King-Sears, 1997), when in fact barriers in the curriculum itself are, in our view, the root of the difficulty.

The insights gained from the special education curriculum and the general education curriculum have been crucial steps toward a new more flexible curriculum—the universally designed curriculum. The idea of creating a flexible environment that serves diverse users originated with the universal design concept in architecture. Retrofitting buildings with ramps and automatic doors to accommodate people with disabilities is costly, marginally effective, and often aesthetically disastrous. Architects have learned that considering the needs of diverse learners when designing buildings saves money and leads to more streamlined, accessible buildings. And as it turns out, universal design works better for everyone:

> The curb cut is the classically cited example. The curb cut was originally designed to better enable those in wheelchairs to negotiate curbs, but they also ease travel for people pushing strollers or riding skateboards, pedestrians with canes, and even the average walker. Commercial product designers also practice universal design, with similar results. Consider television captioning. When these captions first appeared, individuals who were Deaf had to purchase expensive decoder boxes, retrofitting their televisions so that they could access the cap-

tions. Later, decoder chips were built into every television, making captions available to all viewers. This universal design feature now benefits not only the Deaf but also exercisers in health clubs, diners in noisy restaurants, individuals working on their language skills, and couples who go to sleep at different times. Furthermore, as a built in feature, access to television captioning costs a few cents rather than several hundred dollars. (Rose & Meyer, 2002, p. 71)

In the early 1990s, CAST began to apply the concept of universal design to curriculum materials and methods and coined the term Universal Design for Learning, or UDL. The UDL framework helps us see that inflexible curricular materials and methods are barriers to diverse learners, just as buildings with only stairs at the entrance are barriers to individuals with physical disabilities. If curriculum designers recognize the widely diverse learners in current classrooms and build in options to support learning differences from the beginning, the curriculum as inherently designed can work for all learners. In addition, the need to modify, create alternative versions, and employ assistive technologies is greatly diminished. Universally designed curricula include a range of options for accessing, using, and engaging with learning materials—recognizing that no single option will work for all students (Rose & Meyer, 2002). UDL shifts the burden for reducing obstacles in the curriculum away from special educators and the students themselves and leads to the development of a flexible curriculum that can support all learners more effectively.

How can we create a curriculum whose goals, materials, methods, and assessments serve widely diverse learners? To meet that goal, teachers need to offer many alternative ways to access, use, and engage with learning content. In a print-based environment, where there is one "primary" version and others are all alternatives, offering such variety is impractical. Fortunately, digital media and computer technologies make it possible to offer a curriculum that is created once but can be displayed and used in an almost limitless variety of ways. With the power of digital technologies, it is possible to provide a malleable curriculum in which content and activities can be presented in multiple ways and transformed to suit different learners. Thus, with digital content we can provide multiple representations (e.g., image, text, and video), transform one medium to another (e.g., text to speech or speech to text), or modify the characteristics of a presentation (e.g., size and color of text, loudness of sound; Hitchcock, 2001; Rose & Meyer, 2002).

Building a curriculum with inherent flexibility also helps teachers maintain educational integrity and maximize consistency of instructional goals and methods while still individualizing learning. To see how such a curriculum might work, we will highlight key features of UDL goals, materials, methods, and assessments, as derived from CAST's research and development (Hitchcock, 2001; Rose & Meyer, 2002).

Goals in a UDL curriculum provide an appropriate challenge for all students. UDL goals begin with standards and benchmarks that reflect the knowledge and skills all students will strive for and are carefully conceived and expressed to encourage multiple pathways for achieving them. To develop a UDL goal, teachers must first and foremost thoroughly understand what they want students to learn. This sounds simple and obvious, but it is not a given. The language of the goal frequently incorporates a specific means for achievement when that means is not what the student actually needs to learn. In such cases, goals inadvertently specify one acceptable path and exclude all others. Almost any goal can be made inaccessible by unnecessarily limiting the means for reaching it, and conversely, most goals can be achieved if there is flexibility in the means. Human flight is a good example. The goal of human flight is unreachable if the means are limited (e.g., "students will fly using their arms as wings"), but quite attainable if more alternatives are included ("students will fly").

Similarly, if a goal for composition is stated narrowly ("handwrite a 300-word essay about the challenges faced by Lewis and Clark"), then students with motor disabilities and many with learning disabilities are excluded or severely disadvantaged. The same goal stated more broadly ("generate a 300-word essay . . .") allows students with various disabilities to participate and make progress by using word processors, spell-checkers, voice-recognition software, and other scaffolds and supports. This rewording reflects a clearer focus on the purpose of the essay, which is to gather, synthesize, and express certain historical information, not to demonstrate penmanship!

Once the true purpose for learning is understood, various means, media, scaffolds, and supports can be used to help students reach the goal without undermining the challenge and the learning. For example, if the goal is for students to understand a mathematical or scientific relationship, students could reasonably employ a variety of media and approaches for gathering and keeping track of information and expressing knowledge. Graphics, video, or digital text with reading supports could be among the many appropriate routes to achieving this goal.

Clear goals also reduce problems likely to arise from inappropriate accommodations and adaptations. If the goal were clearly focused on learning to decode words, then many kinds of reading supports or accommodations that would be appropriate in a history lesson would eliminate the challenge and opportunity for learning to decode. Clear goals enable us to know when alternative methods and materials are NOT appropriate for reaching those goals.

Materials in a UDL curriculum are provided in a flexible format supporting transformation between media and multiple representations of content to support all students' learning. The critical content of a curriculum—the facts, concepts, information, principles, and relationships that are to be learned—must be rendered in some medium. What medium is best? No single medium is accessible to all students. The UDL curriculum offers built-in "alternate" or "multiple" representations.

With printed books, the content and its display are inextricably linked; the ink of the text or image is embedded in the page. With digital media, the content can be separated from its display. Thus, the content can be provided once and displayed in a variety of ways. For example, text can be displayed in any size on a screen or in print, as speech, in the context of a concept map, or as braille (either printed or on a refreshable braille device). An image can be presented in print or onscreen in any size and with colors modified to increase visibility, as a text or spoken description, or as a summary of the image's importance and implications for the context in which it is found. Furthermore, this same content can potentially be displayed on various electronic devices such as hand-held computers or even telephones.

This adaptability increases accessibility for students with visual, auditory, reading, or motor impairments because they can elect to view and respond to the content in a medium and means that suit their needs. Students may choose the medium or media most effective for them, as long as the learning goal is not undermined.

Digital content makes possible another important kind of flexibility, the flexibility to embed supports and links. Not only can digital content be displayed in different ways, it can also provide optional "smart supports" to be used by individual students as needed. Thus digital documents can include hyperlinks to glossaries, related background information in multiple media, graphics and animations to summarize or highlight key relationships, queries to support strategic thinking, or sequenced supports for step-wise processes, among many others. Embedded supports can also take the form of tools for expression and organization, such as a note pad with capacity to store text, recorded voice, and images, or of a Q&A tool to ask questions of teachers or peers online.

Digital materials for expression are also far more flexible than their print-based cousins. The power of word processing, with its ease of editing and multiple writing tools such as thesauri, spelling and grammar checkers, and dictionaries, is now widely known and used. Tools to track changes and identify the authors of changes, insert annotations, and merge documents elegantly support collaborative composition. Voice-recognition software enables students who are unable to type or who type with difficulty to compose in text. Multimedia tools offer diverse learners alternatives to composing in straight text, including creating an entire communication using images and sound or recorded voice, or, alternately, beginning with images or sound and moving to text once the key ideas are laid out.

Within a UDL curriculum, these alternatives are all viable means of expression. Flexible materials fulfill the promise of UDL because they open doors and circumvent barriers for students with disabilities and also improve learning opportunities for all students. As long as the learning goal is kept in mind and the challenge remains in place, the curriculum should offer rich scaffolds, supports, and alternative ways of obtaining information and expressing ideas. Through these alternatives, all students benefit.

Methods in a UDL curriculum are flexible and diverse enough to provide appropriate learning experiences, challenges, and supports for all students. Good pedagogy is at the core of a good curriculum. The value of instructional design is in elevating the probability that any one child, and every single child, will learn the critical elements of the curriculum. Rather than offering content unsupported and leaving students' success to happenstance, privilege, or random discovery, we teach what is important and we teach it by adopting the most effective methods so that all children will learn.

In a diverse classroom, no single method can reach all learners. Multiple pathways to achieving goals are needed. In a UDL classroom, teachers support those multiple pathways by presenting concepts in multiple ways, offering students multiple means of expressing their knowledge, and providing a variety of options to support each student's engagement with learning. Teachers practicing UDL assume that each student needs his or her own "size" and provide options, scaffolds, and further opportunities for in-depth learning as a matter of course. In the examples that follow, we illustrate what *could* be real, given technologies that exist today, though of course UDL is not yet fully implemented by publishers or by educators.

Using a UDL approach to presenting concepts, teachers offer multiple examples and highlight the critical features that differentiate that concept from others. In a UDL classroom, teachers also assume that students bring varied amounts of background knowledge to a particular concept and offer optional additional background information for those who may lack prerequisite knowledge. Digital technologies could substantially ease this process. Consider, for example, conveying the critical features of a right triangle. With software that supports graphics and hyperlinks, a teacher could prepare a document that shows the following:

- Multiple examples of right triangles in different orientations and sizes with the right angle and the three points highlighted
- An animation of the right triangle morphing into an isosceles triangle or into a rectangle, with voice and onscreen text to highlight the differences
- Links to reviews on the characteristics of triangles and of right angles
- Links to examples of right triangles in various real-world contexts
- Links to pages that students can go to on their own for review or enrichment of the subject

The document could then be projected onto a large screen in front of the class. Thus, the concept is presented not simply by a teacher explaining it verbally or by a textbook or workbook page, but via many modalities and with options for extra support or enrichment.

When supporting strategic learning, teachers using a UDL approach offer models of skilled performance, plentiful chances for students to practice with appropriate supports and ongoing feedback, and opportunities to demonstrate skills in a meaningful social context. These models and supports need to be provided in a number of ways to meet all students' needs. For example, a U.S. history teacher might ask her students to construct an essay that compares and contrasts the industrial North with the agricultural South in the 1800s. Her emphasis is on the thinking behind the essay—the method of comparing and contrasting—as a means to help students develop a deeper understanding of the period and the geographical locations. She emphasizes that there are many different approaches to constructing the essay and offers examples, such as outlines, diagrams, concept maps, digitally recorded "think alouds," and drawings. She uses tools that support each of these approaches, so that students who need extra structure can choose the supports that work for them, and she creates templates with partially filled-in sections and links to more information. Because this is a long-term assignment, the teacher breaks the research and the writing into pieces and builds in group sharing and feedback to help students revise as they work. The teacher also provides models of the process by sharing the work of previous students who approached the problem in varied ways.

Teachers using a UDL approach recognize that each student will engage with learning for different reasons and in different ways. To support these differences, teachers offer students choices of content and media or tools to work with as long as the learning goal is not compromised. To stay interested and committed to the task at hand, students also need an appropriate balance of challenge and support. Vygotsky (1978) describes the ideal balance point as where the goal is just beyond reach but achievable with effort, what he calls the "zone of proximal development" (ZPD). Of course, the ZPD is different for different students, and teachers can lower the bar without compromising the goal by supporting students in areas of need that are not germane to the challenge at hand. Optional scaffolds might include offering concept maps that highlight main points and support details; showing relationships between events or parts of a complex concept; or walking learners through an inquiry process. Tools that help students organize their work, such as templates (visual or textual), highlighting tools that enable students to code and collect content by categories, and many others, can help overcome organizational or motor difficulties. The learning context can also be adjusted so that collaboration, rather than competition, is emphasized, as in cooperative learning (Johnson & Johnson, 1986, 1989; Slavin et al.,

1984). Offering such varied options supports the motivational and emotional involvement of varied learners in a UDL classroom.

Assessment in a UDL curriculum is sufficiently flexible to provide accurate, ongoing information that helps teachers adjust instruction and maximize learning. Effective teaching requires accurate knowledge of progress. To obtain this knowledge, a teacher must separate the skill required to use specific media, such as printed text, from the skill or knowledge being assessed. A test given in a single medium inevitably tests mastery of that medium, rather than progress in learning (Rose & Meyer, 2002). For students with disabilities who may have difficulty with a particular medium, the test poses insurmountable barriers that have nothing to do with the actual skill or knowledge that is supposedly being evaluated.

Like UDL teaching, UDL assessment requires a clear understanding of the learning goal. With that understanding, teachers can provide scaffolds during an evaluation to help students overcome media-related barriers and show what they really know. Even better, evaluation should be embedded in the materials with which students are working, so that ongoing monitoring and feedback can help them stay on track. Thinking Reader, developed by CAST as part of two OSEP-funded literacy projects, offers an early example of embedded assessment. Thinking Reader is a Web-based "supportive reading environment" that embeds strategy supports into digital versions of children's literature (Dalton, Pisha, Coyne, Eagleton, & Deysher, 2001). Students respond to prompts embedded in the text that support strategic thinking, and their responses are saved in a reading log that can be viewed and discussed by students and teachers. This kind of embedded assessment is integral to the learning task and provides the supports that students need while learning. Thus, the focus of the assessment matches the focus of the instruction, and students do not face media-related barriers. Though much more research is required, this direction is promising, and the technology is here to make it possible. (Editors' note: Thinking Reader has since been commercially developed by Tom Snyder Productions.)

Access, Participation, and Progress in the Universally Designed Curriculum

When implemented, the UDL curriculum will be ideally suited to support true access, participation, and progress in the general curriculum for students with disabilities, and to improve learning opportunities for all students. With the premise that each student can benefit from a flexible curriculum offering clear goals, multiple pathways for reaching those goals, and fair and accurate assessment, the UDL curriculum reflects an understanding that each learner is unique.

Access in a UDL curriculum occurs at many levels. Most basically, because students with disabilities are considered from the outset, many barriers found in the general education curriculum are eliminated or greatly reduced. By building in flexible options for teachers to convey concepts and for students to express their knowledge, the UDL curriculum increases access for everyone. Thus the goals, methods, materials, and assessments in a UDL curriculum are accessible to all.

There is a tendency to equate access in a curriculum with access to information or access to activities. But a curriculum is not information or activities, it is a plan for learning, and therefore the learning has to be accessible. After all, the important thing is not whether a particular activity or piece of material (a textbook, a film, a software simulation) is accessible; the important thing is whether the learning for which the material or activity is designed is accessible. That is its purpose in a curriculum. Thus, access needs to be implemented in the context of learning goals. An example will illustrate. Suppose a student is assigned an Aesop's fable to read. The purpose of this assignment determines the appropriate steps for making it accessible. Is the goal to learn to decode text, to learn comprehension strategies for extended passages, to build vocabulary, to learn the moral or point of the fable, to learn the common elements of any fable, to learn how to compare and contrast fables with news reports, or to articulate the relationship between the fable and the overall culture? The scaffolds and supports that might be appropriate depend entirely on the purpose of the assignment.

If, for example, the purpose of the fable assignment were to become familiar with the elements commonly found in fables, then supporting word decoding, vocabulary, and comprehension of the story itself would not interfere with the learning challenge. Supports such as text-to-speech, linked vocabulary, or animations illustrating interactions between characters would support different students but still leave the appropriate kind of challenge for all learners. But if the goal were to provide practice in decoding and reading fluency, providing those same supports could undermine the learning challenge and actually impede access to learning. The reading support would eliminate the students' opportunity to practice and work toward reading independence. Because the alternatives offered in a UDL curriculum could in theory "give away" the point of a lesson, the alternatives and options must be carefully embedded in learning goals in order to preserve true access to learning.

Participation in a universally designed curriculum means true engagement with learning in pursuit of the goal that is defined for the class as a whole. Clearly articulated goals, communicated to and agreed to by students, are the bedrock of a functional UDL curriculum and a prerequisite for true participation. John Dewey long ago articulated the importance of active participation for real learning to take place:

> There is, I think, no point in the philosophy of progressive education which is sounder than its emphasis upon the importance of the participation of the learner in the formation of the purposes which direct his activities in the learning process, just as there is no defect in traditional education greater than its failure to secure the active co-operation of the pupil in construction of the purposes involved in his studying. (Dewey, 1938, p. 67)

To build learners' awareness and commitment to their learning purposes, teachers in a UDL classroom make goals clear and help students focus on them when working in class or on homework assignments.

More than simple content or skills learning, true participation requires learning how to learn. In a universally designed classroom, the heavy emphasis placed on content learning in the general education curriculum classroom is shifted to the mastery of skills and strategies: "Learning how to plan, execute, and evaluate a range of tasks from forming single letters to writing a research paper, directing a video production, or creating a website . . . is highly critical to all aspects of learning" (Rose & Meyer, 2002). Skill development is embedded in all content learning activities to provide opportunities to "learn how to learn."

With digital tools, supports for active learning can be built into curriculum materials themselves. For example, in the CAST prototype of Thinking Reader, features like text-to-speech, leveled prompts, and hints for various strategies are introduced, and a selection of content, challenge, and support help all learners become more strategic, self-aware, and engaged—critical components for participating in the curriculum.

Progress in a UDL curriculum is centered on curricular goals, not on overcoming curricular barriers. The distracting "proxies" for progress—changes in setting or place, increased participation in activities, reduction of barriers, or success in utilizing accommodations and modifications—are no longer the central focus. Measures of progress for students with disabilities become the same measures as for other students: measures of learning.

This emphasis on the goals for learning is possible because the curriculum is designed to eliminate barriers to access and participation. But eliminating those barriers does not eliminate all effort or challenge in reaching goals, which most significant learning requires. On the contrary, Universal Design for Learning requires that the challenge and resistance essential to real learning be preserved, but properly focused (Rose & Meyer, 2002). The goal of UDL is not to reduce all effort, but to reduce extraneous effort—effort that is unrelated, distracting, disabling—because it is expended in overcoming barriers and poorly designed pedagogies. When goals do not needlessly restrict the pathways to success, all students, even those with disabilities, can make progress with them.

For diverse students to work effectively toward a common goal, the goal must be clearly defined so that teachers can easily identify "allowable" scaffolds—scaffolds that do not interfere with learning, that preserve the challenge. In addition, assessment measures need to have the same scaffolds built into them that students use when working in class. Only then is the evaluation a fair and accurate assessment of what students know and can do in relation to that particular learning goal.

Conclusions Regarding the Universally Designed Curriculum

The universally designed curriculum arose in response to a rethinking of a core educational assumption. The assumption that there are two types of learners—those with disabilities and those without disabilities—no longer seemed valid. Simple classroom observations and neuroscience findings show that every learner is unique, rendering these commonly used categorizations artificial and counterproductive. Retrofitting the general education curriculum, although a step forward from the special education curriculum, perpetuated these categorizations and undersold all students, especially those with disabilities.

Drawing on technological advances, especially digital media, UDL builds flexibility into each of the four main components of the general curriculum. Clearly stated goals, centered on the true learning purpose, are the cornerstone. Stripped of unnecessary restrictions, UDL goals can permit multiple pathways to achievement. To support these multiple pathways, students use materials in multiple formats and media, with optional supports and scaffolds; teachers offer not one teaching method but many different methods; and assessment is offered in multiple forms, making use of varied media and scaffolds.

Because every student can benefit from a more flexible learning environment, UDL is ideally suited to supporting access, participation, and progress for all learners, not just those with disabilities. When goals are clear and properly focused and materials, methods, and assessment diversified, access is ensured not merely to information but, more importantly, to learning. Because goals are not overspecified, they are inclusive of all students, enabling whole-class participation. Moreover, they support the broad skills and strategies fundamental to learning how to learn. Progress for students with disabilities is no longer merely a matter of overcoming curriculum barriers. For them, as for all other students, progress is defined as advancement toward curriculum goals.

The technologies, tools, and methods built up through the years since the beginning of IDEA have made it possible to conceive of and to realize UDL. However, there is no such thing as a completely universally designed curriculum—the field is too new and universal design is a process rather than an outcome. The intent in practicing universal design is to engage in a process that creates better and better curricula. That process will improve over time, but there will always be room for improvement, new techniques, and even newly discovered barriers. Consequently, there will always be a need for assistive technologies and other adaptations. Our goal should be to reduce the need for them in favor of better solutions wherever possible.

One erroneous perception is that a UDL curriculum will immediately reduce the cost of education by bringing special education students into participation in the general curriculum and using one general curriculum for all learners. While costs may be reduced in the long run, once the strategies and the accessible, supportive materials are developed and in place, moving from the current state of affairs to a full implementation of UDL will take time and money. Investments in planning, product development, professional development, teacher collaboration, technology, and other aspects of UDL curriculum will be needed in the short run. The allocation of resources to the needs of a special population will result in educational benefits for all students and more than justify the investment.

THE CHANGING FACE OF CURRICULUM

Since the inception of IDEA in 1975, the challenges facing disability educators have progressed from the most basic concerns of access to buildings and classrooms to concerns of equal participation and progress toward high standards of excellence. This progress has been spurred by IDEA's progressive language and amendments that reflect a clear monitoring of the changing landscape in schools for students with disabilities.

The National Center on Accessing the General Curriculum (NCAC) has supported a new underlying assumption for curriculum design, namely that "each learner needs his or her own size." While this may seem radical, this notion is familiar to clothing manufacturers, designers of car seats, and makers of fitness equipment. Resting on this new assumption, UDL offers design principles, technology tools, and implementation strategies for creating one curriculum that is sufficiently flexible to reach all students. Clear goals, flexible methods and materials, and embedded assessments make it possible for students with disabilities to truly access, participate, and progress in the general curriculum.

Each stage of curriculum development has contributed significantly to the knowledge base and tool set that made UDL's conception and implementation possible. The special education curriculum contributed in-depth knowledge of student characteristics and the widely varied techniques and tools needed to reach all students. The general education curriculum contributed the viewpoint that the curriculum itself needed to be adjusted, and the technologies and tools to make these adjustments. Collectively, these insights and techniques form the substance of the flexibility to be embedded in UDL curriculum.

REFERENCES

Dalton, B., Pisha, B., Coyne, P., Eagleton, M., & Deysher, S. (2001). *Engaging the text: Reciprocal teaching and questioning strategies in a scaffolded learning environment.* (Final report to the U.S. Office of Special Education). Peabody, MA: CAST.

Dewey, J. (1938). *Experience and education.* New York: Macmillan.

Hewitt, M. (1999). Inclusion from a general educator's perspective. *Preventing School Failure, 43,* 125–128.

Hitchcock, C. G. (2001). Balanced instructional support and challenge in universally designed learning environments. *Journal of Special Education Technology, 16*(4), 23–30.

Hocutt, A. M. (1996). Effectiveness of special education: Is placement the critical factor? *Future of Children, 6*(1), 77–102.

Hodkinson, K., & Ornato, J. G. (1968). *Wordly wise.* Cambridge, MA: Educators Publishing Service.

Individuals with Disabilities Education Act (IDEA) Amendments. (1997). Retrieved February 16, 2001, from http://www.ideapractices.org

Jackson, R., Harper, K., & Jackson, J. (2001). *Effective teaching practices and the barriers limiting their use in accessing the curriculum: A review of recent literature.* Retrieved September 5, 2001, from http://www.cast.org/publications/index.html

Johnson, D. W., & Johnson, R. T. (1986). Mainstreaming and cooperative learning strategies. *Exceptional Children, 52,* 553–561.

Johnson, D. W., & Johnson, R. T. (1989). *Cooperation and competition: Theory and research.* Edina, MN: Interaction Book.

King-Sears, M. E. (1997). Best academic practices for inclusive practices. *Focus on Exceptional Children, 29*(7), 1–21.

Klingner, J. K., & Vaughn, S. (1999). Students' perceptions of instruction in inclusive classrooms: Implications for students with learning disabilities. *Exceptional Children, 66,* 23–37.

Moody, S. W., Vaughn, S., Hughes, M. T., & Fischer, M. (2000). Reading instruction in the resource room: Set up for failure. *Exceptional Children, 66,* 305–316.

O'Connell, K., & Ruzic, R. (2001). *Informal survey of textbooks.* Retrieved September 5, 2001, from http://www.cast.org/publications/index.html

Office of Special Education and Rehabilitative Services (OSERS). (2001). *Twenty-five years of progress in educating children with disabilities through IDEA.* Washington, DC: U.S. Department of Education, Office of Special Education Programs. Retrieved June 16, 2005, from http://www.ed.gov/policy/speced/leg/idea/history.html

Rose, D. H., & Meyer, A. (2002). *Teaching every student in the digital age: Universal Design for Learning.* Alexandria, VA: ASCD.

Scruggs, T. E., & Mastropieri, M. A. (1996). Teacher perceptions of mainstreaming/inclusion, 1958–1995: A research synthesis. *Exceptional Children, 63,* 59–74.

Slavin, R. E., Madden, N. A., & Leavey, M. (1984). Effects of team assisted individualization on the mathematics achievement of academically handicapped and non-handicapped students. *Journal of Educational Psychology, 76,* 813–819.

Steere, A., Peck, C., & Kahn, L. (1996). *Solving language difficulties.* Cambridge, MA: Educators Publishing Service.

U.S. Department of Education (USDOE). (2000). U.S. Department of Education News, Press Release, November 29, 2000. Retrieved January 22, 2002, from http://www.ed.gov/PressReleases/11-2000/112900.html

Vygotsky, L. S. (1978). *Mind in society: The development of higher psychological processes* (M. Cole, V. John-Steiner, S. Scribner, & E. Souberman, Eds.). Cambridge, MA: Harvard University Press.

This chapter was originally published as Hitchcock, C., Meyer, A., Rose, D., & Jackson, R. (2002). *Technical brief: Access, participation, and progress in the general curriculum.* Peabody, MA: National Center on Accessing the General Curriculum. It has been edited for this volume. This content was developed pursuant to Cooperative Agreement #H324H990004 under CFDA 84.324H between CAST and the Office of Special Education Programs, U.S. Department of Education. However, the opinions expressed herein do not necessarily reflect the position or policy of the U.S. Department of Education or the Office of Special Education Programs, and no endorsement by that office should be inferred.

CHAPTER THREE

What IDEA and NCLB Suggest about Curriculum Access for Students with Disabilities

JOANNE KARGER

n 1975, Congress passed the Education for All Handicapped Children Act (EAHCA), giving children with disabilities the right to a "free appropriate public education" (FAPE)[1] in the "least restrictive environment" (LRE).[2] Before this time, the educational needs of one million children with disabilities were not being fully met (20 U.S.C. § 1400(c)(2)). A primary purpose of the 1975 law was to ensure that all students with disabilities had access to special education and related services designed to meet their unique needs. The statute was reauthorized several times; in 1990 it was renamed the Individuals with Disabilities Education Act (IDEA).

By the early 1990s, many improvements had been made in the education of children with disabilities. Early intervention and early childhood special education services were introduced in 1986, and requirements for transition planning were initiated in 1990. Moreover, the number of children with significant disabilities living in residential institutions had decreased dramatically (U.S. Department of Education, 1995). In addition, more students with disabilities were graduating from high school and obtaining postschool employment (U.S. Department of Education, 1995; Wagner, Blackorby, Cameto, Hebbeler, & Newman, 1993). In spite of these positive changes, however, students with disabilities still faced many obstacles. For example, research showed that students with disabilities tended to fail classes and drop out of school at higher rates than students without disabilities (U.S. Department of Education, 1995). In addition, efforts to include students with disabilities in the regular education classroom—commonly referred to as "mainstreaming" and later "inclusion"—often focused on special education as a place, without sufficient attention to necessary supports and services (Hocutt, 1996). In 1997, Congress summed up the situation as it considered reauthorizing IDEA: "Despite the progress, the promise of the law has not been fulfilled" (H.R. Rep. No. 105-95 [1997]).

The 1997 reauthorization of IDEA (IDEA '97) attempted to address many of these problems, introducing important changes in the provision of educational services for students with disabilities. One of the most significant changes was the new requirement that students with disabilities have access to the general curriculum—for example, the same curriculum as that provided to students without disabilities (34 C.F.R. § 300.347(a)(1)(i)). Expanding on the earlier concepts of FAPE and LRE, the goal was to raise expectations for the educational performance of students with disabilities and to improve their educational results (U.S. Department of Education, 1995). Four years later, in 2001, Congress passed the No Child Left Behind Act (NCLB), the purpose of which was to promote equal opportunity for all children to receive a high-quality education and attain proficiency, at a minimum, on challenging state achievement standards and state assessments (20 U.S.C. § 6301). NCLB includes several requirements that have implications for the participation of students with disabilities in the general curriculum.

On December 3, 2004, President Bush signed into law the Individuals with Disabilities Education Improvement Act of 2004 (IDEA '04) (Pub. L. No. 108-446, 118 Stat. 2647 [2004] [amending 20 U.S.C. §§ 1400 et seq.]). IDEA '04 maintains the emphasis of IDEA '97 on the promotion of access to the general curriculum, while at the same time introducing a number of changes, including various points of alignment with NCLB. IDEA '04 also alters some of the language used in IDEA '97. For example, throughout IDEA '04, Congress replaced the words "general curriculum" used in IDEA '97 with the phrase "general education curriculum," emphasizing the educational component of the general curriculum. This chapter uses the latter phrase found in IDEA '04, unless directly quoting IDEA '97 or NCLB.

This chapter analyzes the concept of access to the general education curriculum as mandated by IDEA and further impacted by NCLB. Through a discussion of the interrelationship between IDEA and NCLB, it addresses the following questions: 1) What are the legal provisions in IDEA and NCLB associated with access to the general education curriculum for students with disabilities? 2) How do these provisions intersect with one another? and 3) How do these provisions translate into educational obligations for states and school districts? By clarifying the interrelationship between IDEA and NCLB and highlighting the legal and educational obligations incumbent upon states and local school districts, this chapter will lead to a more comprehensive understanding of the meaning of access to the general education curriculum.

INDIVIDUALS WITH DISABILITIES EDUCATION ACT

Access to the General Education Curriculum

Congress first introduced the concept of access to the general education curriculum in IDEA '97, stating, "Over 20 years of research and experience has demonstrated that the education of students with disabilities can be made more effective by having high expectations for such children and *ensuring their access to the general curriculum* to the maximum extent possible" (20 U.S.C. § 1400(c)(5)(A) (1997) [emphasis added]). Similarly, the implementing regulations of the U.S. Department of Education (DOE) for IDEA '97[3] defined special education as "specially designed instruction" whose purpose is "to address the unique needs of the child that result from the child's disability; and *to ensure access of the child to the general curriculum,* so that he or she can meet the educational standards within the jurisdiction of the public agency that apply to all children" (34 C.F.R. § 300.26(b)(3) [emphasis added]).

The nonspecific term "general curriculum" was not defined anywhere in IDEA '97 or its implementing regulations but was later described in the regulations as "the same curriculum as for nondisabled children" (*Id.* § 300.347(a)(1)(i)). The statute and regulations essentially left the details of the general curriculum to be filled in by states and local school districts.

IDEA '04 both preserves and extends the above language of IDEA '97 regarding research and access to the general curriculum, stating, "Almost 30 years of research and experience has demonstrated that the education of students with disabilities can be made more effective by having high expectations for such children and ensuring their *access to the general education curriculum in the regular classroom*, to the maximum extent possible" (20 U.S.C. § 1400(c)(5)(A) (2004) [emphasis added]). As noted in the introduction, IDEA '04 replaced the words "general curriculum" with "general education curriculum." Moreover, by adding the words "in the regular classroom," IDEA '04 calls attention to the important relationship between access to the general education curriculum and placement in the regular classroom, highlighting the strong preference of IDEA for education in the LRE.[4]

Beyond these general introductory statements concerning access to the general education curriculum, in other places in the respective reauthorizations both IDEA '97 and IDEA '04 specifically require that students with disabilities be involved in and progress in the general education curriculum. Thus, the overall right to have access to the general education curriculum can, in fact, be viewed as consisting of three interrelated stages: access, involvement, and progress (Hitchcock et al., 2002).

The first stage, access, refers to the accessibility of the curriculum to the student. Involvement, the second stage, can be thought of as the ongoing process of meaningful participation by the student in the general education curriculum and, as such, is an interim phase that links access to progress. Progress in the general education curriculum, the third stage, refers not only to a final outcome, but also to an evaluative measure that can feed back into the earlier stages of access and involvement. The three stages of access, involvement, and progress can therefore be thought of as forming an ongoing cycle (see Figure 1). These stages are not entirely discrete because in certain instances, a provision can arguably fall under more than one rubric. This framework, however, which is used throughout this chapter, is useful in elucidating the various components of access to the general education curriculum and in analyzing the educational issues involved.

The concept of access to the general education curriculum specified in IDEA '97 and IDEA '04 and described above represents a significant advance in the education of students with disabilities, far exceeding the earlier notion of physical access to the school building and access to special education and related services intended by the EAHCA in 1975. Moreover, by incorporating both involvement and progress, the requirement that students have access to the general education curriculum ex-

FIGURE 1   *Cycle of Ensuring Access to the General Education Curriculum*

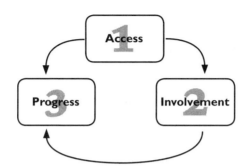

tends well beyond the concepts of mainstreaming and inclusion that developed following 1975 and focused mainly on placement in the regular classroom.

IDEA '04 includes a new provision not found in IDEA '97 that has the potential to bring about improved accessibility of the general education curriculum for students with disabilities—the establishment of a National Instructional Materials Access Center, which will maintain a catalog of print instructional materials prepared in accordance with the National Instructional Materials Accessibility Standard (NIMAS) (20 U.S.C. § 1474(e)(2)). The NIMAS standard, which is "to be used in the preparation of electronic files suitable and used solely for efficient conversion into specialized formats" (*Id.* at § 1474(e)(3)(B)), will help students with print and other disabilities have greater access in a more timely fashion to the print materials that are part of the general education curriculum. IDEA '04 also establishes a process for the preparation, delivery, and purchase of digitized instructional materials for states and school districts that choose to use the voluntary NIMAS standard (*Id.* §§ 1412(a)(23); 1413(a)(6)).

Involvement in the General Education Curriculum

Both IDEA '97 and IDEA '04 contain three requirements pertaining to a student's Individualized Education Program (IEP) that specifically mention involvement in the general education curriculum—the requirements concerning present levels of performance, annual goals, supplementary aids and services, program modifications, and supports for personnel. IDEA '04 maintains the major focus of the provisions found in IDEA '97 while at the same time introducing a number of changes. The provisions appearing in IDEA '04 are as follows:

- The IEP must include a statement of the child's present levels of academic achievement and functional performance, including how the child's disability affects the child's involvement and progress[5] in the general education curriculum.
- The IEP must include a statement of measurable annual goals, including academic and functional goals, designed to meet the child's needs that result from the child's disability in order to enable the child to be involved in and make progress in the general education curriculum.
- The IEP must include a statement of the special education and related services and supplementary aids and services, based on peer-reviewed research to the extent practicable, to be provided to the child, or on behalf of the child, and a statement of the program modifications or supports for school personnel that will be provided for the child to be involved in and make progress in the general education curriculum. (20 U.S.C. §§ 1414(d)(1)(A)(i)(I), (II), (IV))

The above provisions pertain to the IEP, which can be viewed as the central mechanism, both legally and educationally, for ensuring access to the general education curriculum. These three requirements translate into important educational obligations for school districts by laying out specific steps that must be taken by the IEP team in order to enable the student to be involved in the general education curriculum in a meaningful way.

The first provision relates to the child's present levels of performance. Before IDEA '97, the IEP team had to state the student's current level of educational performance. IDEA '97 and IDEA '04, however, add the requirement that the statement describe the specific effect of the student's disability on his or her involvement in and progress in the general education curriculum. Such specification is an important first step in the design of an appropriate educational program for the student. IDEA '04 goes beyond IDEA '97 in requiring not only the level of the student's educational performance but also the level of his or her "functional performance," acknowledging "that for some children, functional performance is also a critical element that should be measured" (Sen. Rep. No. 108-185 (2004)).

The second provision requires the IEP to include annual goals that will enable the child to be involved in and progress in the general education curriculum, as appropriate to the child's needs. IEP goals lay the foundation for a student's educational program and provide a roadmap for the teacher. Before IDEA '97, IEP goals had to be based on the specific needs of the individual student; however, the goals did not necessarily relate to the general education curriculum (U.S. Department of Education, 1995). As with the first provision, IDEA '04 extends the requirement to include "functional goals" in addition to academic goals, again with the intent of recognizing the importance of functional performance for some students with disabilities (Sen. Rep. No. 108-185 (2004)).

IDEA '04 also introduces another change by eliminating the requirement in IDEA '97 for the inclusion of short-term objectives or benchmarks. The report of the Senate Health, Education, Labor, and Pensions (HELP) Committee notes that short-term objectives and benchmarks have contributed to the large paperwork burden associated with IEPs and that elimination of this requirement should facilitate a greater focus on the goals themselves (Sen. Rep. No. 108-185 (2004)). The elimination of short-term objectives and benchmarks, however, does not apply to students who are taking part in alternate assessments aligned with alternate achievement standards (20 U.S.C. § 1414(d)(1)(A)(i)(I)(cc)) (see discussion of alternate achievement standards under "Assessments" under NCLB below).

The third provision specifies that the IEP team must consider the supplementary aids and services, program modifications, and supports for school personnel that will enable the student to be involved in and progress in the general education curriculum. This provision, underscoring the fact that mere physical access to the regular classroom without appropriate support is no longer sufficient under the law, has the potential to lead teachers to consider ways to adapt their instructional practices to enable the student to participate in the general education curriculum. The legislative history leading up to the IDEA '97 explained:

> The new emphasis on participation in the general education curriculum . . . is intended to produce attention to the accommodations and adjustments necessary for disabled children to access the general education curriculum and the special services which may be necessary for appropriate participation in particular areas of the curriculum. (Sen. Rep. No. 105-17 [1997])

IDEA '04 also extends the language of IDEA '97 by specifying that determination of the necessary supplementary aids and services, program modifications, and supports for school personnel should be based on peer-reviewed research, thereby enhancing the quality of supports provided.

Beyond the three requirements pertaining to the IEP cited above that explicitly mention involvement in the general education curriculum, there are two additional requirements in both IDEA '97 and IDEA '04 that, while not specifically mentioning involvement in the general education curriculum, nevertheless have implications for the student's involvement by referring to the "regular class" and the "regular education environment." The provisions in IDEA '04 are as follows:

- The IEP must include an explanation of the extent, if any, to which the child will not participate with nondisabled children in the regular class (20 U.S.C. § 1414(d)(1)(A)(i)(V)).
- The IEP team must include not less than one regular education teacher of such child (if the child is, or may be, participating in the regular education environment); [and] not less than one special education teacher, or where appropriate, not less than one special education provider of such child (*Id.* §§ 1414(d)(1)(B)(ii)-(iii)).[6]

These two requirements also translate into important educational obligations for school districts. According to the first provision, school districts are obligated to provide greater justification for *not* including students with disabilities in the regular class. This provision expands upon IDEA's mandate that students with disabilities be educated in the least restrictive environment to the maximum extent appropriate. The DOE's implementing regulations for IDEA '97 further elaborate that a child cannot be removed from education in age-appropriate regular classrooms solely because of needed modifications in the general curriculum (34 C.F.R. § 300.552(e)). Although these requirements in the statute and regulations do not convey an automatic obligation to place students with disabilities in the regular class, they reinforce IDEA's long-standing preference in favor of such placement.

The second provision concerns the composition of the IEP team. Before 1997, IDEA merely specified that the "child's teacher" had to participate as a member of the IEP team (34 C.F.R. § 300.344(a)(2)(1990)), but did not refer directly to the child's regular education teacher.[7] Both

IDEA '97 and IDEA '04 include the requirement that the child's regular education teacher be a member of the IEP team. The inclusion of the regular education teacher on the IEP team should help regular education teachers to begin to view students with disabilities as part of their responsibility and to think about ways of involving them in the general education curriculum. In addition, this provision has the potential to lead special education and regular education teachers to work together. Because the regular education teacher is the individual who is most familiar with the general education curriculum and who oversees instruction in the regular class, the input of this teacher, in conjunction with special education personnel, can help ensure that the student participates in the general education curriculum in a meaningful way.

Finally, IDEA '04 also includes another requirement that has implications for the student's involvement in the general education curriculum—namely, that special education teachers be highly qualified (20 U.S.C. § 1412(a)(14)(C)). This requirement aligns IDEA with the "highly qualified" requirements in NCLB (see "Teacher Qualifications" under NCLB, below). Specifically, IDEA '04 requires that in order for a special education teacher to be highly qualified he or she must 1) have obtained full state certification as a special education teacher or have passed a state special education teacher licensing examination and hold a license to teach as a special education teacher in the state; 2) have not had special education teacher certification or licensure waived; and 3) hold at least a bachelor's degree (*Id.* § 1401(10)(B)). Moreover, special education teachers must demonstrate subject-matter competence in accordance with the requirements for new and veteran elementary, middle, and high school teachers under NCLB (*Id.* §§ 1412(a)(14)(C)-(D)). IDEA '04 further specifies that nothing in the law can be construed as creating a private right of action for parents to bring a claim for failure of a staff person to be highly qualified (*Id.* § 1412(a)(14)(E)).

Progress in the General Education Curriculum

As described earlier, access to the general education curriculum consists of three interrelated phases forming a cycle, the third of which is progress. Three aspects of progress in the general education curriculum[8] can be delineated: 1) progress toward IEP goals, 2) participation in state and districtwide assessments, and 3) establishment of state-level performance goals and indicators.

The following provisions in IDEA '04 pertain to the first aspect of progress in the general education curriculum, progress toward IEP goals:

- The IEP must include a description of how the child's progress toward meeting the annual goals will be measured and when periodic reports on the child's progress toward meeting the annual goals (such as through quarterly or other periodic reports, concurrent with the issuance of report cards) will be provided (20 U.S.C. § 1414(d)(1)(A)(i)(III)).
- The IEP must be reviewed periodically, but not less frequently than annually, and revised as appropriate to address any lack of expected progress toward the annual goals and in the general education curriculum, where appropriate (*Id.* §§ 1414(d)(4)(A)(i), (ii)(I)).

As with the majority of the requirements pertaining to involvement in the general education curriculum, these two requirements also focus on the IEP, and each translates into specific educational obligations for school districts. The first does not explicitly mention the general education curriculum; however, because IEP goals must address the child's involvement and progress in the general education curriculum (as appropriate to the needs of the child), the measurement of progress toward the attainment of these goals and the reporting of this progress to parents will also be connected to the general education curriculum. The Senate HELP Committee stated that although IDEA '04 eliminated the requirement for short-term objectives and benchmarks, the reauthorization also heightened the reporting requirements regarding progress toward IEP goals.[9] According to the committee, "These progress updates must provide parents with specific, meaningful, and understandable information on the progress children are making" (Sen. Rep. No. 108-185 [2004]).

The following provisions in IDEA '04 pertain to the second aspect of progress in the general education curriculum, the participation of students with disabilities in state and districtwide assessments:

- All children with disabilities must be included in all general state and districtwide assessment programs, including assessments described under NCLB, with appropriate accommodations and alternate assessments where necessary and as indicated in their respective IEPs (20 U.S.C. § 1412(a)(16)(A)).

- The IEP must include a statement of any individual appropriate accommodations that are necessary to measure the academic achievement and functional performance of the child on state and district-wide assessments; if the IEP team determines that the child will take an alternate assessment, the IEP must state why the child cannot participate in the regular assessment and why the particular alternate assessment selected is appropriate (*Id.* § 1414(d)(1)(A)(i)(VI)).
- States and districts must report, and make available to the public, information concerning the number of children with disabilities participating in regular assessments, in regular assessments with accommodations, and in alternate assessments, as well as the performance of children with disabilities on regular assessments and alternate assessments compared with the achievement of all children, including children with disabilities, on those assessments [10] (*Id.* § 1412(a)(16)(D)).

The requirements pertaining to the participation of students with disabilities in state and districtwide assessments were introduced in IDEA '97 in order to increase accountability for the performance of students with disabilities and thereby improve their educational results. As part of the IDEA reauthorization process completed in 1997, the Department of Education (1995) stated,

> When schools are required to assess students with disabilities and report on the results, schools are more likely to focus on improving results for students with disabilities, and students are more likely to have *meaningful access to the general curriculum.* (p. 12, emphasis added).

IDEA '04 not only maintains the emphasis of IDEA '97 on assessments and accountability, but also aligns IDEA with NCLB by stating that the IDEA mandate for the inclusion of students with disabilities in state and districtwide assessments includes assessments described under NCLB. In addition, while IDEA '97 included the phrase "individual modifications in the administration of State or districtwide assessments" (20 U.S.C. § 1414(d)(1)(A)(v)(1997)), IDEA '04 changed the corresponding wording to read "individual appropriate accommodations" (20 U.S.C. § 1414 (d)(1)(A)(i)(VI)(2004)). In the field of special education, an accommodation is generally thought of as an alteration that does not change the content of the curriculum or lower standards. In contrast, a modification is generally considered a change that creates a substantial alteration in the content of the curriculum or lowers standards (e.g., teaching less content or different content; Nolet & McLaughlin, 2000).

The participation of students with disabilities in state and district-wide assessments raises complex educational and psychometric issues with which states and districts must grapple in administering appropriate testing accommodations and alternate assessments. Testing accommodations that are appropriate can be thought of as a "corrective lens" through which "to correct for distortions in a student's true competence caused by a disability unrelated to the construct being measured" (National Research Council [NRC], 1997, pp. 173, 176). There is the risk, however, that the accommodations may over- or undercompensate for such distortions and thereby interfere with the validity of the inferences being drawn from the assessment scores. Although decisions about the use of appropriate accommodations with respect to physical disabilities may be somewhat straightforward, according to the National Research Council (1997), "Most students with disabilities have cognitive impairments that presumably are related to at least some of the constructs tested" (p. 170). Unfortunately, there is little research examining the effects of specific accommodations on the validity of inferences made from the assessment scores of students with different types of disabilities (NRC, 1997, 1999; Sireci, Li, & Scarpati, 2003). IDEA '04 further indicates that states and local school districts should, to the extent feasible, use "universal design principles" in the development and administration of state and districtwide assessments (20 U.S.C. § 1412(a)(16)(E)). According to the National Center on Educational Outcomes, "'Universally designed assessments' are designed and developed from the beginning to allow participation of the widest possible range of students, and to result in valid inferences about performance for all students who participate in the assessment" (Thompson, Johnstone, & Thurlow, 2002).

An alternate assessment is a different measure of the educational progress of students who cannot take part in the regular assessment, even with the help of accommodations. An alternate assessment, for example, may be a portfolio of the student's work. As with the use of accommodations, educational and psychometric issues arise with respect to the use of alternate assessments (see, e.g., Quenemoen, Rigney, & Thurlow, 2002). IDEA '04 includes a new provision specifying that alternate assessments must be aligned with the state's content and achievement standards; if the state has adopted alternate academic achievement standards as permitted under the implementing regulations for NCLB, the alternate assessments must measure the achievement of children with disabilities against those standards (20 U.S.C. § 1412(a)(16)(C)(ii)) (see the discussion of alternate achievement standards under "Assessements" under NCLB, below).

Finally, the following provisions in IDEA '04 pertain to the third aspect of progress in the general education curriculum, the establishment of performance goals and indicators by states. Specifically, states must

- Establish performance goals for children with disabilities that are the same as the state's definition of adequate yearly progress, including the state's objectives for progress by children with disabilities, as specified under NCLB, and address graduation rates and dropout rates, as well as other factors that are consistent, to the extent appropriate, with any other goals and standards for children established by the state;
- Establish performance indicators to assess progress toward achieving the performance goals, including measurable annual objectives for progress by children with disabilities under NCLB; and
- Provide annual reports on the progress of the state, and of children with disabilities in the state, toward meeting the performance goals (20 U.S.C. §§1412(a)(15)(A)-(C)).

These three requirements pertain to states' obligations. As noted with respect to the participation in assessment provisions, these requirements concerning performance goals and indicators are intended to increase accountability for the educational performance of students with disabilities. The first provision, requiring performance goals for students with disabilities to be consistent to the maximum extent appropriate with goals and standards for all children, also underscores the intent of both IDEA '97 and IDEA '04 to raise the level of expectations for the educational performance of students with disabilities. Moreover, it can be seen that IDEA '04 connects the first two provisions to NCLB (see "Accountability" under NCLB, below).

According to the Senate HELP Committee, "Since NCLB already established a system to measure the educational results for all children, including children with disabilities . . . any goals for the performance of children with disabilities should be the same as the State definition of adequately yearly progress, which include the State's objectives for progress by children with disabilities as provided for under NCLB" (Sen. Rep. No. 108-185 [2004]). IDEA '04 also changed the requirement for reporting on progress toward performance goals from every two years (in IDEA '97) to every year.

In summary, IDEA '97 and IDEA '04 lay out specific obligations incumbent on states and districts to ensure that students with disabilities have access to, are involved in, and make progress in the general education curriculum. For many of these obligations, the IEP serves as the central mechanism, both legally and educationally, for ensuring access to the general education curriculum. The next section will discuss the impact of certain provisions in the No Child Left Behind Act of 2001 on the provision of access to the general education curriculum for students with disabilities.

NO CHILD LEFT BEHIND ACT

Four years after the 1997 reauthorization of IDEA, Congress passed the No Child Left Behind Act, the purpose of which was "to ensure that all children have a fair, equal, and significant opportunity to obtain a high-quality education and reach, at a minimum, proficiency on challenging State academic achievement standards and State academic assessments" (20 U.S.C. § 6301). Although NCLB applies to all students, including students with disabilities, and IDEA applies only to students with disabilities, both statutes share the goal of raising expectations for the educational performance of students with disabilities and increasing accountability for their educational results. In several places in the law, NCLB makes explicit reference to IDEA.[11] Moreover, as noted earlier, IDEA '04 aligns a number of requirements in IDEA with those in NCLB.

At the same time, however, the two statutes differ in that IDEA explicitly allows parents to bring individual claims and seek a remedy. A recent federal court case in New York has held that NCLB does not convey to parents or students "individually enforceable rights" (Assoc. of Comm. Organizations for Reform NOW v. New York City Dept. of Educ., 269 F. Supp. 2d 338, 347 (S.D.N.Y. 2003)).

This section will examine various requirements in NCLB that have implications for providing access to the general education curriculum for students with disabilities. NCLB, which was enacted prior to IDEA

'04, uses the earlier phrase found in IDEA '97, "general curriculum," rather than "general education curriculum" as used in IDEA '04. The relevant provisions of NCLB will be discussed under the three rubrics of access, involvement, and progress.[12] In these discussions, "general education curriculum" will be used, except in direct quotes from NCLB.

Access to Challenging Content and Achievement Standards

IDEA, as noted, requires that students with disabilities have access to the general education curriculum—in other words, the same curriculum as that provided to students without disabilities—but does not elaborate further on the meaning of the term "general education curriculum," leaving the details to be filled in by states and school districts. NCLB focuses attention on the general education curriculum by requiring that states develop "challenging" academic standards for both content and student achievement for all children in at least mathematics and reading/language arts and, by the beginning of the 2005–06 school year, science (20 U.S.C. §§ 6311(b)(1)(A)-(C)).[13] The obligation to develop challenging content standards should help states define the general education curriculum. Moreover, the requirement for states to adopt challenging achievement standards has the potential to raise the level of the general education curriculum. The development of standards is thus a point of intersection for the two statutes: IDEA requires that students with disabilities have access to the general education curriculum, according to their individualized needs, while NCLB helps to define and raise the level of the general education curriculum.

It is significant that the applicability of a state's challenging academic standards to all students under NCLB is inclusive of students with disabilities. In the Appendix to the statute's implementing regulations, the DOE states,

> Too often in the past, schools and LEAs have not expected students with disabilities to meet the same grade-level standards as other students. The NCLB Act sought to correct this problem by requiring each State to develop grade-level academic content and achievement standards that it expects all students—including students with disabilities—to meet. (67 Fed. Reg. 71710, 71741)

Thus, IDEA and NCLB converge with respect to expectations for the educational performance of students with disabilities: IDEA requires that students with disabilities have access to the same curriculum (according to their individualized needs) as students without disabilities so that they can meet the educational standards that apply to all children; NCLB establishes the expectation that students with disabilities can meet the same standards as students without disabilities.

Access to a High-Quality Curriculum

In addition to the mandate for states to develop challenging content and achievement standards, NCLB also refers, in a number of places, to the use of a high-quality curriculum, further emphasizing the high level expected of a state's general education curriculum. For example, NCLB discusses the shared responsibility of schools and parents to develop a school-parent compact that describes "the school's responsibility to provide *high-quality curriculum* and instruction . . . that enables the children served under this part to meet the State's student academic achievement standards" (20 U.S.C. § 6318(d)(1) [emphasis added]; see also *Id.* §§ 6311(b)(8)(D), 6312(c)(1)(O)). Thus, NCLB raises the level of the general education curriculum by requiring that a state develop "challenging" content and achievement standards and establish a curriculum that is of a "high quality."

Involvement in the General Education Curriculum

IDEA, as noted, requires that students with disabilities be involved in the general education curriculum. Several provisions in NCLB have implications for such involvement—namely 1) teacher qualifications, 2) professional development, and 3) special programs and services.

Teacher Qualifications

In order to raise the level of the general education curriculum, in addition to a state developing challenging standards and a high-quality curriculum, NCLB also mandates requirements concerning teacher qualifications: Beginning in the 2002–03 school year, all newly hired teachers had to be "highly qualified," and no later than the end of the 2005–06 school year all teachers who teach the "core academic subjects"[14] must be highly qualified (20 U.S.C. § 6319(a)). A teacher who is highly qualified is one who 1) has obtained full state certification or has passed a state teacher licensing examination and holds a license to teach in the state; 2) holds at least a bachelor's degree; and 3) has demonstrated competence in the subjects in which he or she teaches (*Id.* § 7801(23)).[15] Underlying the requirement that teachers be highly qualified is the assumption that such teachers will be better able to teach the general education curriculum established by a state or district.

Although NCLB is silent on the qualifications of special education teachers, IDEA '04 follows the lead of NCLB and requires that special education teachers be highly qualified, as noted earlier. If students with disabilities are to participate in the general education curriculum, it is important for special education teachers to be knowledgeable about the core academic subjects they teach, as well as the impact of the student's disability on development, learning, and behavior.

Professional Development

A second area that can be identified as having the potential to facilitate the involvement of students with disabilities in the general education curriculum is professional development. NCLB calls for professional development, for example, that is aligned with state content and achievement standards, as well as assessments (20 U.S.C. § 7801(34)(A)(viii)). Such alignment has the effect of linking professional development activities to an understanding of the general education curriculum, an important step for teachers who will be helping students with disabilities to be involved in the general education curriculum. In addition, professional development, to the extent appropriate, is to include training in the use of technology that can improve the quality of teaching in the curricula and core academic subjects (*Id.* § 7801(34)(A)(xi)). Providing training in technology for teachers is crucial in helping them integrate technology into their instructional practices. Such integration can also play a significant role in helping students with disabilities have access to and participate in the general education curriculum (Rose & Meyer, 2002). IDEA '04 similarly discusses professional development training that incorporates the integration of technology into curricula and instruction (*Id.* § 1454(a)(2)).

NCLB further specifies that professional development should, among other pedagogical activities, "provide instruction in methods of teaching children with special needs" (20 U.S.C. § 7801(34)(A)(xiii)) and "provide training in how to teach and address the needs of students with different learning styles, particularly students with disabilities" (*Id.* § 6623(a)(3)(B)(ii)). Moreover, NCLB also encourages the development of programs to train and hire regular and special education teachers, including the hiring of special education teachers who will team-teach classes that include students with and without disabilities (*Id.* § 6623(a)(2)(C)(i)). IDEA '04 similarly emphasizes the need to recruit, train, and retain highly qualified special education personnel, and to prepare regular education teachers who provide instruction for students with disabilities.[16] Professional development that is instructive to regular education teachers in promoting an understanding of the needs of students with disabilities in their classroom can help teachers provide more effective instruction to these students. Professional development that trains special education teachers to team-teach with regular education teachers is also important. When regular and special education teachers work together, they can pool their resources and expertise toward the goal of involving students with disabilities in the general education curriculum.

Special Programs and Services

A third area of NCLB that has the potential to facilitate the involvement of students with disabilities in the general education curriculum relates to special programs and services that are available to schools and students, like the Reading First program. Reading First assists states and local districts "in selecting or developing effective instructional materials (including classroom-based materials to assist teachers in implementing the essential components of reading instruction), programs, learning systems, and strategies to implement methods that have been proven to prevent or remediate reading failure" (20 U.S.C. § 6361(4)). This program is targeted at children who, among other criteria, are at risk of being referred to special education or are served under IDEA because of a learning disability (LD) related to reading (*Id.* § 6362(c)(7)(A)(ii)(II)). The goal of this program is to help all children learn to read by the end of the third grade (*Id.* § 6361(1)).

Research has shown that more than half of all students who are identified for special education services are classified as LD (Vaughn & Fuchs, 2003), and approximately 80 percent of children with LD have problems with reading (Lyon et al., 2001). The emphasis on reading in NCLB, particularly as part of the Reading First program, has the potential to lead educators to focus on effective instructional techniques in reading that can help students with disabilities be involved in the general education curriculum. Early identification of struggling readers, followed up with carefully targeted literacy instruction, can reduce the number of students referred to special education. Moreover, effective reading instruction in the early grades can provide the foundation for the establishment of literacy skills that are crucial for later content-area learning in the core curriculum subjects.

NCLB also requires school districts to arrange for the provision of supplemental educational services, from a state-approved provider, for children from low-income families, including children with disabilities, who attend schools that have failed to make "adequate yearly progress" (see "Accountability," below) for three consecutive years (20 U.S.C. § 6316(e)(1)). Such services, defined as "tutoring and other supplemental academic enrichment services," are to be provided outside of the regular school day and are designed to improve the achievement on state assessments of children eligible to receive supplemental educational services and help them attain proficiency in meeting the state achievement standards (*Id.* § 6316(e)(12)(C)). For students with disabilities, the supplemental educational services must be consistent with the child's IEP (*Id.* § 6316(e)(3)(A)); the services, however, do not have to meet the goals of the IEP and are not considered part of the IEP (67 Fed. Reg. 71757).[17] These services have the potential to facilitate involvement in the general education curriculum because they are designed to help students improve their achievement on state assessments and attain proficiency. Moreover, the interactive one-on-one tutoring creates a focus on the specific needs of the child. Finally, because the tutoring is provided outside the regular school day, the services do not take the child out of class.

Progress in the General Education Curriculum

A major focus of NCLB is the area of assessments and accountability. As noted earlier, IDEA '04 aligns the requirements in IDEA pertaining to assessments and accountability with some of the provisions in NCLB.

Assessments

NCLB requires states to institute "high-quality, yearly student academic assessments" that are to be the same for all children and are to be aligned with the state's content and achievement standards (20 U.S.C. §§ 6311(b)(3)(A), (C)(i)-(ii)). The implementing regulations add that the assessments must "be designed to be valid and accessible for use by

the widest possible range of students, including students with disabilities" (34 C.F.R. § 200.2(b)(2)). These assessments must include, at a
minimum, mathematics and reading/language arts (also science, beginning in the 2007–08 school year) and are to be the primary measure to
determine the annual performance of the state, districts, and schools
in helping all children meet the state's achievement standards (*Id.* §
6311(b)(3)(A)).

Beginning in the 2005–06 school year, students must be tested in each
of grades 3 through 8 (*Id.* § 6311(b)(3)(C)(vii)) and at least once in
grades 10 through 12 (34 C.F.R. § 200.5(a)(2)(ii)). Moreover, because
state standards help define the general education curriculum, the assessments under NCLB will also be based on the general education curriculum. This has implications for the provision of access to the general
education curriculum for students with disabilities. If students are to
be evaluated by means of tests that are based on the general education
curriculum, they must first be taught the material that comprises this
curriculum. Therefore, the assessment provisions of NCLB also have a
potential impact on access to and involvement in the general education
curriculum for students with disabilities. As noted, IDEA '04 requires
that students with disabilities participate in assessments mandated under NCLB.

NCLB requires reporting on the results of the assessments and disaggregation by students with disabilities as compared to students without
disabilities. NCLB also provides for an exception to the requirement
for disaggregation when "the number of students in a category is insufficient to yield statistically reliable information or the results would
reveal personally identifiable information about an individual student"
(20 U.S.C. § 6311(b)(3)(C)(xiii)). The implementing regulations add
that each state must determine what constitutes the minimum number of
students that would provide statistically reliable information (34 C.F.R.
§ 200.7(a)(2)). IDEA '04 similarly requires reporting on the assessment
results of students with disabilities as compared to the achievement of
all children, so long as the number of children with disabilities participating is large enough to yield statistically reliable information and reporting will not reveal personally identifiable information (20 U.S.C. §
1412(a)(16)(D)(iv)).

As noted with respect to IDEA, assessing students with disabilities and reporting on the assessment results is intended to hold edu-

cators accountable for the educational performance of these students. NCLB, however, goes beyond IDEA by also requiring that an individual report of each student's performance be provided to parents, teachers, and principals in "a language that parents can understand" (*Id.* § 6311(b)(3)(C)(xii)), thus including an additional layer of accountability that extends to parents.

NCLB further requires that state assessments provide for the participation of students with disabilities (as defined under IDEA) with accommodations (20 U.S.C. § 6311(b)(3)(C)(ix)(II)). The implementing regulations for NCLB add that the accommodations are to be determined by the student's IEP team (34 C.F.R. § 200.6(a)(1)(i)). The references to IDEA and the IEP team again show the intended coordination between the two statutes. In addition, it is significant that neither NCLB nor IDEA '04 addresses the issues concerning the validity of inferences drawn from scores on assessments on which students receive accommodations.[18] As noted, there has been little research on the effect of specific accommodations on the validity of inferences made from the scores of students with different types of disabilities.

NCLB also requires that states allow the use of alternate assessments for children whose IEP team determines that they cannot take part in the assessment, even with appropriate accommodations (34 C.F.R. § 200.6(a)(2)(i)). The NCLB regulations also require that alternate assessments provide results for the particular grade in which the student is enrolled[19] for at least reading/language arts and mathematics, and for science beginning in the 2007–08 school year (*Id.* § 200.6(a)(2)(ii)(A)).

A new aspect added to the implementing regulations of NCLB is the use of alternate achievement standards. The regulations that were published in the Federal Register on December 9, 2003, allow states to develop "alternate academic achievement standards" for students with the most significant cognitive disabilities[20] whose performance is assessed by means of an alternate assessment (34 C.F.R. § 200.1(d)). An alternate achievement standard is "an expectation of performance that differs in complexity from a grade-level achievement standard" (68 F.R. 68698, 68699). It must be "aligned with the State's academic content standards[21]; *promote access to the general curriculum*; and reflect professional judgment of the highest achievement standards possible" (34 C.F.R. §§ 200.1(d)(1)-(3) [emphasis added]). As noted earlier, IDEA '04 refers to the use of alternate achievement standards in several places in the law that pertain to access to the general curriculum: The elimination of short-term objectives and benchmarks does not apply to students being tested against alternate achievement standards; special education teachers of students who are tested against alternate achievement standards must be highly qualified; and alternate assessments must measure the achievement of children with disabilities against the state's content standards or alternate achievement standards.

The implementing regulations for NCLB further specify that a state is not required to use alternate achievement standards; however, if a state chooses to do so, it must first satisfy a number of conditions, including, for example, the establishment of appropriate guidelines for IEP teams to use in determining whether a student's achievement should be based on alternate achievement standards, as well as documentation "that students with the most significant cognitive disabilities are, to the extent possible, *included in the general curriculum and in assessments aligned with that curriculum*" (34 C.F.R. § 200.6(a)(2)(iii) [emphasis added]).

States would be allowed to use the proficient and advanced scores of students with the most significant cognitive disabilities, based on the alternate achievement standards, in determining "adequate yearly progress" (see "Accountability," below), provided that the number of students who attain a proficient or advanced level based on the alternate achievement standards at both the district and state levels[22] does not exceed 1.0 percent of all students in the grades assessed (34 C.F.R. § 200.13(c)(1)(ii)). If the percentage of students attaining a proficient or advanced level based on the alternate achievement standards exceeds the 1.0 percent cap, the state must make sure that the scores of all students with the most significant cognitive disabilities are included but must count the proficient and advanced scores above the cap as "non-proficient" (*Id.* §§ 200.13(c)(4)(i)-(ii)). States can determine which proficient scores based on the alternate achievement scores count as nonproficient, and they must make sure that parents are informed of the actual achievement levels of their children (*Id.* §§ 200.13(c)(4)(iii), (v)). The DOE explained that the 1.0 percent cap was included in order to ensure that alternate achievement standards are used in a thoughtful manner and to protect against the assignment of children to inappropriate assessments and curricula (68 Fed. Reg. 68706). States and districts can ask for an exception permitting them to exceed the 1.0 percent cap if they can show that the incidence of students with the most significant cognitive disabilities is higher than 1.0 percent of all students in the grades assessed, and if they can explain why the incidence is higher (34 C.F.R. §§ 200.13(c)(2)(i)-(ii), (3)(i)). States and districts requesting an exception must also document that they have fully addressed certain conditions (discussed above) associated with the use of alternate achievement standards (*Id.* §§ 200.13(c)(2)(iii), (3)(i)).[23]

The purpose of the new regulations concerning alternate achievement standards is to provide for the inclusion of students with the most significant cognitive disabilities in school accountability systems. According to the DOE,

> these regulations are designed to ensure that schools are held accountable for the educational progress of students with the most significant cognitive disabilities, just as schools are held accountable for the educational results of all other students with disabilities and students without disabilities. (68 Fed. Reg. 68698)

Allowing the use of alternate achievement standards should facilitate the participation of students with significant cognitive disabilities in assessments. At the same time, however, certain policy and psychometric issues remain; for example, how a state should go about setting achievement standards (i.e., determining the meaning of "proficiency").

Accountability

NCLB requires that each state develop a statewide system of accountability to measure whether schools and districts are making adequate yearly progress (AYP) toward enabling all students, including students with disabilities, to meet or exceed the proficiency level on the state assessments no later than 12 years after the end of the 2001–2002 school year (20 U.S.C. §§ 6311(b)(2)(A), (F)). Moreover, AYP also requires states to establish measurable annual objectives, applied separately to students with disabilities,[24] that will specify the minimum percentage of students who must meet or exceed the state's proficiency level on the state assessments (*Id.* § 6311(b)(2)(G)(iii); see also *Id.* § 6311(b)(2)(C)(v)). As noted, IDEA '04 states that performance goals should be the same as the state's definition of AYP and that performance indicators should include measurable annual goals under NCLB. NCLB further specifies that in order for a school or district to make AYP, not less than 95 percent of students with disabilities[25] must participate in the assessments through regular assessments, regular assessments with accommodations, or by means of alternate assessments (*Id.* § 6311(b)(2)(I)(ii)). The regulations add that if a student takes the same assessment more than once, the score from the first administration should be used to determine AYP (34 C.F.R. § 200.20(c)(3)).

In spite of these stringent requirements, it is important to note that NCLB does not attach "high-stakes" consequences to testing results, such as the denial of a high school diploma, to individual students. There are, however, serious consequences for schools and districts, which can weigh heavily on school personnel. As part of a state's accountability system, the district must identify for improvement those schools that have failed to make AYP for two consecutive years (20 U.S.C. § 6316(b)(1)(A)). In addition, the district must allow all students, including students with disabilities, who are enrolled in a school that has been identified for school improvement (i.e., did not make AYP for two consecutive years) the option of transferring to another public school within the district that has not been identified for school improvement (*Id.* §§ 6316(b)(1)(E)-(F)). The regulations add that for students with disabilities covered under IDEA or Section 504, "the public school choice option must provide a free appropriate public education" (34 C.F.R. § 200.44(j)). If the school continues to fail to make AYP after being identified for school improvement, the district must identify the school for "corrective action" and subsequently for "restructuring" (*Id.* §§ 6316(b)(7)-(8)).[26]

The expectation underlying NCLB is that holding schools accountable for the educational performance of students with disabilities will ultimately lead to improvement in the provision of educational services for these students, as well as improved results. At the same time, however, it is also possible that the stringent accountability requirements of NCLB may, in certain respects, have a negative impact on students with disabilities. For example, being identified as a school that has failed to make AYP can lower the morale of both teachers and students, including students with disabilities, especially in light of the fact that sanctions are applied to schools without regard to factors that might contribute to low performance (e.g., lack of resources). Moreover, although NCLB does not attach high stakes for the individual student, such as denial of a high school diploma, many states on their own have done so, with potentially negative consequences for students with disabilities.

CONCLUSION

Since passage of the EAHCA in 1975, significant improvements have been made in the quality of education provided to students with disabilities. Increased numbers of students with disabilities have been attending public schools and participating in classes with students without disabilities. Moreover, attention has shifted from mainstreaming and inclusion to the meaningful participation of students with disabilities in the regular class. IDEA '97 has played a major role in this evolution, with one of the most important innovations being the requirement that students with disabilities have access to the general education curriculum. Four years after the passage of IDEA '97, Congress passed NCLB, which shares the goal of raising expectations for the educational performance of students with disabilities and increasing accountability for their educational results. IDEA '04 has maintained the focus on access to the general education curriculum while at the same time introducing a number of changes, several of which were intended to align IDEA with NCLB.

This chapter has discussed the legal provisions in IDEA '97, IDEA '04, and NCLB associated with access to the general education curriculum, as well as the translation of these provisions into educational obligations for states and school districts. A theoretical framework has been used that conceptualizes the overall right of students with disabilities in IDEA to have access to the general education curriculum as comprising three interrelated stages that form an ongoing cycle: access, involvement, and progress. The educational obligations of states and school districts extend to each of these stages. The first stage, access, requires that the general education curriculum be accessible to students with disabilities. The second stage, involvement, requires that students with disabilities participate in the general education curriculum in an ongoing and meaningful way. The third stage, progress, requires that students with disabilities be able to demonstrate progress in the general education curriculum through improved educational performance.

The first stage of the cycle involves the accessibility of the general education curriculum to students with disabilities. The implementing regulations for IDEA '97 described the general curriculum as the same curriculum as that provided to students without disabilities, but did not elaborate further on the meaning of the term. The NCLB requirement that states adopt challenging academic content and achievement standards, as well as the emphasis on a high-quality curriculum, should help states define and raise the level of the general education curriculum. IDEA '04 includes new provisions pertaining to the establishment of the National Instructional Materials Accessibility Standard and the National Instructional Materials Access Center that should help students with print and other disabilities have greater access in a more timely manner to the print materials that are part of the general education curriculum.

With respect to the second stage, involvement in the general education curriculum, IDEA '04 maintains, for the most part, the obligations of school districts that were introduced in IDEA '97. These obligations, centering around the IEP, include specification in the IEP of how the student's disability affects his or her involvement and progress in the general education curriculum; IEP goals that enable the student to be involved in and progress in the general education curriculum; identification in the IEP of supplementary aids and services, program modifications, or supports for personnel that help the student to be involved in and progress in the general education curriculum; explanation of the extent to which the student will not participate in the regular class; and inclusion of the regular education teacher on the IEP team. These requirements are intended to engage students with disabilities as actual participants rather than passive observers in the regular education class. IDEA '04 also includes a focus on functional performance and functional goals and eliminates the requirement for short-term objectives and benchmarks, except for those students who are taking assessments aligned with alternate achievement standards.

In addition, a number of provisions in NCLB have the potential to facilitate greater involvement in the general education curriculum—namely, the requirement that teachers be highly qualified; professional development that focuses on, for example, strategies for providing instruction to students with disabilities in regular education classes; and programs or services such as Reading First and supplemental educational services. While NCLB is silent regarding the qualifications of special education teachers, IDEA '04 specifically requires that these teachers be highly qualified.

Finally, with respect to the third stage, progress in the general education curriculum, both IDEA '97 and IDEA '04 include requirements concerning progress toward IEP goals, participation in state and districtwide assessments, and the establishment of state performance goals and indicators. In the area of assessments, NCLB mandates that states must establish high-quality, yearly academic assessments for all students, including students with disabilities (with accommodations or by means of alternate assessments), and that these assessments must be aligned with state content and achievement standards. Implementing regulations for NCLB also allows for the development of alternate achievement standards for students with the most significant cognitive disabilities whose performance is based on an alternate assessment. IDEA '04 aligns IDEA with NCLB with respect to assessments by stating that the IDEA mandate for the inclusion of students with disabilities in state and district-wide assessments includes assessments required under NCLB. Moreover, IDEA '04 refers to the use of alternate achievement standards in several places in the statute that pertain to access to the general education curriculum.

NCLB also requires the establishment of a system of accountability to measure whether schools and districts are making adequate yearly progress toward enabling all students, including students with disabilities, to meet or exceed the proficiency level on the state assessments within 12 years. Implementing regulations for NCLB modifies the manner of the inclusion of the performance of students with the most significant cognitive disabilities by permitting the use of alternate achievement standards in determination of AYP, provided that the number of proficient or advanced scores based on the alternate achievement standards counted toward AYP at the district and state levels does not exceed 1.0 percent of all students assessed. IDEA '04 aligns IDEA with NCLB with respect to accountability by stating that performance goals should be the same as AYP and that performance indicators should include measurable annual goals under NCLB.

The accountability system called for under NCLB is intended to increase accountability for the educational performance of all students, including students with disabilities. At the same time, there is also the possibility that the stringent accountability requirements in NCLB, including the threat of sanctions, may in some instances have a negative effect on students with disabilities. For example, the sanctions are applied without taking into account factors such as a lack of resources, and may adversely affect the morale of teachers and students, including students with disabilities. In addition, many states on their own have decided to attach high stakes for the individual student, which can have significant consequences for students with disabilities.

In conclusion, through a discussion of the interrelationship between IDEA and NCLB, this chapter has presented a comprehensive analysis of the concept of access to the general education curriculum. It is significant that IDEA '04 has maintained the majority of the provisions pertaining to access to the general education curriculum found in IDEA '97, while at the same time following in the direction of NCLB with respect to requirements pertaining to highly qualified personnel, assessments, and accountability. The provisions in IDEA '04 concerning access to the general education curriculum have the potential to lead to increased expectations and improved educational outcomes for students with disabilities.

NOTES

1. FAPE is defined as "special education and related services that (A) have been provided at public expense, under public supervision and direction, and without charge; (B) meet the standards of the State educational agency; (C) include an appropriate preschool, elementary, or secondary school education in the State involved; and (D) are provided in conformity with the individualized education program required under [the law]" (20 U.S.C. § 1401(9)).

2. LRE refers to the education of students with disabilities to the maximum extent appropriate in a setting together with students without disabilities (20 U.S.C. § 1412(a)(5)(A)).

3. The DOE is currently in the process of preparing its implementing regulations for IDEA '04, having completed its period for comments and recommendations on February 28, 2005 (69 Fed. Reg. 77968, 77969).

4. For a discussion of this congressional preference, *see, e.g., Oberti v. Board of Educ.*, 995 F.2d 1204, 1214 (3d Cir. 1993); *Daniel R.R. v. State Bd. of Educ.*, 874 F.2d 1036, 1044 (5th Cir. 1989); *Roncker v. Walter*, 700 F.2d 1058, 1063 (6th Cir. 1983).

5. Although the language used by IDEA in these requirements refers to both involvement and progress, the requirements are included here under the rubric of involvement.

6. IDEA '04 further specifies that attendance of a member is not required when the member's area of curriculum or related services is not being modified or discussed, if the parent and Local Educational Agency (LEA) consent. If the meeting involves modification to or discussion of the member's area of the curriculum or related services, the member can be excused from attending the meeting if the parent and LEA consent and the member submits his or her input in writing prior to the meeting (20 U.S.C. § 1414(d)(1)(C)).

7. In addition, IDEA '97 and IDEA '04 specify that the IEP team must include a representative of the LEA who is knowledgeable about the general education curriculum and about the availability of resources of the LEA (20 U.S.C. §§ 1414(d)(1)(B)(iv)(II)-(III)).

8. In addition, the implementing regulations for IDEA '97 require that when a student with a disability is placed in an "interim alternative educational setting," the setting must be selected so as to enable the child to continue to progress in the general curriculum (34 C.F.R. § 300.522(b)(1)).

9. As with the elimination of short-term objectives and benchmarks, in an effort to help reduce the paperwork associated with IEPs, IDEA '04 authorizes the secretary to approve no more than 15 proposals from states to develop a comprehensive multiyear IEP, not to exceed three years, designed to coincide with the natural transition points for the child (20 U.S.C. § 1414(d)(5)(A)).

10. States are only required to report on the performance of students with disabilities "if the number of children with disabilities participating in those assessments is sufficient to yield statistically reliable information and reporting that information will not reveal personally identifiable information about an individual student" (20 U.S.C. § 1412(a)(16)(D)(iv)).

11. For example, NCLB mandates that in order to receive Title I funds, the plan of a state or district must be coordinated with the requirements of IDEA (20 U.S.C. §§ 6311(a)(1), 6312(a)(1)).

12. NCLB is a vast statute with many components. This chapter includes only select provisions that relate specifically to access to the general education curriculum for students with disabilities.

13. Content standards are to "specify what children are expected to know and be able to do; contain coherent and rigorous content; and encourage the teaching of advanced skills" (20 U.S.C. § 6311(b)(1)(D)(i)). Achievement standards are to be aligned with a state's content standards and describe at least two levels of high achievement (proficient and advanced), as well as a third level of achievement (basic) (*Id.* § 6311(b)(1)(D)(ii)).

14. NCLB defines the core academic subjects as follows: "English, reading or language arts, mathematics, science, foreign languages, civics and government, economics, arts, history, and geography" (20 U.S.C. § 7801(11)).

15. The specific requirements differ somewhat for elementary and middle/secondary teachers and for newly hired and veteran teachers.

16. Although IDEA '04 eliminated the requirement found in IDEA '97 for states to develop a comprehensive system of personnel development, IDEA '04 replaced the State Improvement Grant program with the State Personnel Preparation and Professional Development Grant program, in which states receive funds to provide professional development training for regular and special education teachers and administrators (20 U.S.C. § 1454(a)(1)).

17. The state and district must make sure that at least some of the available providers are able to provide services to students with disabilities and students covered under Section 504, including necessary accommodations; if no provider is able to make such accommodations, the district has to provide the services with the necessary accommodations "either directly or through a contract" (67 Fed. Reg. 71757-58).

18. The regulations do state that assessments should "be designed to be valid and accessible for use by the widest possible range of students, including students with disabilities" (34 C.F.R. § 200.2(b)(2)).

19. The one exception is for students with the most significant cognitive disabilities whose performance is measured against alternate achievement standards (*see*

discussion of alternate achievement standards below under NCLB) (34 C.F.R. §
200.6(a)(2)(ii)(B)).

20. A previous NPRM (March 20, 2003) had defined students with the most significant
disabilities as those "whose intellectual functioning and adaptive behavior are three
or more standard deviations below the mean" (68 Fed. Reg. 13796, 13801). The final regulations do not include this definition, leaving greater flexibility to the states
(68 Fed. Reg. 68697, 68700).

21. According to the DOE, alignment with a state's content standards refers to a "con-
nection between the instructional content appropriate for non-disabled students and
the related knowledge and skills that may serve as the basis for a definition of proficient achievement for students with the most significant disabilities" (68 Fed. Reg.
68703).

22. The 1.0 percent cap applies only at the state and district levels, not at the school level, and should be based on the number of students enrolled in the particular grade(s)
being tested (68 Fed. Reg. 68706).

23. The DOE has explained, however, that the use of alternate achievement standards
at the school level is not unlimited and that it is to be expected that not more than
9.0 percent of all students with disabilities will be tested relative to the alternate
achievement standards (68 Fed. Reg. 68700).

24. Disaggregation is not required when the number of students in the category is so
small that the results would not be statistically reliable or would reveal identifiable
information about the students (20 U.S.C. § 6311(b)(2)(C)(v)).

25. The 95 percent rule does "not apply in a case in which the number of students in a
category is insufficient to yield statistically reliable information or the results would
reveal personally identifiable information about an individual student" (20 U.S.C. §
6311(b)(2)(I)(ii)).

26. Corrective action may include such measures as replacing staff, implementing a new
curriculum, appointing an outside expert, or extending the school year or school day
(20 U.S.C. § 6316(b)(7)(C)(iv)). Restructuring may include reopening the school as
a public charter school, replacing all or most of the school staff, or turning over op-
eration of the school to the state or a private contractor (*Id.* § 6316(b)(8)(B)).

REFERENCES

Association of Community Organizations for Reform NOW v. New York City Department of Education, 269 F. Supp. 2d 338 (S.D.N.Y. 2003).

Daniel R.R. v. State Board of Education, 874 F.2d 1036 (5th Cir. 1989).

Heubert, J. P., & Hauser, R. M. (Eds.). (1999). *High stakes: Testing for tracking, promotion, and graduation* (National Research Council, Committee on Appropriate Test
Use). Washington, DC: National Academy Press.

Hitchcock, C., Meyer, A., Rose, D., & Jackson, R. (2002). Providing new access to the
general curriculum: Universal Design for Learning. *Teaching Exceptional Children,
35*, 8–17.

Hocutt, A. M. (1996). Effectiveness of special education: Is placement the critical factor?
Future of Children, 6(1), 77–102.

H.R. Rep. No. 105-95 (1997).

Individuals with Disabilities Education Act Amendments of 1997, 20 U.S.C. §§ 1400 *et seq.* (amended 2004); 34 C.F.R. §§ 300.1 *et seq.* (2003).

Individuals with Disabilities Education Improvement Act of 2004, Pub. L. No. 108-446, 118 Stat. 2647 (2004) (amending 20 U.S.C. §§ 1400 *et seq.*).

Lyon, G. R., Fletcher, J. M., Shaywitz, S. E., Shaywitz, B. A., Torgesen, J. K., Wood, F. B., Schultz, A., & Olsen, R. (2001). Rethinking learning disabilities. In C. E. Finn, A. J. Rotherman, & C. R. Hokanson (Eds.), *Rethinking special education for a new century* (pp. 259–287). Washington, DC: Thomas B. Fordham Foundation and the Progressive Policy Institute.

McDonnell, L. M., McLaughlin, M. J., & Morison, P. (Eds.). (1997). *Educating one and all: Students with disabilities and standards-based reform* (National Research Council, Committee on Goals 2000 and the Inclusion of Students with Disabilities). Washington, DC: National Academy Press.

National Research Council, Committee on Appropriate Test Use. (1999). *High stakes: Testing for tracking, promotion, and graduation* (J. P. Heubert & R. M. Hauser, Eds.). Washington, DC: National Academy Press.

National Research Council, Committee on Goals 2000 and the Inclusion of Students with Disabilities. (1997). *Educating one and all: Students with disabilities and standards-based reform* (L. M. McDonnell, M. J. McLaughlin, & P. Morison, Eds.). Washington, DC: National Academy Press.

No Child Left Behind Act, 20 U.S.C. §§ 6301 *et seq.* (2002); 34 C.F.R. §§ 200.1 *et seq.* (2003).

Nolet, V., & McLaughlin, M. J. (2000). *Accessing the general curriculum: Including students with disabilities in standards-based reform.* Thousand Oaks, CA: Corwin Press.

Oberti v. Board of Education, 995 F.2d 1204 (3d Cir. 1993).

Office of Elementary and Secondary Education, U.S. Department of Education. (2002, December 2). *Title I—Improving the academic achievement of the disadvantaged: Analysis of comments and changes.* 67 Fed. Reg. 71710, 71739-71771.

Office of Elementary and Secondary Education, U.S. Department of Education. (2003, March 20). *Title I—Improving the academic achievement of the disadvantaged: Notice of proposed rulemaking.* 68 Fed. Reg. 13796-13801.

Office of Elementary and Secondary Education, U.S. Department of Education. (2003, December 9). *Title I—Improving the academic achievement of the disadvantaged: Background and analysis of comments and changes.* 68 Fed. Reg. 68698-68701, 68703-68708.

Office of Elementary and Secondary Education, U.S. Department of Education. (2004, January 16). *Improving teacher quality state grants (Title II part A): Non-regulatory guidance.* Retrieved June 7, 2004, from http://www.ed.gov/programs/teacherqual/guidance.pdf

Office of Special Education and Rehabilitative Services, U.S. Department of Education. (2004, December 29). *Notice of request for comments and recommendations on regulatory issues under the Individuals with Disabilities Education Act (IDEA), as amended by the Individuals with Disabilities Education Improvement Act of 2004.* 69 Fed. Reg. 77968-77969.

Quenemoen, R., Rigney, S., & Thurlow, M. (2002). *Use of alternate assessment results in reporting and accountability systems: Conditions for use based on re-*

search and practice (Synthesis Report 43). Minneapolis: University of Minnesota, National Center on Educational Outcomes. Retrieved June 7, 2004, from http://education.umn.edu/NCEO/OnlinePubs/Synthesis43.html

Roncker v. Walter, 700 F.2d 1058 (6th Cir. 1983).

Rose, D. H., & Meyer, A. (2002). *Teaching every student in the digital age: Universal Design for Learning.* Alexandria, VA: ASCD.

Sen. Rep. 105-17 (1997).

Sen. Rep. 108-185 (2004).

Sireci, S. G., Li, S., & Scarpati, S. (2003). *The effects of test accommodations on test performance: A review of the literature* (Center for Educational Assessment Research Report no. 485). Amherst: University of Massachusetts, School of Education. Retrieved June 7, 2004, from http://education.umn.edu/nceo/OnlinePubs/TestAccommLitReview.pdf

Thompson, S. J., Johnstone, C. J., & Thurlow, M. L. (2002). *Universal design applied to large scale assessments* (Synthesis Report 44). Minneapolis: University of Minnesota, National Center on Educational Outcomes. Retrieved March 25, 2005, from http://education.umn.edu/NCEO/OnlinePubs/Synthesis44.html

U.S. Department of Education. (1995). *Individuals with Disabilities Education Act amendments of 1995: Reauthorization of the Individuals with Disabilities Education Act (IDEA).* Washington, DC: Author.

Vaughn, S., & Fuchs, L. S. (2003). Redefining learning disabilities as inadequate response to instruction: The promise and potential problems. *Learning Disabilities Research and Practice, 18,* 137–146.

Wagner, M., Blackorby, J., Cameto, R., Hebbeler, K., & Newman, K. (1993). *The transition experiences of young people with disabilities.* Palo Alto, CA: SRI.

This report was originally published as Karger, J. (2005). *Access to the general curriculum for students with disabilities: A discussion of the interrelationship between IDEA and NCLB.* Wakefield, MA: CAST. This report was written with support from the National Center on Accessing the General Curriculum (NCAC) and a cooperative agreement between the Center for Applied Special Technology (CAST) and the U.S. Department of Education, Office of Special Education Programs (OSEP), Cooperative Agreement No. H324H990004. Although the U.S. Department of Education has reviewed this document for consistency with the IDEA and NCLB, the contents of this document do not necessarily reflect the views or policies of the U.S. Department of Education, nor does mention of other organizations imply their endorsement of this report.

CHAPTER FOUR

Teacher Planning for Accessibility: The Universal Design of Learning Environments

RICHARD JACKSON AND KELLY HARPER

Teaching is both an art and a science. At times it can be an impassioned performance with no manner of predictable outcome. At other times, teaching can be a carefully scripted series of interactions between student and teacher. The art and science of teaching most often have highly profitable results. However, as we all know, not all children succeed. This chapter is about teachers and how they can work together to teach *all* children effectively, including those with disabilities. We believe many teachers are lifelong learners who manifest an intense desire to share what they know with others. (Additionally, teachers view children not as mere vessels but as vibrant creatures, full of potential and wondrous possibilities.)

We speak of teachers generically here because we take the stance that general educators, special educators, compensatory educators, remedial educators, and educators of students who are gifted or talented equally share a commitment to and responsibility for the success of all learners (Friend, 2000a). Teachers also contribute their own special talents, interests, passions, and, of course, areas of expertise. When teachers find ways to work together—both formally and informally—to plan, implement, monitor, and evaluate student learning, the complex realities of the classroom are better understood and managed through their multiple perspectives. As Vaughn, Bos, and Schumm (2000) argue, teaching students who are exceptional, diverse, or otherwise at risk requires careful planning and collaborative decisionmaking.

Teachers confront many challenges as they set about each day deciding what and how to teach children. They now face increasing numbers of students with disabilities within their general education classrooms (U.S. Department of Education, 1999). Their schools, particularly in urban centers, are increasingly made up of students from diverse cultural, ethnic, and linguistic backgrounds (U.S. Department of Education, 2000). Due to greater national and state emphasis on standards and high-stakes testing, teachers find more of their students at risk of failure and dropping out (Rumberger & Thomas, 2000).

Challenges for teachers may be the barriers to learning for their students. This chapter illustrates how teacher planning can be enhanced and barriers to effective instruction can be overcome by pursuing a new framework for reform called Universal Design for Learning (UDL; Rose & Meyer, 2002). Before discussing teacher planning, however, we would like to explore why a new framework is needed.

Under IDEA and No Child Left Behind, the same emphasis on accountability for educating nondisabled students is now extended to include students with disabilities, with raised expectations for success and participation in large-scale assessment (e.g., districtwide and state-level standards-based measures). All students with disabilities are now tested against state standards, and they and their families require various services and resources to meet these standards. Teams of general and special education personnel determine each student's current level of performance in the general curriculum and in disability-specific areas as well. Goals are set for advancing in the general curriculum and for mitigating the impact of disability. This may require specially designed instruction to address targeted needs. Where instruction or assessment activities do not match up with the student's functional capabilities, accommodations must be made explicit. Where standards or expectations prove unreasonable, curriculum modifications are put into place.

Standards are not changed for students with disabilities; only the means for learning and for demonstrating proficiency are altered. Students who receive accommodations in instruction must also receive comparable treatment during the assessment process. For students whose needs are intensive, alternate instruction and assessment may be required. Standards remain in the context of the general curriculum but are altered to match the student's level of entry. Assessment accommodations or alternate instruction and assessment procedures are based on the objectives contained in the student's Individualized Education Program (IEP).

A brief glance at history reveals a substantial change in perspective when considering curriculum and assessment for students with disabilities. There has been a significant shift from "fix the student"—the student does not fit the school or the curriculum—to "fix the curriculum and school" to meet the needs of *all* learners. Placing instructional targets in the context of the general curriculum allows all children to access core subject areas. Accountability for results now cuts across the previously separate worlds of general and special education through shared responsibility.

As with all change in education, some challenges will persist. Issues of time to work together in planning, pacing lessons to meet the needs of all learners, and increased student diversity in the classroom may be difficult for educators at the building and classroom levels. IEP requirements from IDEA stipulate that both general and special education personnel engage in a planning process that aims at accessing the general curriculum. Thus, collaboration becomes key to this process.

Adopting the framework of Universal Design for Learning can mitigate these constraints. A thematic unit applying UDL currently in use in a Boston-area elementary school is presented here. This illustrates how the various elements of a unit can be transformed by following the logic of UDL.

COLLABORATIVE PLANNING AND INSTRUCTIONAL DECISIONMAKING

The shift toward access for all implies a partnership between general and special education—a partnership that embodies shared responsibility, commitment, resources, and accountability (O'Shea & O'Shea, 1997). The coordinated planning that occurs among general and special educators may take many forms as teachers take on new roles to help improve the education of all learners in today's classrooms.

On the surface, it would appear that these new requirements make the task of educating students with disabilities all the more daunting, since needs arising as a result of the disability must continue to be addressed. Paper books, resource materials, and magazines that cannot be read, videos that are not captioned, chalkboard renderings that cannot be copied, words and numbers that cannot be handwritten, stories that can be neither spoken nor heard are the mainstays of classrooms that for many are inaccessible and inconsiderate. Today, teachers can access new forms of media such as digital text, digital images, digital audio, digital video, digital multimedia, and networked environments. A digital curriculum holds the promise of increased flexibility and the capacity to align content and tools more precisely with a wide range of students' strengths and needs. Without a digital curriculum, the transformations and adaptations classroom materials and activities must undergo to permit participation in the general curriculum are onerous. However, with digital media and the technology tools enabling access to and manipulation of the curriculum, teams of educators can function with greater efficiency and effectiveness.

Teacher collaboration can take many forms in schools today (Friend, 2000b). Partnerships required in collaboration require professionals to take on new roles (Pugach & Johnson, 1995) in order to accomplish the kind of teacher planning necessary to improve outcomes for all learners. A necessary condition for successful collaboration is the willingness of all parties to participate in earnest and with the expectation that all will derive benefit from the negotiated arrangements. A variety of models exist for collaborative teaching and collaborative consultation (Walther-Thomas, Korinek, McLaughlin, & Williams, 2000). There are models for building support teams, teacher-assistance teams, and interprofessional teams. The types of personnel who engage in interactive teaming vary greatly. In sum, accessing the general curriculum for students with disabilities requires teacher collaboration; collaboration results in planning; and opportunities for planning must never be assumed but designed.

Teacher planning can be quite complex in that it can and should occur prior to, during, and following instruction. Collaborative planning should be carried out over time throughout the year, involving course planning, unit planning, and lesson planning, while always taking into account the individual needs of all learners. Special education and general education teachers often contribute different but complementary perspectives to the process. In planning a unit, for example, the teachers might choose a theme integrating several subject areas. They would examine standards across the subject-matter areas to ensure that the unit's "big ideas" were in alignment. The special educator would contribute his or her understanding of the student's abilities and disabilities, based on formal and informal assessment and the student's IEP. They may also identify necessary accommodations and adaptations for diverse learners in the classroom. The team would jointly plan unit activities that maximally engage students with content and peer-to-peer arrangements. The general education teacher would have a feel for how the units and lessons connect with prior knowledge, make available resource materials, and create activities to enrich the learning environment and measure student outcomes. If expectations for standards need to be modified, the special educator would design an authentic means of benchmarking progress within the curriculum area.

Ensuring that all students achieve should not require that teachers completely abandon the instructional practices for which they have developed some level of comfort. Rather, teachers should reflect on their preferred practices, carefully and critically examining how these practices may be made more flexible, malleable, and considerate of learners with diverse skills and disabilities. Teachers have a personal sense of ownership over what they feel works in their classrooms. While they become more comfortable in collaborative arrangements, it will prove far more beneficial to start where teachers find themselves—in the units and lessons they have come to know well and find effective (Tomlinson & Allan, 2000). The challenge then becomes one of modifying or extending existing practices in order to accommodate diversity and attain greater results for students with disabilities. Together, teachers will transform instruction to meet the needs of all learners in the classroom.

THE UDL FRAMEWORK

Transforming what teachers already know and do into more accessible and considerate lessons is best accomplished when collaborative teams apply the principles of Universal Design for Learning. The UDL framework builds on what teachers already do well for the purpose of extending curriculum and instructional opportunities to learners traditionally ignored or left out of classroom instruction. Based on the work of Rose and Meyer (2002), the UDL framework sets forth three operative principles for guiding the development of flexible teaching approaches and curriculum resources. These principles are derived from brain research and new understandings of how neuroscience informs our appreciation of learning and knowing (Rose & Meyer, 2000). The brain regions that take part in learning can be grouped roughly into three interconnected networks, each with a fundamental role in the classroom: 1) "recognition" networks are specialized to receive and analyze information (the "what" of learning); 2) "strategic" networks are specialized to plan and execute actions (the "how" of learning); and 3) "affective" networks are specialized to evaluate and set priorities (the "why" of learning; Dolan & Hall, 2001; Rose & Meyer, 2000, 2002).

To put this all into practice, we now have principles for what a universally designed learning environment must provide in order to be accessible to *all* learners. These correspond to three neural networks in the brain: the recognition system, the strategic system, and the affective system.

1. To support diverse *recognition* networks, provide multiple, flexible methods of presentation. For example, when introducing students to a new concept or unit, the teacher may provide multiple structures to present the information, such as a lecture, digitized text, activity-based exploration, or demonstration.
2. To support diverse *strategic* networks, provide multiple flexible methods of expression and apprenticeship. For example, when the teacher requests student responses to demonstrate understanding and knowledge, they could provide a range of tools that allow students to respond in various formats, such as written, oral, slide show, video, drawing.
3. To support diverse *affective* networks, provide multiple flexible options for engagement. Allow students to select an area of interest within the topic or concept to research or study. For example, they select rather than be assigned one of the natural resources in a geographic area under study and obtain in-depth information.

The three principles of UDL have strong intuitive appeal when applied to the design of curriculum media and materials. High-quality curriculum resources contain multiple means of representing information. They allow the student multiple ways of expressing what he or she knows or can do, and they contain multiple options for engaging in the task or activity. The three principles also have practical and ethical appeal in that application endeavors to increase instructional effectiveness, and simultaneously extend this effectiveness to all learners.

How might these principles be applied to teaching practices? All instructional plans lead learners somewhere. They must explicitly state a purpose, goal, or objective, and these must be aligned with standards. Lessons developed from the UDL framework embrace standards that could be attained from multiple, authentic means of expression. For example, evidence of one's ability to construct a carefully crafted narrative need not depend on one's ability to put pen to paper. Using assistive technology, many alternative tasks can be designed to demonstrate attainment of a standard to create prose. Goals for universally designed lessons, therefore, should not contain verbs that unnecessarily confine the demonstration of competence to a single task. As collaborative teams plan units and lessons, team members should envision many ways of demonstrating knowledge and skill, recognizing content, and engaging with the lesson. Goals are best designed when written in a broad manner to permit flexible options for demonstrating mastery. When goals are too tightly tied to methods, the logical result is that some students encounter barriers that prevent them from working toward these goals and others are not offered an appropriate level of challenge (Rose & Meyer, 2002).

Universally designed lessons maximize opportunity for *participation*. The use of flexible grouping schemes (Radencich & McKay, 1995) proactively sets up interactions between teachers and students, and between groups of students, to provide the opportunity to create multiple means of representation, expression, and engagement within the social context of the classroom.

Rubrics, defined as performance descriptions of a given task, are a tool that can help to implement UDL instruction and evaluation in numerous ways. By using rubrics, teachers may set forth a set of guidelines that may be precisely defined or described and used to judge or score student work. Rubrics also may be used to specify accommodations or conditions under which learners can demonstrate skills. The structure may be implemented for teachers and students to allow multiple means of expression. For example, the teacher in the planning process may indicate a range of means by which students may make selections and create responses or products. Finally, rubrics used as a scoring procedure are highly flexible and help teachers to reveal authenticity and product quality (Taggart, Phifer, Nixon, & Wood, 1998).

DESIGNING CURRICULUM FOR ALL LEARNERS THROUGH UDL: A MODEL

To see how UDL might play out in teacher planning and decisionmaking, the following unit plan for fifth grade students attending a suburban elementary school near Boston is presented (Table 1). The intent is to build a structure, identify resources, and design activities that would reach all learners in the classroom. The unit was designed following best practices in general education and the principles of UDL. Flexibility is built into the unit in a variety of ways, but the specific tailoring of lessons for students with disabilities would need to be refined in collaboration with special education teachers and related services personnel as discussed above.

This model unit focuses on Endangered Species: Causes and Ways to Address Threats to Their Survival. The topic of this thematic unit is of high social value and is capable of engaging learners at multiple levels of social consciousness. Content for the unit is drawn from a variety of disciplines (e.g., science, math, and language arts), bringing traditionally separate subject-matter areas together and making connections explicit and relevant to promote understanding. The unit is consistent with project-based learning, emphasizing a number of features that make it highly effective (Carr & Jitendra, 2000; Laffey, Tupper, Musser, & Wedman, 1998).

- The unit contains options for student choice, allowing students to go as deep into the topic as they choose and developing higher-order thinking skills.
- Goals for the unit are stated in the form of questions, thus making the unit inquiry based.
- Larger goals are kept in mind as the unit builds.
- The unit is systematically planned, yet not regimented. It focuses on building from activity to activity.
- Outcomes are anticipated but not standardized.

- Students have an opportunity to go beyond the curriculum frameworks.
- Student progress is monitored through consistent feedback, use of self-monitoring checklists, and individual writing conferences.
- The evaluations and assessment are authentic in that students are evaluated using rubrics applied to products they actually create.
- The unit content is aligned with curricular (learning) standards.

DESIGNING DAILY LESSONS FROM UNIT ACTIVITIES

When developing individual lessons from unit plans consistent with the UDL framework, the following assumptions should be acknowledged:

1. Classrooms today are both culturally and academically diverse.
2. Students in classrooms are heterogeneously grouped.
3. Teachers vary widely in their approach to pedagogy. Many may use direct instruction in which presentations are carefully scripted and controlled. Others may follow constructivist notions of teaching that emphasize the discovery of meaning through shared interaction.
4. Teachers vary widely in their approach to lesson planning; some opt for developing daily lesson plans while others are more comfortable with resource unit development.
5. Both explicit and implicit approaches have advantages in classrooms using UDL. These advantages often depend on students' particular needs, abilities, and levels.

Heterogeneous classrooms contain high-, average-, and low-achieving students and also students with disabilities (Lenz, 1993). The advantage of this inquiry- and project-based unit is that it gives students options to demonstrate what they know and what they can do. It also encourages all students to go beyond what is required and to carry what they have learned into the future through active involvement and life-long learning. Consequently, the unit can sustain the interests and motivation of the most talented and at the same time target instruction on students who need the most support.

However, it should be understood that input from special education and related services personnel is critical to make this unit and lesson planning engage students with and without disabilities. As teachers

TABLE 1   Thematic Unit: "Endangered Species: Causes and Ways to Address Threats to Their Survival"

This unit was designed to be taught over the course of several weeks and contains four phases. Phase I establishes purpose and motivation through exploration. Phase II actively involves the student by providing experiences that make the topic personally relevant. Phase III helps students to construct meaning to achieve understanding, and Phase IV reaches closure through a process of debriefing, concluding, and culminating.

	Unit Plan	Considerations during Teacher Collaboration in Planning for Universal Design for Learning
Goals	Students will develop awareness of both natural and man-made causes that impede endangered species of our world. Students will use this knowledge to convince human forces to change. Guiding questions: 1. Who or what is responsible for the endangerment of various plant and animal species throughout our world? What problems have remained consistent over time? 2. What global changes can be made to protect the vulnerable animals at risk of extinction? 3. How much control do we really have? 4. What ways can we make ourselves heard? 5. Where do we go from here?	Evaluate: Define instructional goal(s) for all learners, separating the means from the goal & aligning the lesson to the standard(s).

Materials	Resources:
	• Rain Forest Rap–video by World Wildlife Fund
	• The Great Kapok Tree by Lynne Cherry
	• Local or national newspaper clippings about animals in danger of extinction
	• Ranger Rick magazines, Nature Conservancy and Sierra Club newsletters
	• Houghton Mifflin Grade 5 Reading Anthology Theme Unit on "Operation Wildlife"
		Consider multiple means of access:
		• Make available digitized texts and resource materials, students make accessible with text information in format different from print using:
		  – Text-to-speech
		  – Enlarged font, greater color contrasts, etc.
		  – Enhanced graphics
		  – Alternative tags
		• Assure that video is available with captioned soundtrack for

• Internet resources such as World Wildlife Fund (wwf.com) for current information on endangered species throughout the world
• Other research resources: Encyclopedias on CD, nonfiction picture books of endangered animals
• "Rain Forest Live" unit sponsored by Ocean Challenge, Inc.
 	
Tools:
• Inspiration software by Tom Snyder
• Projection unit for computer on classroom screen
• Computers with word processing software
• Pens, pencils
	• Access newspapers/journals/magazines electronically available.
	• Assistive technology devices as necessary.
	  – Toggle switches
	  – Pointers
	  – Response recording
	  – Keyboarding alternatives

Procedures		
Phase 1	*Introduction: Purpose, Motivation, Exploration, Gathering* • The unit is introduced to the whole class using oral presentation. • Focus students' attention on the purpose of the lesson. • Motivate student interest. • Offer exploration of the topic. • Emphasize information gathering as a foundation for application. *Thinking Cap Question (local term used to engage children in reflective thinking):* Can we be optimistic about the situation in our rain forests today? Why or why not? *Activity 1* Students view the video *Rain Forest Rap*, by World Wildlife Fund, includes footage of rain forest either being burned or cut down. When left alone, the rain forest is thriving, it is home to hundreds and thousands of species. A six-minute clip, with musical interlude, a rap song about the tropical rain forest, offers optimism as more people become aware and proactive.	• Student engagement can be optimized with the use of graphic organizers as visual aids. • Consider prior knowledge students bring to the unit (e.g., rain forest, endangered, habitat, species). • Identify students for whom it is appropriate to pre-teach concepts if not covered in previous units. • Consider supports for listening and hearing during lecture presentation. • Universally designed videos are closed-captioned and verbally described to benefit a full range of students including visually and hearing impaired children. • Provide scaffolds with note-taking devices to assist students in recalling important information. • Offer scaffolds such as pre-video questioning for learners to hear or see for specific information during the viewing.

TABLE 1 Thematic Unit: "Endangered Species: Causes and Ways to Address Threats to Their Survival"

Unit Plan	Considerations during Teacher Collaboration in Planning for Universal Design for Learning
Activity 2 Teacher and students discuss reactions, concerns, and feelings about what was learned from the video. Lead a discussion regarding why animals are endangered (e.g., loss of habitat) and add to the K-W-L chart "Why Animals are Endangered."	• Positioning of students in front of the display screen to optimize viewing for students with low vision or hearing impairments in need of speech reading/sign language. • Positioning to prompt students with attention issues. • K-W-L charts help children be focused, organized, & engaged. • Some students may require individual charts to follow the flow of group problem solving and discussion.
Activity 3 Teacher reads aloud the story *The Great Kapok Tree*, by Lynne Cherry. Children pay attention to the various and numerous kinds of animals, plants, and insects that are indigenous to the tropical rain forest. Ask children to choose one animal and respond to the *Thinking Cap Question* in writing: "If you were an animal in this forest and had the opportunity to give the story character Senhor a message, what would you say?" Option for students to share their messages with the class.	• Class "read aloud" provides students with a model of oral fluency and prompts students with comprehension difficulties to listen with purpose. • Provide options for creating different responses to question (e.g., screen readers, voice recognition) to support this activity. • Students with written or expressive language difficulties could note message using a range of modes (e.g., PowerPoint and synthesized speech).
Activity 4 From a collection of sources (Scholastic newspapers, *Boston Globe* articles, and *Nature Conservancy/Sierra Club* newsletters), the teacher will share information about animals that are extinct or endangered, and those returning to the wild. Consider jigsaw cooperative groups of four, so each group will become expert storytellers of one animal's fate or fortune.	• Make available a broad selection of articles in digital format for students with disabilities. • The formation of expert cooperative groups requires a distribution of roles within each group to examine the literature & develop a story to tell about their particular animal. • Students cooperate to study available resources and gather information (photos, drawings, and text).

Activity 5 Introduce "Operation Wildlife," a unit in anthology book that looks at three success stories of animals endangered by human intervention (harbor seal, polar bear cub, and pelican). • Read each story. • Add to K-W-L chart. • Begin a new graphic organizer with three columns: (1) Animal that is endangered, (2) Why it is endangered, (3) Why people can do to help. • Indicate where animal lives: (1) land, (2) sea, and (3) air. • Research each section in conjunction with animal habitat.	• If the anthology book were digitized, it could be accessed using multiple formats (e.g., font size, contrasts, TTS). • Content of text could be enhanced using outlines & concept maps. • Offer supports during independent reading, decoding, fluency, and comprehension. • Cooperative reading groups could share ideas and skills in use of tools and accommodations. • Provide supports for K-W-L chart use and completion. • Consider supports/tools to support making graphic organizer. • Provide supports and assistance in researching animal habitat.
Activity 6 Provide a current list of endangered animals from the WWF Web site. • Students choose several animals from list of interest. • Student selects an animal to explore for remainder of unit. (Consider a unique animal for each child so collectively, the class studies variety of endangered species.)	• Determine needed supports when moving into this more independent phase of the unit. • Review the K-W-L charts and have students make their animal selection. • Determine need for access tools. • Working in pairs may help some students with organizational challenges. • Scaffold decisionmaking. • Provide prompts to remind students of animal choice.
Activity 7 Students develop a series of questions about their animal as a guide for research to be conducted.	• Questions may be recorded using a variety of writing or voice recording alternatives. • Provide guidelines: number/type of question (how, what, where). • Scaffold question development. • Provide multiple means of recording questions (writing, word processing, audio recording). • Consider use of Inspiration software to create concept maps to aid students in question generating. (Inspiration software is a tool that can create word webs, mind maps, and other graphic organizers to help organize thinking.)

TABLE 1   Thematic Unit: "Endangered Species: Causes and Ways to Address Threats to Their Survival"

Unit Plan	Considerations during Teacher Collaboration in Planning for Universal Design for Learning
Activity 8 "Class, brainstorm the different possible categories in which the questions could fit." • Students record questions. • Examine the lists and abstract common characteristics. • Organize lists (folders, files, bins, graphic organizer). • Categories could be located in subfolders. • Create a poster to depict categories of endangered animals. *Thinking Cap Question:* What issues contribute most to the endangerment of your particular endangered species?	• Students with print disabilities could listen to a rapid reading of questions and then be asked to think about what questions were similar and what questions were different. • Consider multiple methods to record and "file" questions. • Access using various input/output combinations. • Brainstorming template in Inspiration could also be used during the whole class discussion. • Consider multiple methods for poster creation. • Scaffold poster development.
Activity 9 Research and explore: • Students find facts and information about animal in available resources (may recommend minimum number of resources). • Record findings under the appropriate category. • Form the basis for categorization.	• Assure that research resources are accessible. • Support with scaffolds and tools as students locate facts and information, record, and categorize. • Make available resources such as the Internet, encyclopedia books or CDs, newspapers and magazines. • Scaffold categorizing activities. • Consider multiple means of expression to record facts/information.
Activity 10 Outlining: • Demonstrate skill of outlining (usually new to 5th grade). • Recommended theme book *Peregrine Falcons*. • Provide multiple examples and tools (e.g., word processor, chalkboard, paper, graphic organizers).	• Access issues to "view" teacher demonstrations must be considered. • The program Inspiration could be helpful for some children that benefit from alternative approaches to outlining. Inspiration can provide both linear and graphical outlines of the same information. • Monitor student behavior; ask frequent questions about strategy or procedures during demonstrations.

Phase II		
	Experience: Active Involvement and Personal Relevance—Application and Further Analysis Actively involve students and encourage them to raise concerns, consider issues, develop questions, or seek solutions using active participation and interactive processing.	• Monitor to assure engagement in activities. • Provide multiple means to respond and express ideas and information about the topic.
	Activity 11 Develop an awareness of words that persuade: • Demonstrate meaning of persuasive and not persuasive language. • Students identify sentences that use persuasive language, e.g. "People searching for oil and minerals threaten to destroy the polar bear's environment," or "People searching for oil and minerals are changing the polar bear's environment."	• Provide multiple means of representation when presenting sentences or words. • Consider starting exercise with single words and moving to sentence level. • Scaffold from easy to more difficult the discrimination between sentences. • Consider more than two sentences to make task more complex; make less complex by providing simpler sentence structure.
	Activity 12 Students apply use of persuasive language in communications: • Students brainstorm words in the English language that are persuasive, especially action words. • Teacher introduces concept of bias in writing. • Individual students record word list in their research folder.	• Scaffold with examples/counter-examples of persuasive words • Consider computer software Inspiration to use as a tool to record brainstorming. • Offer multiple means for students to record and store their lists of persuasive words. • Provide background language information, i.e., action words, bias, persuasive.

TABLE 1 Thematic Unit: "Endangered Species: Causes and Ways to Address Threats to Their Survival"

Unit Plan	Considerations during Teacher Collaboration in Planning for Universal Design for Learning
Activity 13 • Present facts from both sides of the issue of "Mountain Lion vs. Cattle Rancher," e.g., "Mountain lions sometimes kill sheep and cattle that belong to ranchers" vs. "People are building housing developments, ranches, and highways on land that once was the mountain lion's habitat." • Students work independently to determine which side they support most strongly and write a persuasive paragraph defending their reasoning. • Students representing the two sides of the issue will meet separately and collaboratively to build their arguments, in preparation for a debate. • Students conduct mock debate to practice persuasive skills. • Class comment on degree of persuasiveness, encourage ideas for improvement. • Add this activity product to student folders.	• The task requires combining facts/issues with persuasive language maintained in each student's folder. • Consider compare/contrast graphic organizer to present activity. • Consider need for scaffolding activity in writing. • Consider alternative presentation structures for independent activity. • Support/encourage students to communicate opinions with group. • Demonstrate strategy to create persuasive paragraph. • Support collaboration which is needed to identify and list common views. • Consider scaffolding procedures to organize common views. • Support participation in groups and debate. • Provide options for multiple means of expression in both activities. • Encourage help among team members.

Activity 14
Endangered Species Ongoing/Long-Term Writing Process Project
• Students prepare introductions from three different points of view, e.g., from the animal itself, a scientist, a hunter, another animal, or their own idea. Students will demonstrate critical thinking using persuasive writing style.
• Assign students to working pairs.
• Students share leads with a partner and choose one.
• Students integrate critical elements into their writing such as the behavior of the animal, threats to its survival, and ways man can intervene to protect it.
• Students choose from categories in resource files and decide placement in their story: Beginning, Middle, or End.
	• Apply strategies from peer mediated instruction and interventions for this activity.
	• Provide scaffolds with graphic organizers or writing templates to prompt components of persuasive writing.
	• Provide alternative means of expression in addition to traditional paper and pencil tools, such as word processing, electronic presentation, oral presentation, video, etc.
	• Scaffold thinking and writing with a series of prompting questions:
	  – What type of behaviors does your animal exhibit?
	  – What is being done to help your animal?
	  – Are there products made from this endangered species?
	  – What words describe your feelings about this animal?

Phase III		
	Experience: Construction of Meaning: Understanding Whole Class and Individual Activities • The students will individually choose one of the four options that are presented here for application, synthesis and evaluation. • Provide students with the opportunity to construct meaning from knowledge and experience. Emphasize critical and creative thinking.	• Provide students with options for responding, reacting, demonstrating knowledge. • Options to engage that promote self-determination and focus attention. • Provide supports for decisionmaking and options selection.

	Option 1: Persuasive Commercial with Artistic Expression
	Create a persuasive commercial containing the following elements:
	• A written script from the point of view of the animal containing:
	  – Information about the animal itself
	  – Reasons for its risk of extinction
	  – Ways to prevent extinction or to help save the animal
	• Script must be persuasive, with appropriate language so that viewers commit to efforts.
	• Be prepared to answer questions; memorize the script in order to be videotaped, and plan to be dressed as selected animal.
	
	Artistic Expression:
	Choose one idea brainstormed in class to present during videotaping.
		• Provide structures for demonstrating knowledge in a persuasive structure and to prepare learners for audience. For example:
		  – Be prepared to answer questions
		  – Memorize the script in order to be videotaped
		  – Plan to be dressed as your animal
		• Consider options for presentation mode. Traditionally, we think of standing in front of the class and speaking. Options:
		  – Computer slide presentation
		  – Make and show video
		  – Create a poster session
		• Provide scaffolding of persuasive presentation components.
		  – State position
		  – Present facts and opinions to support position
		  – Present alternate arguments
		  – Argue why alternate positions are not good
		  – Concluding statement of position

	Option 2: Create a Set and Role Play
	Put on a skit complete with background.
	• Create a background set, props, etc. to depict an accurate image of your endangered animal in its habitat.
	• Emphasize unique characteristics (beyond its being "cute").
	• Describe importance in our ecosystem.
	• Demonstrate problems facing this animal.
	• Address how enthusiasts can join the cause.
	• Provide specific information on how to protect animal.
	• Invite classmates to play a part in production.
	• Skit to be word processed so that work may be reviewed.
		• Provide options for methods to create materials to enhance presentation:
		  – Draw
		  – Computer images
		  – Collage
		  – Projected image versus paper
		• Provide scaffolds for students to prepare a play set.
		• Provide scaffolds to put on a play/skit.
		• Consider options for skit script other than word processing (e.g., recorded, concept map, drawings).

TABLE I   Thematic Unit: "Endangered Species: Causes and Ways to Address Threats to Their Survival"

Unit Plan	Considerations during Teacher Collaboration in Planning for Universal Design for Learning
Option 3: Write a Letter to a Congressional Representative Research information on your animal in great detail. Write a persuasive (word processed) business letter to your congressional representative. • Report number of endangered species left compared to how many there used to be. • Report where are they located geographically. • Determine if they are safe in some areas and not in others. • Report what protection programs are in place, if any. • Determine if programs are working and report if they need additional attention or revision. • Based on estimates of their disappearance rate, project the population changes for this animal in the next ten years. • Illustrate facts with detailed graphic presentation. • Convince your congressional representative to save your endangered animal.	• Provide alternate means by which students could communicate with authorities (e.g., recording, concept map, electronic letter). • Scaffold task with prompts for critical elements. • Create rubric using the steps of option as a structure. • Scaffold and support estimation. • Consider using graphics programs such as Tabletop, Sr., or The Graph Club. • Consider template for persuasive letter writing. • Provide alternate means for graphic representation of facts.
Option 4: Create a Brochure about Your Animal Create a brochure that includes facts about your animal. Options include: • List of identifying characteristics • World map showing regions it inhabits • Description of behavior • Threats to survival • Include illustrations Get others to join and support your efforts. Options include: • Specific ways individuals can help	• Provide options for means of expression: word processing, computer, paper, audio, video, etc. • Scaffold how to obtain resources from previous work. • Multiple means for obtaining and displaying illustrations. • Clarify, assist, set procedure to select options for items included in brochure.

	• Addresses of organizations • Information on "adopting" the animal, if applicable • Make brochure attractive to capture attention	• Effective strategies include: open discussion, small group processing, written comments, student presentations, Q/A discussion, "what-if" questions, and written evaluation. Options for display of projects: • School library • Endangered Species Awareness breakfast for families • Student body • Showcase brochures • Show the persuasive commercials • Display graphs and letters (and any responses) to representatives • Skit backdrops can form display
Phase IV	*Closure: Debrief, Conclude, Culminate* Teacher, complete the objectives of lesson and relate findings to concepts. Debrief: • Students will complete the K-W-L chart in a whole-class discussion. • Students will openly discuss satisfaction about progress our world is making in helping endangered species to survive. Conclude: • Facilitate students' sharing of products and results, drawing conclusions about concepts, or developing new problems to study. • As visitors view the displays, they may opt to hear non-fiction stories. The children will read their book to listeners. • Opportunities to pair up with a student from another class will be provided to give students the opportunity to read before a live audience. Culminate: • Offer opportunity to do creative, independent activities, extending knowledge into creative production. • Students establish long-term commitments to endangered animals and seek opportunities to remain involved. • Discuss/brainstorm ways students could continue learning. • Introduce "Rain Forest Live," by Ocean Challenge, Inc. Link to the School for Field Studies (SFS) Center for Rain Forest Studies in Queensland, Australia. Newsletter about discoveries and new information. Students may write questions at any time throughout the year.	

FIGURE 1 *Template for Collaborative Planning with UDL*

Lesson Planning Form

Unit: _____ Phase: _____ Lesson: _____

Lesson Objective(s): _____

Materials	Evaluation

Accommodations Available	UDL Features

Pyramid   Agenda

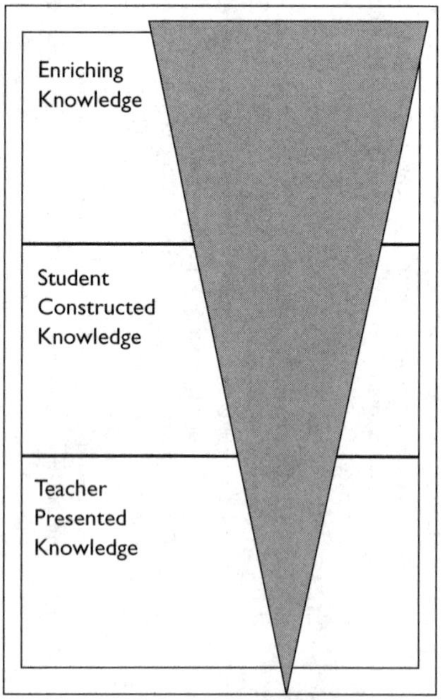

Enriching
Knowledge

Student
Constructed
Knowledge

Teacher
Presented
Knowledge

collaborate, they are able to assess the classroom profile with regard to the level of prior knowledge and requisite skill requirements. They can help with the identification of accommodations that do not substantially alter the outcomes or standards. They can also help to identify modifications that maximize the child's participation in the general curriculum.

Through collaboration, school-based teams may find it helpful to employ a UDL lesson design template presented at the end of this report. This template is intended to facilitate teacher planning for accessing the general curriculum. It is modified from the "planning pyramid" used in various forms by scholars and researchers in instructional design (Lenz et al., 1995; Vaughn et al., 2000). This particular template allows the collaborative planning team to specify the UDL features of the lesson, along with the appropriate accommodations specified in the child's IEP. The inverted pyramid allows the team to specify instructional objectives to be taught explicitly (see Figure 1). At the same time, the other two levels of the pyramid allow the team to raise expectations as to what the student can accomplish with appropriate supports, accommodations, and UDL features.

CONCLUSION

Access to the general curriculum for all students, including students with disabilities, is now a national priority. The UDL unit herein illustrates one approach in translating research and theory into practice. Universal Design for Learning can and does work. The principal means for teacher planning and instructional decisionmaking is collaboration. The educational emphasis now focuses on improving student results through the attainment of standards and the raising of expectations for students with disabilities. Efforts to design instruction that include supports and multiple means of representation, response, and expression for a range of students will create greater access for students and result in greater student outcomes. Today, teams of special and general educators are increasingly called upon to collaborate and create solutions for meeting the educational needs of diverse learners. UDL thus serves as a framework for facilitating teaching practices.

REFERENCES

Carlberg, C., & Kavale, K. A. (1980). The efficacy of special versus regular class placement for exceptional children: A meta-analysis. *Journal of Special Education, 14*, 295–309.

Carr, T., & Jitendra, A. K. (2000). Using hypermedia and multimedia to promote project-based learning of at-risk high school students. *Intervention in School and Clinic, 36*(1), 40–45.

Cegalka, P. (1995). An overview of effective education for students with learning problems. In P. T. Cegelka & W. H. Berdine (Eds.), *Effective instruction for students with learning difficulties* (pp. 1–18). Boston: Allyn & Bacon.

Dolan, R. P., & Hall, T. E. (2001). Universal Design for Learning: Implications for large-scale assessment. *IDA Perspectives, 27*(4), 22–25.

Eisner, E. H. (2001). What does it mean to say a school is doing well. *Phi Delta Kappan, 82*, 367–373.

Friend, M. (2000a). Myths and misunderstandings about professional collaboration. *Remedial and Special Education, 21*, 130–141.

Friend, M. (2000b). *Interactions: Collaborative skills for school professionals.* New York: Addison Wesley Longman.

Laffey, J., Tupper, T., Musser, D., & Wedman, J. (1998). A computer-mediated support system for project-based learning. *Educational Technology Research and Development, 46*(1), 73–86.

Lenz, B. K. (1993). *The course planning routine: A guide for inclusive planning.* Lawrence: University of Kansas Center for Research on Learning.

Lenz, B. K., Shumaker, J., Deshler, D., Vaughn, S., Schumm, J., & Fuchs, D. (1995). *Planning for academic diversity in America's classrooms: Windows on reality, research, change, and practice.* Lawrence: University of Kansas Center for Research on Learning.

O'Shea, D. J., & O'Shea, L. J. (1997). Collaboration and school reform: A twenty-first century perspective. *Journal of Learning Disabilities, 30*, 449–462.

Pugach, M. C., & Johnson, L. J. (1995). *Collaborative practitioners, collaborative schools.* Denver: Love.

Radencich, M. C., & McKay, L. J. (Eds.). (1995). *Flexible grouping for literacy in the elementary grade.* Boston: Allyn & Bacon.

Rose, D., & Meyer, A. (2000). Universal design for individual differences. *Educational Leadership, 58*(3), 39–43.

Rose, D. H., & Meyer, A. (2002). *Teaching every student in the digital age: Universal Design for Learning.* Alexandria, VA: ASCD.

Rumberger, R. W., & Thomas, S. L. (2000). The distribution of dropout and turnover rates among urban and suburban high schools. *Sociology of Education, 73*(1), 39–69.

Taggart, G. L., Phifer, S. J., Nixon, J. A., & Wood, M. (Eds.). (1998). *Rubrics: A handbook for construction and use.* Lancaster, PA: Technomic.

Thurlow, M. L. (2000). Standards-based reform and students with disabilities: Reflections on a decade of change. *Focus on Exceptional Children, 33*(3), 1–16.

Tomlinson, C. A., & Allan, S. D. (2000). *Leadership for differentiating schools and classrooms.* Alexandria, VA: ASCD.

U.S. Department of Education. (1999). *The twenty-first annual report to Congress on the implementation of the Individuals with Disabilities Education Act.* Washington, DC: U.S. Government Printing Office.

U.S. Department of Education. (2000). *The condition of education, 2000.* Washington, DC: National Center for Education Statistics.

Valdez, K., Williamson, B., & Wagner, M. (1990). *The national longitudinal study of special education students: Statistical almanac* (Vol. 1). Menlo Park, CA: SRI.

Vaughn, S., Bos, C. S., & Schumm, J. S. (2000). *Teaching exceptional, diverse, and at-risk students in the general education classroom.* Boston: Allyn & Bacon.

Walther-Thomas, C., Korinek, L., McLaughlin, V. L., & Williams, B. T. (2000). *Collaboration for inclusive education: Developing successful programs.* Boston: Allyn & Bacon.

The authors wish to thank Tracey Hall for her invaluable contributions in editing and revising this paper.

This report was first published as Jackson, R., & Harper, K. (2001). *Teacher planning and the Universal Design for Learning environments.* Peabody, MA: National Center on Accessing the General Curriculum. It has been revised and edited for this volume. The content of this report was developed pursuant to Cooperative Agreement #H324H990004 under CFDA 84.324H between CAST and the Office of Special Education Programs, U.S. Department of Education. However, the opinions expressed herein do not necessarily reflect the position or policy of the U.S. Department of Education or the Office of Special Education Programs, and no endorsement by that office should be inferred.

CHAPTER FIVE

Teaching for Accessibility: Effective Practices, Classroom Barriers

RICHARD JACKSON, KELLY HARPER,
AND JANNA JACKSON

C hanges in federal law have opened up great opportunities for students with disabilities by mandating their access, participation, and progress in the general education curriculum. However, these opportunities have been difficult to realize, in part due to the persistence of predominantly print-based curricula, suitable perhaps to most learners but a barrier to significant numbers. Increasingly, general education classrooms will undergo rapid changes with the introduction of new forms of media, such as digital text, digital images, digital audio, digital video, digital multimedia, and networked environments (Dolan & Hall, 2001; Rose & Meyer, 2000, 2002).

A digital curriculum holds the promise of increased flexibility and the capacity to develop instructional goals, methods, materials, and assessments that accommodate students' diverse strengths and needs and promote genuine learning (Rose & Meyer, 2002). As accessible digital media become ubiquitous in schools and classrooms, the National Center on Accessing the General Curriculum (NCAC) envisions collaborative teams of general educators, special educators, and other school personnel able to function with increased efficiency, less stress, and greater effectiveness. These educators can raise expectations and improve results for all students by providing greater access to the curriculum. To maximize the likelihood that future curriculum will be accessible, interactive, and promote student progress, NCAC suggests using Universal Design for Learning (UDL) as a blueprint (Rose & Meyer, 2002).

Based on new insights from brain research and new understandings about the complexities of individual differences, UDL advances three guiding principles for the design of learning opportunities (Rose & Meyer, 2000, 2002):

1. Provide multiple, flexible methods of presentation in order to support diverse recognition networks. For example, the content of a lesson on endangered species could be presented as printed text, text in digital format (with an option for text-to-speech, braille, and variable display formats), images, video, or as an online simulation.
2. Provide multiple, flexible methods of expression and apprenticeship in order to support diverse strategic networks. For example, when testing understanding of the characteristics of mammals, a teacher could offer flexible options for demonstrating knowledge or skill, including answering multiple-choice questions, composing an essay, selecting critical features from a picture series, composing a scrapbook of mammalian exemplars, or giving an oral presentation.
3. Provide multiple, flexible options for engagement in order to support diverse affective networks. For example, a lesson about state government could allow the students to select a state of interest to them and learn about the state's government by reading, searching the Web, interviewing government officials, etc. Additionally, for some learners, an extrinsic motivation structure could support their affective networks, much like the system of paychecks does for working adults.

Developments in digital media and UDL cannot move ahead without an understanding of the related contexts of schools and classrooms. With the intent of contributing to such an understanding, this chapter summarizes the results of a review of the research literature from 1996 to 2001 concerning barriers that impede student access to the general curriculum and the support structures and teaching practices that hold particular promise for improving access for students who have high-incidence disabilities.

In recent years, the U.S. Department of Education, through its Office of Special Education Programs (OSEP), has supported numerous efforts to examine the knowledge base in special education and identify practices that are supported by the research literature. The results of these efforts have been disseminated through a host of professional publications in the form of meta-analyses, research syntheses, state-of-the-art reports, and various seminal works by recognized leaders in the field. This review encompasses works published between 1996 and 2001 that address curriculum barriers and teaching practices in K–12 schools. The authors acknowledge, however, that without more foundational research predating 1996, the field would not be where it is at this time (e.g., Fuchs & Fuchs, 1994; Lipsky & Gartner, 1997; Stainback & Stainback, 1992; Stainback, Stainback, & Forest, 1989).

BARRIERS LIMITING ACCESS TO THE GENERAL CURRICULUM

Teachers employ a variety of instructional methods in classrooms. Many of these methods are well grounded in an educational pedagogy and constitute validated classroom practices. Moreover, these teaching practices are most often applied for the intended purpose of producing the best possible results. However, classroom research indicates that within and outside classrooms, both students and teachers face a number of barriers that block access to and impede progress in the general education curriculum. These barriers touch on practical issues, such as physical and instructional access, as well as pedagogical theory. The following sections address the barriers most frequently noted in the literature.

Differing Interpretations of Inclusion

The laws and regulations requiring access to the general curriculum for all students have resulted in a trend toward inclusion. A problematic and fundamental starting point for the discussion of curriculum barriers is that the term "inclusion" has many interpretations (e.g., Fuchs & Fuchs, 1994; Hewitt, 1999; Kauffman & Hallahan, 1995; Stainback & Stainback, 1992; Will, 1986). Some teachers view inclusion as dichotomous teaching—teaching special needs students and general education students in the same classroom but at different times, in different spaces, and with different lessons. Many would argue that this is as exclusive as teaching students with disabilities in a separate classroom. In other adaptations of inclusion, the school simply provides a place for special needs students among their peers without variation of instruction.

This kind of whole-class instruction without individualization frequently presents problems for learners with disabilities (Elbaum, Vaughn, Hughes, & Watson-Moody, 1999). For example, Moody, Vaughn, Hughes, and Fischer (2000) reported that most teachers taught reading much like they were instructing a whole class of students with the same abilities. These teachers provided little instruction that addressed word recognition or specific reading comprehension strategies for the students who were less proficient, including students with disabilities.

Supporters of full inclusion propose that all students should be educated in the general education classroom, but overemphasis on full inclusion "runs the risk of over-generalizing an ideology quite detached from the realities of classrooms" (Chow, Blais, & Hemingway, 1999, p. 464). Chow et al. question whether some advocates of full inclusion are respecting the nature and severity of disabilities or possibly seizing a "golden opportunity" to cut back on costly special education services.

The NCAC has adapted the definition of inclusion introduced by York and Tundidor (1995). Inclusion means that students with disabilities are (a) attending the same schools as siblings and neighbors, (b) have membership in general education classrooms with age-appropriate peers, (c) have individualized, relevant learning objectives, and (d) are provided with the means to access classroom curriculum materials. Defined as such, inclusion leads to a greater number of students participating in the general education classroom. However they define inclusion, teachers today are increasingly confronted with the expectation that they must meet the needs of all learners.

Curriculum Standards and Availability

Meeting every student's needs becomes a challenge in general education classrooms where students with disabilities are integrated to the fullest extent possible. Moody et al. (2000) note that current reform movements are stressing higher, more specific, and more inflexible academic performance requirements. The need to align curriculum and instruction more carefully with standards to improve academic achievement as measured by broad-scale assessment systems leaves less time and opportunity for teachers to accommodate and adapt instruction for students with disabilities (Deschenes, Cuban, & Tyack, 2001; King-Sears & Cummings, 1996; Klingner & Vaughn, 1999). King-Sears (1997) questioned the extent to which general educators can differentiate instruction. Unfortunately, adaptations to meet all students' needs are not feasible given the other demands placed on teachers. The overall cultures in schools (Mamlin, 1999) and teachers' unfamiliarity with the standards-based reform movement (Maccini & Gagnon, 2000) are also not particularly conducive to the consideration of all learners. Nolet and McLaughlin (2000) state that for many special education teachers, access to the general education curriculum is more rhetorical than practical. Moreover, they provide case study examples of general education teachers and administrators who ask what it means to provide access to the general education curriculum and "why should they want to do this?" (p. 9). Clearly, meeting all students' needs whenever possible in the general education setting is a challenge that must be carefully addressed in all academic settings, as teachers and schools work to comply with standards-based reforms and legal requirements.

Increased Practitioner Responsibilities

The obligation to meet the needs of individual students creates challenges for all teachers but particularly for those with large classes. The large caseloads carried by teachers in diverse classroom settings prevent them from individualizing instruction (Moody et al., 2000). As teachers' responsibilities continue to grow, they are nevertheless increasingly called on to assess and accommodate every student's individual approach to learning (Schumm, Vaughn, Gordon, & Rothlein, 1994; Schumm et al., 1995).

Inevitably, both general and special educators must adjust to taking on additional classroom responsibilities. They must assume new roles, develop new competencies, and become more aware of the philosophy and process of inclusion (Benner, 1998; Chow et al., 1999; Pugach & Johnson, 1995). These new roles include, but are not limited to, assessing and accommodating individual academic, intellectual, and emotional needs. Students must be prepared for participation in standards-based assessments, and teachers must adjust the curriculum and instructional approach accordingly. Teachers must also understand how to identify and access resources and support systems and further recognize the importance of positive attitudes toward students with disabilities (Chow et al., 1999). All of these expectations are set in a context of increasing concern with having all students meet the same standards through broad-scale assessment systems.

Practitioner Attitudes toward Shifting Roles and Expectations

As responsibilities expand and expectations increase, teachers' attitudes toward challenges vary. Negative attitudes can emerge among special educators (Cook, Semmel, & Gerber, 1999) when their validated practices do not transfer easily to general education classrooms (Chow et al., 1999). When special educators are unfamiliar with the general education structure and curriculum, the coordination of special and general education teacher roles and responsibilities is made all the more problematic (Nolet & McLaughlin, 2000). Such unfamiliarity may make special educators reluctant to embrace the philosophy of inclusion (Hewitt, 1999). Moreover, when working in the general education classroom, special education teachers are noted in the research to, in some cases, be taking on the role of an instructional aide rather than that of a fully qualified teacher. This lack of parity or mutuality provokes ill feelings about the situation. Additionally, this structure leaves special education teachers with less time for special education students (Hewitt, 1999). Klingner and Vaughn (1999) observe that these constraints can ultimately inhibit progress for students with learning disabilities. In fact, King-Sears (1997) states that inclusive practices may limit students with learning disabilities to "just getting by" from day to day.

Negative attitudes also develop among general practitioners, reflecting their frustration with systemic obstacles to effective instruction and inclusion. Many of the reviewed studies examined the factors that make general education teachers more or less receptive to inclusion, finding that the more teachers feel overworked and overwhelmed with trying to meet students' individual needs, the more resistant they become to inclusion (Soodak, Podell, & Lehman, 1998). Soodak et al. found that teachers are more receptive to those with physical disabilities because the disabilities are seen as involuntary. In contrast, students with cognitive and behavior disorders may be viewed, inappropriately, as "blamable."

Thus, attitudinal shifts on the part of both special and general educators need to occur in order for curriculum access to be successful. Clearly, there is need for professional development that would help teachers from both special and general education to clarify roles, responsibilities, and beliefs about the inclusion of students with disabilities in general education classrooms. Teachers need time to learn new skills, but more importantly they need the opportunity to identify mutual and complementary skills. They need to feel empowered so that all teachers come to this new, shared responsibility from a stance of real purpose and commitment.

Issues of Time, Skills, and Training

Some of the barriers that have been identified appear to be beyond the classroom level, relating to the resources needed by general educators to increase curriculum access. General education teachers frequently report having inadequate training, time, and personnel resources for meeting the needs of students with disabilities (Scruggs & Mastropieri, 1996a). This is not surprising, given that many states and teacher-training programs do not require general education majors to enroll in even a single class with a focus on students with disabilities. Neither preservice nor in-service teacher-preparation programs emphasize the preparation of general education teachers for working with the diversity of students currently enrolled in general education classrooms (Nolet & McLaughlin, 2000; Schumm et al., 1994). The outcome of these current training practices is that many teachers enter the workforce with no formal education regarding students with disabilities. Consequently, they are largely unprepared to work with special needs populations (Hewitt, 1999). This is likely to affect the quality of education they can provide to students with disabilities and, secondarily, these students' access to curricula.

Teachers also report that insufficient time is available to plan, design adaptations, consult, and collaborate with special education teachers (Boon & Mastropieri, 1999; Dev & Scruggs, 1997; Scruggs & Mastropieri, 1996b). Teachers experience frustration with the lack of time to give students with learning disabilities what they need and may give up lunch periods to do so (Moody, Vaughn, Hughes, & Fischer, 2000). Thus, teacher planning and collaboration time is critical for the successful implementation of an inclusion model.

Teacher and Student Perceptions of Curriculum Adaptations

A frequent concern voiced by many general education teachers is that of "fairness." Adaptation may be necessary to meet the needs of all students. When presented with the same lesson, some students report that the pace of instruction is too fast and difficult, while others report that it is too slow and easy (Moody et al., 2000). Students who have difficulty keeping pace with the class often require instructional accommodations.

For example, some students with learning disabilities are greatly aided by tools such as spelling and grammar checkers to manage the writing process due to language difficulties or lack of knowledge in the writing process (DeLaPaz, 1999). Adapting the curriculum in such a manner may be perceived as giving students with disabilities an unfair advantage (Vaughn et al., 1996).

This perceived unfairness on the part of general education students may not itself be particularly problematic; research suggests that general education students do not interpret adaptations for students with disabilities as interfering with their own learning (Klingner & Vaughn, 1999). The real concern may rest with teachers, who in general place too much emphasis on the student as a problem (King-Sears, 1997). Universal Design for Learning turns this perception on its head by remedying curricular barriers to student access instead of seeing the student as the site of change.

POTENTIAL STRATEGIES FOR OVERCOMING BARRIERS

As illustrated throughout this chapter, there are numerous and significant barriers limiting student access to the curriculum. How might teachers and students overcome these barriers? To answer this question, we look again to the research literature and examine studies that report on current practices attempting to overcome these barriers. These practices include implementing systemic reform, clarifying instructional goals, and providing administrative support, teacher support, and equal opportunities for students. In addition to the research outlined below, more research is needed to assess the best ways to implement these support structures. Specifically, integrating UDL among these means of overcoming barriers is an area calling for more examination.

Systemic Reform

Overcoming barriers tied to federal, state, and local coordination calls for systemic educational reform. Osborne and DiMattia (1995) urge school officials to take a more active role in restructuring educational systems so that the integration of special and general education becomes more of a reality (Chow, Blais, & Hemingway, 1999). One approach important to consider is a "bottom-up" method of generating and implementing policy and providing the resources, conditions, and time necessary to make such an integration successful (Cook, Semmel, & Gerber, 1999). Additionally, the ownership for change should be from all levels—administrative, teacher, and parent (Osborne & DiMattia, 1995).

Instructional Goals

The key ingredient to effective instruction for all learners is instruction itself and not merely placement. The integration of students with disabilities in general education classrooms requires carefully targeted and skillfully guided instructional practice (Kuhn & Stahl, 1998). Targeted instruction for students with disabilities will involve both changes in curriculum and changes in pedagogy (Hewitt, 1999). In all cases, the focus needs to be on intensive, direct, and specially designed instruction (Moody, Vaughn, Hughes, & Fischer, 2000). Each of these ingredients has an impact on the objectives in teachers' lesson plans. Goals for instruction need to align with the instructional episode, including lesson introduction, teaching/learning activities, and lesson assessment.

One promising way to address every student's needs in the classroom is to assess students' "zone of proximal development (ZPD)" (Vygotsky, 1978). Vygotsky coined this phrase to describe "the distance between the actual developmental level as determined by independent problem-solving and the level of potential development as determined through problem-solving under adult guidance or in collaboration with more capable peers" (p. 86). Thus, teachers should encourage students to work toward accomplishments just beyond their current capacity. This is possible with UDL. *Universally designed instructional goals contain the following components: they are clearly stated, observable, measurable, separate from the means and performance criteria, and connected to the curriculum standards.* When goals are clearly stated and do not needlessly restrict means and performance criteria, students have the leeway to work within their ZPD and, consequently, a greater chance to make optimal progress.

Administrative Support

Administrators must be more aware and supportive of the needs of general and special education teachers working with students identified as having special needs. One proactive procedure by which this can be accomplished is for administrators to take a more active role in providing continuing in-service training for general education teachers. Additionally, by encouraging active collaboration between special and regular education teachers, administrators can make implementations of school change more successful (Pugach & Johnson, 1995). Administrators can foster collaboration by scheduling shared or common planning time between these educators. When all personnel establish and act upon the instructional goals, the needs of all students are better met (Snyder, 1999). Additional guidance regarding the benefits of administrative support can be found in the effective school and site-based management literature (Darling-Hammond, 1997; Meier, 1995; Wohlstetter & Mohrman, 1996).

Teacher Support

The integration of students with disabilities into general education classrooms can burden already overworked teachers with extra responsibilities. If support is not provided for these teachers, integration of diverse learners is almost certain to fail. Support can take the form of professional development, opportunities for collaboration, extra personnel, more time, and higher salaries (Pugach & Johnson, 1995). Snyder (1999) advises that "administrators and special educators need to be more aware and supportive of the needs of the general education teachers who are working with special education students" (p. 180). The more professional development in the area of special education, the more understanding teachers become of student needs and the more positive their attitudes toward general curriculum access (O'Shea, 1999). Professional development is highly instrumental in general education teachers being able to meet the needs of students with disabilities (Snyder, 1999), particularly because it introduces them to new instructional practices.

Systemic changes can also support teachers. Decreasing class size allows teachers to work individually with all students, especially those who have special needs. Collaboration and team teaching can greatly reduce apprehension about inclusion. Liberman, quoted by Snyder (1999), stated that inclusion "is like a wedding in which we, as special educators, have forgotten to invite the bride (general educators)" (p. 173). Snyder suggests that general educators need to be involved early and at all stages of planning in order to increase access to the general education curriculum.

Equal Opportunities for Students

"Equifinality," the assurance that all students have an equal opportunity to access education in an environment conducive to learning, can maximize individual development (Chow et al., 1999). Equifinality results when students reach the same outcomes whether their instruction occurs in an inclusive classroom or a substantially separate special class. Access to the general curriculum need not require full immersion in the regular classroom. Chow et al. (1999) stress that debate over inclusion may in the long run sacrifice the desire for the attainment of equal opportunity for the sake of equal treatment. They further advise that student voices should be considered as teachers make decisions about instructional routines (Vaughn, Bos, & Schumm, 2000). By adapting the curriculum and instruction to the needs of learners with disabilities instead of attempting to "fix" the student, barriers to equal learning opportunity can be eliminated.

Teachers incorporating the principles of UDL into their lesson plans can move toward this goal. Traditionally, curriculum followed a developmental skills progression in which students were not given the opportunity to write until they learned to read; they were not given the opportunity to solve problems until they learned to calculate. These practices were largely driven by the static nature of curriculum resources and efficiency models of grouping. Lessons that allow students to "read" using synthesized speech or discover problem-solving strategies by using a calculator bring more students into the activity, yielding improved and more equal results.

IMPLEMENTATION OF EFFECTIVE TEACHING PRACTICES FOR ACCESSING THE GENERAL CURRICULUM

Efforts to integrate students with disabilities into the least restrictive milieu promote improvements in self-concept, social awareness, and overall cognitive functioning. Chow et al. (1999) suggest that combining general education and special education techniques can provide the best of both worlds, benefiting all learners. They conclude that while some opponents of inclusion believe it is unrealistic and downright harmful to children, the literature has in many cases illuminated benefits. For example, Klingner and Vaughn's (1999) study found that most students did not perceive the instructional adaptations and accommodations to meet the special needs of selected students as problematic. In fact, the majority of students believed that these adaptations and accommodations could facilitate their own learning. Yet, Snyder (1999) and Mercer, Jordan, and Miller (1996) caution that inclusion is not necessarily the best approach for all students with disabilities. Forness, Kavale, Blum, and Lloyd (1997), as well as Mercer et al. (1996), express concern that research material in the area of inclusion is becoming dated and recommend further research.

Zigmond, Jenkins, Fuchs, and Fafard (1995) present the Vanderbilt Model Integration Project as an example of a comprehensive program incorporating an array of effective practices, and thus holding great promise for the future. The program increases the capacity of general education to accommodate student diversity, boosts meaningful participation, and improves the achievement outcomes of students with learning disabilities. These goals are achieved by relying on ongoing assessment, intensive instruction for students with learning disabilities, trans-environmental programming to increase the similarity between special and general education settings (instruction, motivational strategies, curriculum materials, expectations for classroom behavior), and frequent structured meetings between special and general education teachers.

Inherent in successful instructional methods is built-in flexibility that allows teachers to address the needs of a diverse student body. While some of the best practices are those that are tried and true, others are just now gaining popularity and merit further research.

COLLABORATION AMONG STAKEHOLDERS

All general education professionals, administrators, and parents of students with disabilities need to be involved in the conceptualization and implementation of increasing access to the general curriculum. Collaboration with a great deal of face-to-face communication and planning should be the foundation of all efforts to focus on the general curriculum. Collaboration among these groups can help to shape and realize the most appropriate learning environment for each student. For example, in working with students with behavior disorders, King-Sears (1997) recommends a proactive student behavior–management approach consistent across the school, along with frequent and positive communications with families and collegial teams that support individual teachers and students. Such an approach contributes to the success of responsible inclusion.

Involving all perspectives allows for the consideration of how the demands of schooling affect all students, not just students with learning problems. Preparing administrators and teachers before modifying practices and incorporating teacher input into meeting the needs of students with disabilities can pave the way for success (Mamlin, 1999). Miller, Brownell, and Smith (1999) also suggest strong administrative leadership with shared decisionmaking.

Parental Involvement

Instructional practices that promote meeting the needs of all learners in the general classroom can be further supported in the home environment. Involving parents in the education of their children and encouraging them to take an active role in their children's academic program maximizes learning time, builds students' self-esteem, and focuses resources for individualized instruction (Hewitt, 1999; Kauffman, 1993). One of the most obvious roles parents can take is to help students with supplemental instruction such as homework (Swanson, 1999). Regardless of the degree of involvement on the home front, communication between school and home is essential for progress (Nelson, Epstein, Bursuck, Jayanthi, & Sawyer (1998).

Teacher Collaboration

Teamwork among educators with no territorial attitude between general and special educators is also a constructive feature of successful curriculum access. Cooperative teaching and consultant services between general and special education teachers help move students at a successful pace academically, emotionally, and socially into the least restrictive environment (Cook et al., 1999). Together, general and special education teachers can offer a range of services rather than a continuum of placements (Barry, 1994). By using cooperative teaching, teachers develop the potential for transforming how concepts or skills may ordinarily be taught, what materials are used to support content, and how to apply methods and strategies (Hewitt, 1999)

An aspect of collaborative teaching that is most important, but also most neglected, is co-planning (Downing, Eichinger, & Williams, 1997; Hewitt, 1999; McLeskey, Henry, & Axelrod, 1999; O'Shea, 1999;

Salend & Duhaney, 1999). Common planning time enables more than just an opportunity to hammer out the nuts and bolts of instruction; it is a collaborative process, where teachers develop a shared vision. This shared vision actively involves educators in all steps of the change process, including adoption or initiation and implementation of strategies for effective instruction.

Managing a Self-Directed Learning Environment

Self-regulated strategies (goal-setting, self-instruction, self-monitoring) assist students in learning how to compose, plan, and revise their work. For example, Field and Hoffman (1994) propose a self-determination model for students. Van Reusen, Deshler, and Schumaker (1989) found that high school students with learning disabilities who were taught to self-advocate during their Individual Education Program (IEP) conferences contributed important and relevant information. Their input accounted for 86 percent of the goals on their IEPs.

Mastropieri, Scruggs, and Shiah (1991) compared the effect that different goal-setting conditions (self-set goals, assigned goals, and no goals) would have on 30 sixth-grade students with learning disabilities. Students in the self-set condition had to decide how many pages to complete for the day. These students performed higher than students in both the "assigned goals" and "no goals" groups on all three measures. Thus, when students are involved and empowered to be meta-cognitive about their skills and abilities, they take ownership of their learning and work. This leads to self-directed learning that enriches their life skills, preparing them to participate fully as citizens and valuable contributors in the workplace.

It must be emphasized that self-directed learning is not unstructured learning. Generalization techniques—that is, applying skills and knowledge beyond the classroom—are instrumental in applying the framework. Educators should know "where they are taking a class," as well as where they are taking every individual student in relation to the instructional goal (what they will learn, why they are learning that information, and how it applies in real-world living).

When the primary focus is the needs of the individual child, providing a learning environment that can address those needs is crucial (Hewitt, 1999). According to King-Sears (1997), differentiated instruction, which includes accommodation, adaptation, parallel instruction, and overlapping instruction, has been shown to be effective for this purpose. Moreover, if students are kept apprised of their performance capabilities, engagement increases, and they can self-select incremental individualized goals as stepping stones to achieving the overarching aims set by the teacher. Strategy instruction is another effective means to promote self-directed learning. Combined with scaffolding, strategy instruction is a key ingredient for self-directed learning (King-Sears, 1997; Scanlon, Deshler, & Schumaker, 1996). Teachers can use strategy instruction to create an environment conducive to learning for all students by allowing for different levels of challenge and different kinds of engagement, thus keeping students in their ZPDs.

Peer Support Structures

Peer supports can allow learners to act as both teachers and learners in the classroom. Peer-mediated instructional strategies or peer-mediated instruction and intervention serve as alternative classroom arrangements in which students take an instructional role with classmates or other children (King-Sears, 2001). Acting as a teacher allows students to consolidate and refine their own learning. To be most effective, students must be taught roles in the instructional episode and to be systematic, elicit responses, and provide feedback (Fulk & King, 2001; Utley, Mortweet, & Greenwood, 1997). Research supports the use of these approaches as alternative practice activities; however, it does not support the use of peers for providing instruction in "new" instructional content (Greenwood, Arreaga-Mayer, Utley, Gavin, & Terry, 2001; Harper, Maheady, Mallette, & Karnes, 1999; Mastropieri et al., 2001).

Many approaches have been developed in which students may work in pairs or small groups. Collaborative/cooperative learning (Cook, Semmel, & Gerber, 1999) or small-group learning, particularly student pairing (Elbaum, Vaughn, Hughes, & Watson-Moody, 1999), is effective when students receive appropriate help from a group member. This is best accomplished when the teacher structures cooperative learning groups. Defining specific roles for each participant helps the students achieve clearly stated goals (Gillies & Ashman, 2000). Haring and Breen (1992) note that forming and supporting social networks is a more effective, efficient, and natural way for students with disabilities to learn how to participate in nonstructured contexts. Direct adult support is not necessary to initiate and maintain the interactions, as students rely more on peer-controlled than adult-controlled situations (King-Sears, 1997).

Both peer learning and teacher-facilitated instruction tap into a student's ZPD. ZPD has a direct bearing on practice in psychological testing and school instruction. Potentially, a student may extend his or her ZPD through peer-mediated activities (Gindis, 1999). The examined literature supports Vygotsky's (1978) theory of the social construction of knowledge, as cooperative learning was by far the most popular effective teaching strategy studied by researchers—although it is one not necessarily employed by special educators.

Flexible Grouping

When students with learning disabilities are in smaller learning communities in inclusive settings, they contribute greatly to group efforts and complete assigned tasks (King-Sears, 1997). On the other hand, homogeneous grouping can also support academic success for these students when instructional materials are varied to meet the needs of different groups of students (Moody, Vaughn, Hughes, & Fischer, 2000). Flexible grouping allows students to work in a variety of configurations to best meet their current needs and promote socially constructed knowledge opportunities (Soodak et al., 1998). King-Sears and Cummings (1996) recommend using assessment data to form four groups of students within a classroom: "H" for high achievers, "A" for average or typical students, "L" for low achievers, and "O" for other students or students with disabilities—thus, HALO. Scores across HALO should indicate that all students are progressing (King-Sears, 1997).

Explicit and Implicit Instruction Continuum

The research literature frequently pits explicit (direct) instruction against implicit (indirect) instruction. Explicit instruction may be teacher directed and carefully scripted and sequenced, whereas implicit instruction may be project based or activity centered. While explicit instruction may focus on skill acquisition, implicit instruction may promote more open-ended and (possibly) authentic learning outcomes. Both types of instruction can be beneficial. In the early stages of learning, as students begin to acquire skills, they may benefit from explicit instruction. During later stages they may benefit more from implicit instruction, working on projects where they demonstrate how to apply what they have learned.

A fundamental component of explicit instruction is scaffolding. Scaffolding is the provision of temporary support or guidance to students during initial learning in the form of steps, tasks, and materials, with the ultimate goal of self-directed learning. By providing students with building blocks for future learning, scaffolding helps ensure that new material is reduced in complexity. When a new task is structured into manageable chunks, the odds of successful task completion are increased (Simmons & Kameenui, 1998). The degree of scaffolding changes with the abilities of the learner, the goals of instruction, and the complexities of the task. Scaffolds are gradually removed as the learner becomes more successful and independent at task completion. Thus, the purpose of scaffolding is to allow all students to become successful in independent activities considered to be more implicit (DeLaPaz, 1999). The process of scaffolding brings out the abilities that have been emerging and developing, and thus reveals the hidden potential of a child, which is crucial for prognosis and diagnosis (Gindis, 1999).

Inclusive or heterogeneous classrooms may present curriculum differentially to students, depending on how much direct or explicit instruction and how much opportunity for application an individual student requires. Mercer and Mercer (2000) recommend that teachers consider the notion of a continuum from explicit to implicit, which could prove useful in models of collaboration, such as coteaching between general educators and special educators.

Thus, both explicit and implicit instructional practices have an important role in all classrooms with all learners. It is a disservice to students to provide too much scaffolding or structure throughout the learning process, just as it is unrealistic to expect learners to complete tasks without guidance. Therefore, a continuum of services from high to low levels of support is recommended (e.g., DeLaPaz, 1999; Simmons & Kameenui, 1998; Rosenshine & Stevens, 1986).

Formative Evaluation

The results of all instructional efforts can be measured in an authentic way by using formative evaluation. This frequently used curriculum-based technique indicates to teachers the extent to which their methods are resulting in desirable achievement gains for individuals or groups of students. It is a useful tool for shaping future instruction. When assessing instructional methods, it is important to bear in mind the argument of Gersten, Keating, and Irvin (1995) that assessment is only valid if it results in improved learning; it should guide teachers' decisionmaking during learning, not solely or primarily at the end. Assessments should be not only frequent but varied. Because students engage in and express learning outcomes in various ways, varied assessments more accurately capture the progress individual students make on self-set and teacher-set goals (Stainback & Stainback, 1992; Zigmond et al., 1995). This research underscores the need to offer students multiple means to demonstrate skill and knowledge, which is one of the tenets of UDL.

CONCLUSION

The collaborative process among teachers and other school personnel to plan what and how to teach is very likely the most important activity in which teachers engage. The national priority of "leaving no child behind" implies that educational resources must extend to meet the needs of students who are at risk, are from diverse backgrounds, or have a disability. However, both structural and ideological barriers to curriculum access are well established in schools and classrooms. This chapter identified several of these barriers and then presented teaching practices that have been demonstrated to reduce their impact on students' opportunities for making effective progress. In an era of standards-based reform, where great emphasis is placed on schooling outcomes, scientifically validated instructional interventions and teaching approaches must be made palpable so that practitioners can apply them in their own learning environments. The practices identified here are known to work under the conditions in which they were developed and investigated. The realities of classrooms and the residuals of barriers, however, suggest that to solve these longstanding challenges, students, teachers, and administrators must invest heavily.

Techniques used in both general and special education settings frequently complement one another to produce environments and create opportunities conducive to optimal learning. As described at the outset of this report, technology tools and digital media will increase curriculum flexibility enormously. Application of the principles of UDL will ensure that digital curriculum will be accessible by the widest possible range of students. But new technologies and new digitally based media will not replace teachers. Rather, UDL will reform curriculum so that the challenges of teaching all students will become a more joyful and doable undertaking.

In summary, the literature findings point to the need for flexibility in planning instructional routines, selection of media and materials, and design of learning activities in order for instruction to be considerate of the learner. These studies support the underlying principles of UDL: multiple means of representation, multiple means of engagement, and multiple means of expression.

REFERENCES

Barry, A. (1994). The staffing of high school remedial reading programs in the United States since 1920. *Journal of Reading, 38*(1), 14–22.

Benner, S. M. (1998). *Special education issues within the context of American society.* Belmont, CA: Wadworth.

Boon, R., & Mastropieri, M. A. (1999, March). *Inclusion: What do teachers in the trenches really think?* Paper presented at the annual meeting of the Learning Disabilities Association, Atlanta, GA.

Chow, P., Blais, L., & Hemingway, J. (1999). An outsider looking in: Total inclusion and the concept of equifinality. *Education, 119,* 459–464.

Cook, B. C., Semmel, M. L., & Gerber, M. M. (1999). Attitudes of principals and special education teachers toward the inclusion of students with mild disabilities: Critical differences of opinion. *Remedial and Special Education, 20*(4), 199–207.

Darling-Hammond, L. (1997). *The right to learn: A blueprint for creating schools that work.* San Francisco: Jossey-Bass.

DeLaPaz, S. (1999). Teaching writing strategies and self-regulation procedures to middle school students with learning disabilities. *Focus on Exceptional Children, 31*(5), 1–16.

Deschenes, S., Cuban, L., & Tyack, D. (2001). Mismatch: Historical perspectives on schools and students who don't fit them. *Teachers College Record, 103*(4), 525–547.

Dev, P. C., & Scruggs, T. E. (1997). Mainstreaming and inclusion of students with learning disabilities: Perspectives of general educators in elementary and secondary schools. In T. E. Scruggs & M. A. Mastropieri (Eds.), *Advances in learning and behavioral disabilities* (Vol. 11, pp. 135–178). Greenwich, CT: JAI Press.

Dolan, R. P., & Hall, T. E. (2001). Universal Design for Learning: Implications for large-scale assessment. *IDA Perspectives, 27*(4), 22–25.

Downing, J., Eichinger, J., & Williams, L. (1997). Inclusive education for students with severe disabilities: Comparative views of principals and educators at different levels of implementation. *Remedial and Special Education, 18,* 133–142, 165.

Elbaum, B., Vaughn, S., Hughes, M., & Watson-Moody, S. (1999). Grouping practices and reading outcomes for students with disabilities. *Exceptional Children, 65,* 399–415.

Evans, R. (1993). Special education needs: Rhetoric and reality. *Early Child Development and Care, 89,* 87–100.

Field, S., & Hoffman, A. (1994). Developmental of a model for self-determination. *Career Development for Exceptional Individuals, 17,* 159–169.

Forness, S. R., Kavale, K. A., Blum, I. M., & Lloyd, J. W. (1997). Mega-analysis of meta-analyses. *Teaching Exceptional Children, 19*(6), 4–9.

Fuchs, D., & Fuchs, L. S. (1994). Inclusive schools movement and the radicalization of special education reform. *Exceptional Children, 60,* 294–309.

Fulk, B. M., & King, K. (2001). Classwide peer tutoring at work. *Teaching Exceptional Children, 34*(2), 49–54.

Gersten, R., Carnine, D., & Woodward, J. (1987). Direct instruction research: The third decade. *Remedial and Special Education, 8*(6), 48–56.

Gersten, R., Keating, T., & Irvin, L. K. (1995). The burden of proof: Validity as improvement of instructional practice. *Exceptional Children, 61,* 510–519.

Gillies, R. M., & Ashman, A. F. (2000). The effects of cooperative learning on students with learning difficulties in the lower elementary school. *Journal of Special Education, 34*(1), 19–27.

Gindis, B. (1999). Vygotsky's vision: Reshaping the practice of special education for the 21st century. *Remedial and Special Education, 20*(6), 32–64.

Greenwood, C. R., Arreaga-Mayer, C., Utley, C. A., Gavin, K. M., & Terry, B. (2001). Classwide peer tutoring learning management system: Applications with elementary level English language learners. *Remedial and Special Education, 22,* 34–47.

Haring, T. G., & Breen, C. G. (1992). A peer-mediated social network intervention to enhance the social integration of persons with moderate and severe disabilities. *Journal of Applied Behavior Analysis, 25,* 319–333.

Harper, G. E, Maheady, L, Mallette, B., & Karnes, M. (1999) Peer tutoring and the minority child with disabilities. *Preventing School Failure, 43,* 45–51.

Hewitt, M. (1999). Inclusion from a general educator's perspective. *Preventing School Failure, 43,* 125–128.

Kauffman, J. M. (1993). How we might achieve the radical reform of special education. *Exceptional Children, 60,* 6–16.

Kauffman, J. M., & Hallahan, D. P. (Eds.). (1995). *The illusion of full inclusion: A comprehensive critique of a current special education bandwagon.* Austin, TX: PRO-ED.

King-Sears, M. E. (1997). Best academic practices for inclusive practices. *Focus on Exceptional Children, 29*(7), 1–21.

King-Sears, M. E. (2001). Institutionalizing peer mediated instruction in schools. *Remedial and Special Education, 22*(2), 89–103.

King-Sears, M. E., & Cummings, C. S. (1996). Inclusive practices of classroom teachers. *Remedial and Special Education, 17,* 217–225.

Klingner, J. K., & Vaughn, S. (1999). Students' perceptions of instruction in inclusive classrooms: Implications for students with learning disabilities. *Exceptional Children, 66,* 23–37.

Kuhn, M. R., & Stahl, S. A. (1998). Teaching children how to learn word meanings from context: A synthesis and some questions. *Journal of Literacy Research, 30*(1), 119–138.

Lipsky, D. K., & Gartner, A. (Eds.). (1997). *Inclusion and school reform: Transforming American classrooms.* Baltimore: Brookes.

Maccini, P., & Gagnon, J. C. (2000). Best practices for teaching mathematics to secondary students with special needs. *Focus on Exceptional Children, 32*(5), 1–22.

Mamlin, N. (1999). Despite best intentions: When inclusion fails. *Journal of Special Education, 33*(1), 36–49.

Mastropieri, M. A., Scruggs, L., Mohler, L., Beranek, M., Spencer, V., Boon R. T., & Talbott, E. (2001). Can middle school students with serious reading difficulties help each other and learn anything? *Learning Disabilties Research & Practice, 16,* 18–27.

Mastropieri, M. A., Scruggs, T. E., & Shiah, S. (1991). Mathematics instruction for learning disabled students: A review of research. *Learning Disabilities Research & Practice, 6,* 89–98.

McLeskey, J., Henry, H., & Axelrod, M. I. (1999). Inclusion of students with learning disabilities: An examination of data from reports to Congress. *Exceptional Children, 66,* 55–66.

Meier, D. (1995). *The power of their ideas: Lessons for America from a small school in Harlem.* Boston, MA: Beacon Press.

Mercer, C. D., Jordan, L., & Miller, S. P. (1996). Constructivistic math instruction for diverse learners. *Learning Disabilities Research & Practice, 11,* 147–156.

Mercer, C. D., & Mercer, A. R. (2000). *Teaching students with learning problems* (4th ed.). Columbus, OH: Prentice Hall.

Miller, M. D., Brownell, M. T., & Smith, S. W. (1999). Factors that predict teachers staying in, leaving, or transferring from the special education classroom. *Exceptional Children, 65,* 201–218.

Moody, S. W., Vaughn, S., Hughes, M. T., & Fischer, M. (2000). Reading instruction in the resource room: Set up for failure. *Exceptional Children, 66,* 305–316.

Nelson, J. S., Epstein, M., Bursuck, W. D., Jayanthi, M., & Sawyer, V. (1998). The preference of middle-school students for homework adaptations made by general education teachers. *Learning Disabilities Research & Practice, 13,* 109–117.

Nolet, V., & McLaughlin, M. J. (2000). *Accessing the general curriculum: Including students with disabilities in standards-based reform.* Thousand Oaks, CA: Corwin Press.

Osborne, A. G., & DiMattia, P. (1995). IDEA's LRE mandate: Another look. *Exceptional Children, 61,* 582–584.

O'Shea, D. J. (1999). Tips for teaching: Making uninvited inclusion work. *Preventing School Failure, 43,* 179–180.

Pugach, M. C., & Johnson, L. J. (1995). *Collaborative practitioners, collaborative schools.* Denver: Love.

Rose, D., & Meyer, A. (2000). Universal design for individual differences. *Educational Leadership, 58*(3), 39–43.

Rose, D. H., & Meyer, A. (2002). *Teaching every student in the digital age: Universal Design for Learning.* Alexandria, VA: ASCD.

Rosenshine, B., & Stevens, R. (1986). Teaching functions. In M. Wittrock (Ed.), *Handbook of research on teaching* (3rd ed., pp. 376–391). New York: Macmillan.

Salend, S. J., & Duhaney, L. M. G. (1999). The impact of inclusion on students with and without disabilities and their educators. *Remedial and Special Education, 20,* 114–126.

Scanlon, D., Deshler, D. D., & Schumaker, J. B. (1996). Can a strategy be taught and learned in secondary inclusive classrooms? *Learning Disabilities Research & Practice, 11,* 41–57.

Schumm, J. S., Vaughn, S., Gordon, J., & Rothlein, L. (1994). General education teachers' beliefs, skills, and practices in planning for mainstreamed students with learning disabilities. *Teacher Education and Special Education, 17,* 22–37.

Schumm, J. S., Vaughn, S., Haager, D., McDowell, J., Rothlein, L., & Saumell, L. (1995). General education teacher planning: What can students with learning disabilities expect? *Exceptional Children, 61,* 335–352.

Scruggs, T. E., & Mastropieri, M. A. (1996a). Quantitative synthesis of survey research: Methodology and validation. In T. E. Scruggs & M. A. Mastropieri (Eds.), *Advances in learning and behavioral disabilities* (Vol. 10, pp. 209–223). Greenwich, CT: JAI.

Scruggs, T. E., & Mastropieri, M. A. (1996b). Teacher perceptions of mainstreaming/inclusion, 1958–1995: A research synthesis. *Exceptional Children, 63,* 59–74.

Scruggs, T. E., Mastropieri, M. A., & Boon, R. (1998). Science education for students with disabilities: A review of recent research. *Studies in Science Education, 32,* 21–44.

Simmons, D., & Kameenui, E. J. (1998). *What reading research tells us about children with diverse learning needs: Bases and basics.* Mahwah, NJ: Lawrence Erlbaum Associates.

Snyder, R. (1999). Inclusion: A qualitative study of in-service general education teachers' attitudes and concerns. *Education, 120*(1), 173–180.

Soodak, L. C., Podell, D. M., & Lehman, L. R. (1998). Teacher, student, and school attributes as predictors of teachers' responses to inclusion. *Journal of Special Education, 31,* 480–497.

Stainback, S., & Stainback, W. (1992). *Curriculum considerations in inclusive classrooms: Facilitating learning for all students.* Baltimore: Brookes.

Stainback, S., Stainback, W., & Forest, M. (1989). *Educating all students in the mainstream of regular education.* Baltimore: Brookes.

Swanson, H. L. (1999). Instructional components that predict treatment outcomes for students with learning disabilities: Support for a combined strategy and direct instruction model. *Learning Disabilities Research & Practice, 14,* 129–140.

Utley, C. A., Mortweet, S. L., & Greenwood, C. R. (1997). Peer-mediated instruction and interventions. *Focus on Exceptional Children, 29*(5), 1–23.

Van Reusen, A. K., Deshler, D. D., & Schumaker, J. B. (1989). Effects of a student participation strategy in facilitating the involvement of adolescents with learning disabilities in the individualized educational program planning process. *Learning Disabilities, 1*(2), 23–34.

Vaughn, S., Bos, C. S., & Schumm, J. S. (2000). *Teaching exceptional, diverse, and at-risk students in the general education classroom.* Boston: Allyn & Bacon.

Vaughn, S., Schumm, J. S., Jallad, B., Slusher, J., & Saumell, L. (1996). Teachers' views of inclusion. *Learning Disabilities Research & Practice, 11,* 96–106.

Vygotsky, L. S. (1978). *Mind in society.* Cambridge, MA: Harvard University Press.

Will, M. C. (1986). Educating children with learning problems: A shared responsibility. *Exceptional Children, 52,* 411–416.

Wohlstetter, P., & Mohrman, S. A. (1996). *Studies of education reform: Assessment of school-based management.* Washington, DC: U.S. Department of Education.

York, J., & Tundidor, M. (1995). Issues raised in the name of inclusion: Perspectives of educators, parents, and students. *Journal of the Association for Persons with Severe Handicaps, 20*(1), 31–44.

Zigmond, N., Jenkins, J., Fuchs, L. S., & Fafard, M. B. (1995). Special education in re-structured schools: Findings from three multi-year studies. *Phi Delta Kappan, 76,* 531–540.

The authors wish to acknowledge the valuable contributions to this revised version by Tracey Hall, Ph.D., and Nicole Strangman, Ph.D., of CAST.

This paper was originally published as Jackson, R., Harper, K., & Jackson, J. (2001). *Effective teaching practices and the barriers limiting their use in accessing the curriculum: A review of recent literature.* Peabody, MA: National Center on Accessing the General Curriculum. It has been edited for this volume. The original content was developed pursuant to Cooperative Agreement #H324H990004 under CFDA 84.324H between CAST and the Office of Special Education Programs, U.S. Department of Education. However, the opinions expressed herein do not necessarily reflect the position or policy of the U.S. Department of Education or the Office of Special Education Programs, and no endorsement by that office should be inferred.

CHAPTER SIX

UDL Implementation: Examples Using Best Practices and Curriculum Enhancements

TRACEY HALL, ANNE MEYER, AND NICOLE STRANGMAN

A primary goal of the National Center on Accessing the General Curriculum (NCAC) has been to identify effective, research-based classroom practices and enhancements that ensure that students of all abilities are actively engaged in learning—that is, that the subject matter is cognitively challenging to them and they are appropriately supported, regardless of their developmental level. This chapter demonstrates some of the ways Universal Design for Learning (UDL) can be implemented in classrooms using proven practices and enhancements.

The chapter specifically addresses (a) differentiated instruction, (b) background knowledge instruction, (c) graphic organizers, and (d) virtual reality/computer simulations, and how these tools can be incorporated into a UDL framework. These practices and enhancements do not alone constitute UDL implementation; for example, differentiated instruction by itself does not equal a universally designed approach, nor does the use of graphic organizers or digital technologies. But these can be effective and promising strategies and tools to help realize a UDL curriculum.

A REVIEW OF UDL TEACHING METHODS

Universal Design for Learning is a theoretical framework developed by CAST to guide the development of curricula that are flexible and supportive of all students (Dolan & Hall, 2001; Meyer & Rose, 1998; Rose & Meyer, 2000a, 2000b, 2002). The concept of UDL was inspired by the universal design movement in architecture. This movement calls for the design of structures that anticipate the needs of individuals with disabilities and accommodate these needs from the outset. Similarly, but uniquely, UDL calls for the design of curricula with the needs of all students in mind, so that methods, materials, and assessment are usable by all. Traditional curricula present a host of barriers that limit some students' access to information and learning. Of these, printed text is particularly notorious. In a traditional curriculum, a student without a well-developed ability to see, decode, attend to, or comprehend printed text is compelled to adapt to its ubiquity as best they can. In contrast, a UDL curriculum is designed to be innately flexible and enriched with multiple media so that alternatives can be accessed whenever appropriate. A UDL curriculum takes on the burden of adaptation so that students don't have to, thus maximizing student access to both information and learning.

The UDL framework guides the development of adaptable curricula by means of three principles (see Table 1). These three principles parallel three fundamentally important learning components and three distinct learning networks in the brain: recognition, strategy, and affect (Rose & Meyer, 2002). The common recommendation of these three principles is to select goals, methods, assessments, and materials in a way that will minimize barriers and maximize flexibility. In this manner, the UDL framework structures the development of curricula that fully support every student's access, participation, and progress in all three essential facets of learning.

For teachers wondering *how* to customize the curriculum, CAST has devised three sets of broad teaching methods that support each of the three UDL principles (see Table 2). These teaching methods draw on knowledge of the qualities of digital media and how the brain's recognition, strategic, and affective networks operate. For example, the first teaching method to support recognition learning is to *provide multiple examples*. This teaching method takes advantage of the fact that recog-

TABLE 1   *Principles of Universal Design for Learning*

Principle 1:   To support recognition learning, and provide multiple, flexible methods of presentation

Principle 2:   To support strategic learning, and provide multiple, flexible methods of expression and apprenticeship

Principle 3:   To support affective learning, and provide multiple, flexible options for engagement

TABLE 2   *Teaching Methods to Support UDL Principles*

To support diverse recognition networks:

    Provide multiple examples

    Highlight critical features

    Provide multiple media and formats

    Support background context

To support diverse strategic networks:

    Provide flexible models of skilled performance

    Provide opportunities to practice with supports

    Provide ongoing, relevant feedback

    Offer flexible opportunities for demonstrating skill

To support diverse affective networks:

    Offer choices of content and tools

    Offer adjustable levels of challenge

    Offer choices of rewards

    Offer choices of learning context

Source: Rose & Meyer, 2002.

nition networks can extract the defining features of a pattern and differentiate it from similar patterns simply by viewing multiple examples. Although the presentation of multiple examples might be challenging in a classroom limited to printed text and hard-copy images, digital materials enable the assembly, storage, and maintenance of a large collection of examples in the form of digital text, images, sound, or video—all in the limited space of a classroom.

This is one example of how digital materials and UDL teaching methods can facilitate the successful implementation of UDL. While UDL is not a technology-based approach per se, digital materials can be critical to its implementation because their inherent flexibility enables them to be modified in a host of ways. This flexibility makes it feasible to customize learning materials and methods to each individual, depending on the needs of the student.

The UDL Teaching Methods outlined here will anchor the upcoming discussion that highlights ways to support individualized instruction of recognition, strategic, and affective learning.

Of course, curriculum planning and delivery is critical to making these Teaching Methods work. To begin, we recommend that teachers have a basic understanding of UDL and a commitment to make the curriculum and learning accessible for all learners. While keeping in mind the three principles of UDL based on recognition, strategic, and affective networks, we have found the following process useful in designing lessons. The process includes four steps, based on the principles and concepts of UDL, proven professional development strategies, and effective

FIGURE I

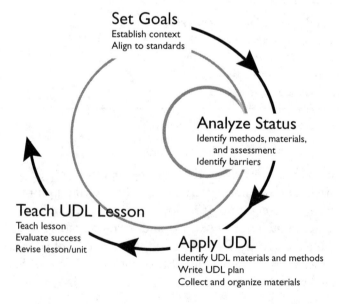

Set Goals
Establish context
Align to standards

Analyze Status
Identify methods, materials,
and assessment
Identify barriers

Teach UDL Lesson
Teach lesson
Evaluate success
Revise lesson/unit

Apply UDL
Identify UDL materials and methods
Write UDL plan
Collect and organize materials

teaching practices: 1) Set Goals, 2) Analyze Status, 3) Apply UDL, and 4) Teach the UDL Lesson.

To Set Goals, teachers may want to establish the context for instruction. Context is usually driven or based on state standards, followed by the design of goals for the instructional episode. We recommend that all teachers closely evaluate these to assure alignment and a clear separation between goals and standards and the means for attaining them.

Next, when designing a UDL lesson, teachers will find it useful to Analyze the Current Status of the instructional episode. What are the current methodologies, assessments, and materials used to teach the lesson? Do all students have access to the materials? Are students able to express themselves with the current methods and materials?

Step three is to Apply UDL to the Lesson/Unit. This includes the goals, methods, assessments, and materials used to implement the lesson. Teachers will want to create a UDL lesson plan that is grounded in the learning goals, classroom profile, methods and assessment, and materials and tools. They then will work to collect and organize materials that support the UDL lesson.

In the final step, Teach the UDL Lesson/Unit, teachers minimize barriers and realize the strengths and challenges each student brings to learning, rely on effective teaching practices, and apply challenges appropriate for each learner. In this way, instructors can engage more students and help them all to progress. When teaching and evaluating students' work, they should also evaluate and revise the lesson/unit to assure student access and success.

Additional information and models of UDL practice are available in the book *Teaching Every Student in the Digital Age* by David H. Rose and Anne Meyer (ASCD, 2002), and at the companion website, www. cast.org/teachingeverystudent.

*   *   *   *   *

DIFFERENTIATED INSTRUCTION

Not all students are alike. Based on this knowledge, differentiated instruction applies an approach to teaching and learning that gives students multiple options for taking in information and making sense of ideas. Differentiated instruction is a teaching theory based on the premise that instructional approaches should vary and be adapted in relation to individual and diverse students in classrooms (Tomlinson, 2001). The model of differentiated instruction requires teachers to be flexible in their approach to teaching and to adjust the curriculum and presentation of information to learners, rather than expecting students to modify themselves for the curriculum. Many teachers and teacher educators have recently identified differentiated instruction as a method of helping more students in diverse classroom settings experience success.

This section examines information on the theory and research behind differentiated instruction and its intersection with Universal Design for Learning, a curriculum design approach to increase flexibility in teaching and decrease the barriers that frequently limit student access to materials and learning in classrooms (Rose & Meyer, 2002). After an introduction to the components, features, and applications of differentiated instruction, we link UDL and differentiated instruction both in theory and with a specific lesson example.

Elements of Differentiated Instruction

According to the authors of differentiated instruction, several key elements guide differentiation in the education environment. Tomlinson (2001) identifies three elements of the curriculum that can be differentiated: content, process, and products. These are described in the following three sections, which are followed by several additional guidelines for forming an understanding of and developing ideas around differentiated instruction.

Content

- *Several elements and materials are used to support instructional content.* These include acts, concepts, generalizations or principles, attitudes, and skills. The variation seen in a differentiated classroom is most frequently in the manner in which students gain access to important learning. Access to the content is considered key.

- *Align tasks and objectives to learning goals.* Designers of differentiated instruction view the alignment of tasks with instructional goals and objectives as essential. Goals are most often assessed by many state-level high-stakes tests and frequently administered standardized measures. Objectives are often written in incremental steps, resulting in a continuum of skills-building tasks. An objectives-driven menu makes it easier to find the next instructional step for learners entering at varying levels.

- *Instruction is concept focused and principle driven.* The instructional concepts should be broad based, not focused on minute details or unlimited facts. Teachers must focus on the concepts, principles, and skills that students should learn. The content of instruction should address the same concepts with all students, but the degree of complexity should be adjusted to suit diverse learners.

Process

- *Flexible grouping is consistently used.* Strategies for flexible grouping are essential. Learners are expected to interact and work together as they develop knowledge of new content. Teachers may conduct whole-class introductory discussions of content "big ideas" followed by small group or paired work. Student groups may be coached from within or by the teacher to complete assigned tasks. Grouping of students is not fixed. As one of the foundations of differentiated instruction, grouping and regrouping must be a dynamic process, changing with the content, project, and ongoing evaluations.

- *Classroom management benefits students and teachers.* To effectively operate a classroom using differentiated instruction, teachers must carefully select organization and instructional delivery strategies. In her book, *How to Differentiate Instruction in Mixed-Ability Classrooms*, Carol Tomlinson (2001) identifies 17 key strategies for teachers to successfully meet the challenge of designing and managing differentiated instruction.

Products

- *Initial and ongoing assessment of student readiness and growth are essential.* Meaningful preassessment naturally leads to functional and successful differentiation. Incorporating pre- and ongoing assessment informs teachers so they can better provide a menu of approaches, choices, and scaffolds for the varying needs, interests, and abilities that exist in classrooms of diverse students. Assessments may be formal or informal, including interviews, surveys, performance assessments, and more formal evaluation procedures.

- *Students are active and responsible explorers.* Teachers respect the fact that each task put before the learner will be interesting, engaging, and accessible to essential understanding and skills. Each child should feel challenged most of the time.

- *Vary expectations and requirements for student responses.* Items to which students respond may be differentiated so that different students can demonstrate or express their knowledge and understanding in different ways. A well-designed student product allows varied means of expression and alternative procedures, and offers varying degrees of difficulty, types of evaluation, and scoring.

Additional Guidelines

- *Clarify key concepts and generalizations.* Ensure that all learners gain powerful understandings that can serve as the foundation for future learning. Teachers are encouraged to identify essential concepts and instructional foci to ensure that all learners comprehend.

- *Use assessment as a teaching tool to extend rather than merely measure instruction.* Assessment should occur before, during, and following the instructional episode, and it should be used to help pose questions regarding student needs and optimal learning.

- *Emphasize critical and creative thinking as a goal in lesson design.* The tasks, activities, and procedures for students should require that they understand and apply meaning. Instruction may require supports, additional motivation, varied tasks, materials, or equipment for different students in the classroom.

- *Engaging all learners is essential.* Teachers are encouraged to strive for the development of lessons that are engaging and motivating for a diverse class of students. Vary tasks within instruction and across students. In other words, one session for students should not consist only of drill and practice, or any other single structure or activity.

- *Provide a balance between teacher-assigned and student-selected tasks.* A balanced working structure is optimal in a differentiated classroom. Based on preassessment information, the balance will vary from class to class, and from lesson to lesson. Teachers should ensure that students have choices in their learning.

Effectiveness as a Classroom Practice and Applications in General Education

According to proponents of differentiation, the principles and guidelines are rooted in years of educational theory and research. For example, differentiated instruction adopts the concept of "readiness"; that is, the difficulty of skills taught should be slightly ahead of the child's current level of mastery. This is grounded in Lev Vygotsky's (1978) concept of a "zone of proximal development" (ZPD) in which each student's learning takes place. Classroom research strongly supports the ZPD concept (Tomlinson, 2001). Other practices noted as being central to differentiation have been validated in the effective-teaching research conducted since the mid-1980s. These practices include effective management procedures, grouping students for instruction, and engaging learners (Ellis & Worthington, 1994).

While differentiation is a compilation of many research-based theories and practices, the "package" itself is lacking empirical validation. Nevertheless, there are a generous number of testimonials and classroom examples that authors of several publications and websites provide. Tomlinson (2001) reports on individual settings in which the full model of differentiation was very promising, and teachers using differentiation have written about improvements in their classrooms.

Many authors of publications about differentiated instruction strongly recommend that teachers adapt the practices slowly, perhaps one content area at a time. These experts also agree that teachers should share the creative load by working together to develop ideas and menus of options for students. A number of websites have been created that include lessons to illustrate what teachers have created for instruction using the model of differentiated instruction.

The initial application of differentiated instruction was with students considered gifted but who perhaps were not sufficiently challenged by the content provided in the general classroom setting. As classrooms have become more diverse, differentiated instruction has been applied at all levels for students of all abilities. Thus, differentiated instruction has excellent potential to have a positive impact on learning by offering teachers a means to provide instruction to a range of students in today's classrooms.

Differentiated Instruction and UDL Principles

Differentiated instruction is well received as a classroom practice that may be well suited to the three principles of UDL. The following section looks at the three network-appropriate teaching methods—recognition, strategic, and affective—in order to address the ways in which differentiated instruction coordinates with UDL theory.

UDL Principle 1: Recognition Learning

The theory of differentiated instruction incorporates some guidelines that can help teachers support critical elements of recognition learning in a flexible way and promote every student's success. Each of the three key elements of differentiated instruction—content, process, and product—supports an important UDL Teaching Method for individualized instruction of pattern recognition.

The content guidelines for differentiated instruction support the first UDL Teaching Method for recognition networks—provide multiple examples—in that they encourage the use of several elements and materials to support instructional content. A teacher following this guideline might help students in a social studies class understand the location of a state in the union by showing them a wall map or a globe, projecting a state map, or describing the location in words.

Also, while preserving the essential content, a teacher could vary the difficulty of the material by presenting smaller or larger, simpler or more complex maps. For students with physical or cognitive disabilities, such a diversity of examples may be vital in order for them to access the pattern being taught. Other students may benefit from the same multiple examples by obtaining a perspective that they otherwise might not. In this way, a range of examples can help to ensure that each student's recognition networks are able to identify the fundamental elements of a pattern.

This same use of varied content examples supports a second recommended practice in UDL methodology: provide multiple media and formats. A wide range of tools for presenting instructional content are available digitally; thus, teachers may manipulate size, color, contrast, and other features to develop examples in multiple media and formats.

These can be saved for future use and flexibly accessed by different students, depending on their needs and preferences.

The content guidelines of differentiated instruction also recommend that content elements of instruction be kept concept focused and principle driven. This practice is consistent with a third UDL Teaching Method for recognition: highlight critical features. By avoiding any focus on extensive facts or seductive details and reiterating the broad concepts (a goal of differentiated instruction), teachers are highlighting essential components, thus supporting recognition more effectively.

The fourth UDL Teaching Method for recognition is to support background knowledge, and in this respect, the assessment step of the differentiated instruction learning cycle is instrumental. By evaluating student knowledge about a construct before designing instruction, teachers can better support students' knowledge base, scaffolding instruction in a very important way.

UDL Principle 2: Strategic Learning

People find for themselves the most desirable method of learning strategies; therefore, teaching methodologies need to be varied. This need for flexibility is reflected in the four UDL Teaching Methods. Differentiated instruction can support these teaching methods in valuable ways. Differentiated instruction recognizes the need for students to receive flexible models of skilled performance. As noted above, teachers implementing differentiated instruction are encouraged to demonstrate information and skills multiple times and at varying levels. As a result, learners enter the instructional episode with different approaches, knowledge, and strategies for learning.

When students are engaged in initial learning on novel tasks or skills, supported practice should be used to ensure success and eventual independence. Supported practice enables students to split up a complex skill into manageable components and fully master these components.

Differentiated instruction promotes this teaching method by encouraging students to be active and responsible learners, and by asking teachers to respect individual differences and scaffold students as they move from initial learning to practiced, less well-supported mastery of skills.

In order to successfully demonstrate the skills they have learned, students need flexible opportunities to demonstrate skill. Differentiated instruction directly supports this UDL Teaching Method by reminding teachers to vary requirements and expectations for learning and expressing knowledge, including the degree of difficulty and the means of evaluation or scoring.

UDL Principle 3: Affective Learning

Supporting affective learning through flexible instruction is the third principle of UDL and an objective that differentiated instruction supports effectively. Differentiated instruction theory reinforces the importance of effective classroom management and reminds teachers of the challenges of effective organizational and instructional practices. Student engagement is vital to success. Differentiated practices bear much in common with UDL Teaching Methods for affective learning: offer choices of content and tools, provide adjustable levels of challenge, and offer a choice of learning context. Teachers are encouraged to offer a choice of tools, adjust the level of difficulty of the material, and provide varying levels of scaffolding to gain and maintain learner attention during the instructional episode. By providing varying levels of challenge when differentiating instruction, students have access to varied learning contexts and choices about their learning environment.

An Example of UDL Application Using Differentiated Instruction

In previous sections, we described ways in which differentiated instruction supports UDL principles and aligns with UDL teaching practices. Here we present an actual lesson plan (see Table 3) that exemplifies applications of UDL in differentiated instruction. The example, "Gathering Evidence: The Life Cycle of Plants," was produced by a school that

TABLE 3
UDL Features of the CAST Lesson Plan
"Gathering Evidence: Life Cycle of Plants"

UDL Teaching Method	Supportive Differentiated Instruction Feature(s)
Provide multiple examples.	In preparation for this lesson, the teacher created multiple examples of finding and identifying seeds. The teacher also provided several examples of finding appropriate texts to complete the assignment. Students have multiple examples of texts in which to find information about the life cycle of seeds. As another example, fast-growing seeds were planted in the classroom, giving students the opportunity to observe the seed life cycle.

Highlight critical features.	The teacher provides critical information for the lesson through oral presentation and highlights critical features in written form, then monitors students to check their focus on important features of the lesson. Additionally, by having texts available in digital format, the teacher or students could literally highlight critical features of the text while preparing lesson assignments.
Provide multiple media and formats.	The teacher located several (4–5) resources, in this case books of different reading difficulty, containing the same science constructs on seed life cycles. The books were then made available digitally as well as on audio tape for flexible accessibility.
Support background context.	Several levels of preparation were designed to support background context: • Before this assignment the teacher and students found seeds in a variety of vegetables and fruits. In this way, the concept of seeds was brought out of the abstract; students had experiences seeing and finding seeds from a range of plants. • Careful instruction was organized to teach students the concept of finding a book that is "just right," helping them find a book that is challenging yet not too difficult. This helped keep students in their "zone of proximal development" when obtaining background information for the lesson.
Provide opportunities to practice with support.	• Students had the option to work in selected pairs as they searched for answers to the science questions. • During guided and independent practice portions of each lesson, the teacher provided supports by checking and prompting.
Offer flexible opportunities for demonstrating skill.	The design of this lesson allowed students varied approaches throughout the lesson. Students could select their best or preferred type of working situation and means of responding.
Offer choice of content and tools.	The teacher organized the lesson at multiple points for choice of tools: • Choice of resource materials. • Choice of access (text, digital, audio). • Choice of response style.
Offer adjustable levels of challenge.	The teacher offered multiple texts, representing a range of difficulty levels, and different means to access these texts. This helped ensure that researching the answers to science questions was appropriately challenging for each student. For example, if decoding was challenging, the student could use a simpler text and/or access the information via audio or digital read-aloud.
Offer choice of learning contexts.	Throughout the lesson the teacher organized several choices that helped diversify the available learning contexts: • Students could select from a variety of methods to respond to the science questions (written, scribed, recorded). • Students could opt to work independently or with a partner during the assignment completion portion of the lesson. • Students could select the "right book" based on difficulty and/or interest.

is working with CAST.[1] This lesson is a two-day instructional plan that is a part of a larger unit designed by a first-grade teacher for a diverse class of students. The lesson plan addresses Mid-Continent Research for Education and Learning (McREL) and Massachusetts state standards in science and English language arts by teaching students the necessary environmental variables about growth in plants.

Before teaching the lesson, the teacher introduces students to science concepts relating to the growth of seeds through oral presentation and in-class experiments. This lesson enables the teacher to discuss, display, and increase student understanding of the science content and concepts. Student choice and access flexibility in the lesson exemplify applications of UDL. Table 3 lists UDL features made possible by elements of differentiated instruction employed in this lesson.

Conclusion

Differentiated instruction, although still developing somewhat in educational settings, has received significant recognition. When combined with the practices and principles of UDL, differentiated instruction can provide teachers with both theory and practice to appropriately challenge the broad scope of students in classrooms today. Although educators are continually challenged by the ever-changing classroom profile of students, resources, and reforms, practices continue to evolve, and the relevant research base should grow. And along with it grows the promise of differentiated instruction and UDL in educational practices.

BACKGROUND/PRIOR KNOWLEDGE INSTRUCTION

Research shows that students who lack sufficient background knowledge or are unable to activate it may struggle to access, participate, and progress throughout the general curriculum. This section examines the research on instructional approaches to support students' use of background knowledge and explores points of intersection with Universal Design for Learning. UDL offers a framework and context to help teachers make their background knowledge instruction more broadly effective. By aligning the implementation of background knowledge instruction with UDL, teachers can make a greater impact on student learning, improving the learning experience for every student in the classroom.

The terms "background knowledge" and "prior knowledge" are generally used in the research literature interchangeably—as they are throughout this chapter. For example, Stevens (1980) defines background knowledge quite simply as "what one already knows about a subject" (p. 151). Biemans and Simons' (1996) definition is slightly more complex: "All knowledge learners have when entering a learning environment that is potentially relevant for acquiring new knowledge" (p. 6). Regarding prior knowledge, Dochy and Alexander (1995) describe it as the whole of a person's knowledge, including explicit and tacit knowledge, metacognitive and conceptual knowledge—a definition quite similar to Schallert's (1982).

Our survey of the literature shows that there is a well-established correlation between background/prior knowledge and reading comprehension (Langer, 1984; Long, Winograd, & Bridget, 1989; Stevens, 1980). In addition, high correlations have been found between prior knowledge and speed and accuracy of study behavior (reviewed in Dochy, Segers, & Buehl, 1999), as well as student interest in a topic (Tobias, 1994). Thus, prior knowledge is associated with beneficial academic behaviors and higher academic performance.

Developing Background Knowledge, Activating Prior Knowledge

The most frequently researched approach to building background knowledge is direct instruction, which has been shown to significantly improve students' comprehension of relevant reading material (Dole, Valencia, Greer, & Wardrop, 1991; Graves & Cooke, 1983; Graves, Cooke, & Laberge, 1983; McKeown, Beck, Sinatra, & Loxterman, 1992; Stevens, 1982). For example, Dole et al. found that students who were taught important background ideas for an expository or narrative text performed significantly better on comprehension questions than did those with no prereading background knowledge instruction.

Indirect approaches to building background knowledge, such as immersing students in field experiences, may also have merit, though the data are too preliminary to clearly establish the effectiveness of the approach or clarify its most valuable elements. Research does show, however, that by building students' background knowledge, teachers may also be able to indirectly influence other aspects of academic performance, such as writing. For example, Davis and Winek (1989) found that students felt better prepared to write a research paper when they took part beforehand in an extended course of building background knowledge through individual research and in-class sharing and discussion. While this study does not show any direct impact on writing quality, it might be expected that improving students' sense of preparedness might raise their engagement and/or motivation, translating into better performance.

As a whole, the research base provides good evidence to support the use of strategies for activating prior knowledge (Pressley, Johnson, Symons, McGoldrick, & Kurita, 1989). Effective strategies include:

1. *Reflection and recording.* That is, prompting students to bring to mind, state, write down, or otherwise record what they already know about the topic (Carr & Thompson, 1996; Peeck, van den Bosch, & Kreupeling, 1982; Smith, Readence, & Alvermann, 1983; Spires & Donley, 1998; Walraven & Reitsma, 1993).

2. *Interactive discussion.* Student reflection can be supplemented with interactive discussion. For example, Dole et al. (1991) designed an intervention where students reflected on and recorded their prior knowledge on a topic, then engaged in a group discussion during which the teacher encouraged them to contribute knowledge to complete a semantic map. This approach proved to be effective at promoting reading comprehension.

3. *Answering questions.* Research suggests that teachers can facilitate student activation of background knowledge by having them answer questions before and/or while they read new material (Rowe & Rayford, 1987), and that this can increase reading comprehension (Hansen & Pearson, 1983; King, 1994; Pflaum, Pascarella, Auer, Augustyn, & Boswick, 1982).

4. *The K-W-L strategy.* Ogle (1986) developed a strategy for helping students access important background information before reading nonfiction. With K-W-L (accessing what I Know, determining what I Want to find out, recalling what I did Learn), students and teacher begin by reflecting on their knowledge about a topic, brainstorming a group list of ideas about the topic, and identifying categories of information. Next, the teacher helps highlight gaps and inconsistencies in students' knowledge, and students list things that they want to learn

or questions they want answered. Then, students read new material and share what they have learned. Informal evaluations indicate that the K-W-L strategy increases the retention of read material and improves students' ability to make connections among different categories of information, as well as increasing their enthusiasm for reading nonfiction (Ogle, 1986). The approach has been recommended by teaching professionals (Bean, 1995; Carr & Ogle, 1987; Fisher, Frey, & Williams, 2002), but it has not been rigorously tested.

5. *Computer-assisted activation.* Biemans and colleagues (2001) investigated the computer-assisted approach CONTACT-2, which assists students in searching for preconceptions, comparing and contrasting these preconceptions with new information, and formulating, applying, and evaluating new conceptions. Their research findings suggest that a computer-assisted approach to integrating new information with prior knowledge can be successful.

Of course, a number of factors affect whether such strategies for developing background knowledge or activating prior knowledge will work, including grade level. But research has clearly established the importance of background/prior knowledge and suggests the importance of considering learners' unique strengths, weaknesses, and preferences when selecting instructional approaches.[2]

Background Knowledge Instruction and the UDL Principles

Background knowledge instruction and UDL have a mutually supportive relationship. Supporting background context is itself a UDL teaching method and therefore directly supports students' diverse recognition abilities and preferences. In addition, the incorporation of UDL teaching methods into background knowledge instruction can help to improve its effectiveness. In the sections that follow, we provide some specific examples.

UDL Principle 1: Recognition Learning

The knowledge students bring to a new situation varies in both quantity and kind—as does their ability to call on this knowledge appropriately. Weaknesses in these areas can present a barrier to recognition learning. Thus, teachers need to help students fill in gaps in their background knowledge and activate this knowledge in response to new information.

When providing background knowledge instruction, it is important to take a flexible approach that can adapt to individual students' strengths, weaknesses, and preferences.

Implementing UDL teaching methods can help teachers individualize background knowledge instruction effectively. For example, providing students multiple examples of a pattern helps them to extract the key features of a pattern and offers them the chance to select and focus on the examples that are most effective for them. A teacher providing direct instruction of background knowledge for a text on mammals, for example, might present examples that draw from a range of mammalian species. When presenting these examples, a teacher might also directly highlight the critical features, perhaps using a graphic organizer or pictures to demonstrate meaningful commonalities.

This raises another important point, which is that students vary in their ability to process different patterns, making it essential that teachers use different media and formats during background knowledge instruction. This might mean showing students text, images, and video, as well as immersing students in field experiences. To help students activate background knowledge, we have seen that both text-based approaches and an image analysis approach (Croll, Idol-Maestas, Heal, & Pearson, 1986) can be effective. A teacher could implement both approaches to ensure that students who might struggle with text or images have an effective means to activate background knowledge.

UDL Principle 2: Strategic Learning

Students' strengths, weaknesses, and preferences in the area of strategic learning vary as widely as they do for recognition learning. Thus, it is equally important to offer multiple, flexible methods of expression and apprenticeship. As students work to generate new background knowledge or activate prior knowledge, they may find different models most effective. Just as students can extract critical features of a pattern from multiple examples, so can they extract the critical features of a process when viewing multiple models. Thus, when modeling background knowledge activation, it is beneficial for teachers in diversifying their examples.

Another UDL Teaching Method to bear in mind is providing opportunities to practice with supports. Complex skills are difficult to master unless students have a chance to focus on individual steps one at a time.

Teachers can facilitate the automation of background knowledge activation by offering students the chance to practice with scaffolds. Depending on the learner's level of need and his or her preferences, scaffolds could take the form of guide sheets explaining the procedure, a one-on-one review with the teacher, access to a peer expert, or a simplifying step such as dividing the topic area into subtopics to be dealt with one at a time.

As students continue to practice, it is also essential to provide ongoing, relevant feedback. This, too, could take a variety of forms to meet different students' needs and preferences: one-on-one teacher or peer feedback, a group discussion to reveal gaps in knowledge or misconceptions, or perhaps a self-test. Last, when asking students to demonstrate background knowledge, offer flexible opportunities for demonstrating skill, such as an oral presentation, composition, hands-on demonstration, or collage. This helps to ensure that strengths and weaknesses unrelated to the background knowledge itself do not confound students' performance.

UDL Principle 3: Affective Learning

Students vary widely in their preferences and inclinations, making it important to give students the flexibility to pursue their own interests and provide multiple, flexible options for engagement. Offering choices of content and tools is one way for teachers to fuel every student's enthusiasm for developing and activating background knowledge. Although by design the content area is often restricted, in some cases there is leeway to offer students choice. For example, when developing background knowledge on a fairly general topic, such as poetry or war, students could be given the option of focusing on particular examples of interest. With respect to tools, students might be given the option of working with pictures or text, or of recording knowledge on computer, on paper, or on tape.

Challenge is another factor influencing students' motivation to learn. When challenged too much or too little, students tend to disengage. But by providing adjustable levels of challenge, teachers can help ensure that each student is optimally motivated. During background knowledge instruction this can be accomplished by offering flexible supports that can be optionally accessed. Computer programs would be particularly useful in this regard, as they could incorporate a range of supports that could be accessed or not, depending on the individual. Students might also select from teacher and peer support, templates for recording knowledge, and graphic organizers for keeping track of and organizing knowledge.

A third advantageous method for engaging students is offering a choice of learning context. Students thrive in different contexts—minimally or maximally structured, individual or group settings, inside or outside the classroom. Background knowledge instruction can be effective in all of these contexts, and students benefit from having a choice. For example, a student could learn by reading a book in class or taking a field trip outside the classroom. One student might pair up with a peer, another might work by himself, and yet another might engage in large-group discussion. By diversifying the options, teachers can reduce affective barriers to success.

Classroom Examples

The section above highlights many ways that background knowledge instruction supports the three UDL principles and aligns with UDL teaching practices. This next section goes a step farther, showing that this can work not only in theory but in practice as well. Here we present two examples of UDL application of background knowledge instruction, one from CAST's work and one from CyberBee, written by Linda C. Joseph of the Columbus (Ohio) Public Schools. For the CAST example, we highlight the ways that background knowledge supports converge with UDL teaching methods. For the outside example, we identify general UDL features in the lesson and then highlight ways that background knowledge instruction could be better integrated with UDL to reduce lingering barriers.

Example 1: CAST's Universally Designed Hypertexts to Improve Reading Comprehension

With funding from the U.S. Department of Education, Office of Special Education Programs, and private foundations, CAST has investigated the benefits of a computer-supported reading environment to help students develop reading comprehension strategies and learn to read for understanding.[3] Merging reciprocal teaching (Palincsar & Brown, 1986) and UDL, CAST's research prototypes provide comprehension strategy instruction in engaging and supported digital environments (Dalton,

TABLE 4

UDL and Background Knowledge Applications of
Thinking Reader Research Prototype

UDL Teaching Method	Supportive Lesson Feature(s)
Provide multiple examples.	The multimedia glossary offers multiple photo illustrations for vocabulary words. Web links to resources offer students multiple examples of key facts and concepts.
Highlight critical features.	The Maps, Timeline, and Character Journey highlight critical features of the text related to setting and characters. The Power-Point and Web links to resources highlight other critical features related to the text.
Provide multiple media and formats.	The multimedia glossary offers text and illustrations. The Video- and Photo-Essays provide redundant information in multiple media and formats. Maps and Character Journey present story information in another medium and format. Vocabulary support is provided in English and Spanish in Thinking Reader.
Provide opportunities to practice with supports.	All the background knowledge aids provide optional support for students, who can access them or not, as they wish.
Offer adjustable levels of challenge.	Students can adjust the level of challenge by varying their consultation of the background knowledge supports.
Offer choices of content and tools.	The variety of background knowledge aids provide students with the opportunity to choose among different content and tools.

Pisha, Coyne, Eagleton, & Deysher, 2001). These prototypes embed reading comprehension strategy instruction directly into literature. As students read with the option of using text-to-speech to access content, they encounter prompts to stop and apply reading comprehension strategies. Instruction is individualized through leveled supports and optional scaffolds, which include background knowledge aids. Table 4 shows different background knowledge supports in Thinking Reader, mapped to UDL teaching strategies.

Example 2: "Building Prior Knowledge" Lesson Plan from CyberBee[4]

Kathleen Waugamann, a fourth grade teacher, developed this lesson plan for her social studies curriculum. The main content objective is responding to the text, in this case the book *Teammates* by Peter Golenbock, a story about the friendship between Brooklyn Dodgers Jackie Robinson and Pee Wee Reese in an era of segregation. As a prelude to reading the book, students visit websites to explore baseball, segregation, the Klu Klux Klan, violence against blacks, and changes made during the civil rights movement. After reading and discussing the book, they return to the Web to retrieve more information, create a Venn diagram to compare the black and white baseball leagues, and produce presentations to show their understanding of the story. This lesson plan supports UDL principles in some fundamental ways, most prominently by using multimedia technology to help students build and activate background knowledge (see Table 5).

There are additional ways to minimize barriers in this lesson using a combination of UDL teaching methods and background knowledge instruction. For example, understanding Web content requires a kind of Internet literacy that can be a recognition barrier for some students. Teachers can reduce this barrier by providing students with rudimentary knowledge about how the Web is organized, types of content it contains, and common Web vocabulary. Table 6 gives additional examples of how UDL can be applied to background knowledge instruction to reduce recognition, strategic, and affective barriers.

For students to succeed throughout the curriculum, they must develop appropriate background knowledge and the ability to use it. Research studies show that helping students to build and activate background knowledge significantly improves their comprehension of expository texts, thereby facilitating content-area learning. Effective instructional approaches include direct instruction of background knowledge and instruction to reflect on and record prior knowledge. These approaches have the added advantage of directly supporting UDL and students' diverse abilities and preferences for recognizing patterns. In this way, they can help minimize barriers to content-area learning and optimize every student's chance to succeed. The ideas and examples shared in this chapter can help educators capitalize on the mutually supportive relationship between background knowledge instruction and UDL, and better ensure that every student is a literacy success.

TABLE 5
Existing UDL Elements in "Building Prior Knowledge" Lesson Plan

UDL Teaching Method	Supportive Lesson Feature(s)
Provide multiple examples.	To identify with the notion of being a baseball player, students visit multiple websites to view multiple examples of baseball cards. Multiple websites are preselected for later in the lesson, when students retrieve more information relevant to the story. Multiple examples are used to illustrate the topic of segregation in the PowerPoint slideshow.
Highlight critical features.	The teacher highlights critical features of the story with a thematic PowerPoint slideshow.
Provide multiple media and formats.	The teacher provides background information in the form of website material, printed text, images, and digital photographs.
Support background context.	The teacher develops and activates student background knowledge in a variety of ways (visiting websites, making baseball cards, viewing a slideshow, consulting other resources, generating Venn diagrams).
Provide opportunities to practice with supports.	The teacher scaffolds the research process by providing suggested Web resources.
Provide ongoing, relevant feedback.	Students have the opportunity to get feedback on their knowledge state during group discussion of the PowerPoint presentation.
Offer choices of content and tools.	Students can choose among websites and library resources and have the latitude to focus on different aspects of the story.

TABLE 6
Strategies to Make Background Knowledge Instruction in "Building Prior Knowledge" Lesson Plan More in Line with UDL

Barrier	UDL Strategy
Recognition Barriers	
Need for conceptual knowledge about what a website is and how to navigate it, as well as familiarity with Web terminology.	Provide students with background knowledge on websites and Web terminology and a way for accessing this background knowledge while using the Web.

TABLE 6   *continued*

Barrier	UDL Strategy
Seeing or decoding the text and/or images on the preselected websites.	Provide students who cannot see or read the text/images on the websites—or who do not like this presentation mode—with the option of using a screen reader to access the content as speech. Preselect websites with different reading levels of text and assign them accordingly. Offer the option of using other media such as video and audio recordings.
The amount of material on the websites is overwhelming and there are too many distractors (advertisements, unrelated text, flashing icons).	Give students the option of bringing in their favorite baseball cards instead of finding them/viewing them on the Web. Provide supports to help keep students on task when reading on the Web and choose between relevant and irrelevant parts of a Web page.
Strategic Barriers	
Keeping track of information.	Provide students with note-taking tools for researching on or off the Web.
Creating a Venn diagram.	Provide scaffolds for students who need them, such as a partially filled-in Venn diagram, the opportunity to work with a peer coach, or models of expert performance.
Lack of awareness of how well they are succeeding with research tasks.	Provide students with regular feedback.
Affective Barriers	
Research process is boring.	Provide students with the option of finding their own resources, such as video and interviews with older relatives who lived during segregation. Challenge students who are adept researchers with finding the answer to a difficult question.
Reading material on the websites and in the Harcourt Brace fourth-grade anthology biographies is too easy or too difficult.	Offer students a broader range of research materials, representing a broader range of reading levels.
Difficulty maintaining focus, attention, and involvement during the classwide PowerPoint presentation and discussion.	Offer students the chance to view the PowerPoint presentation a second time by themselves or in pairs at the computer. Present the PowerPoint to smaller groups of students at one time.

GRAPHIC ORGANIZERS

One way to help make a curriculum more supportive of students and teachers is to incorporate graphic organizers. Graphic organizers have been widely researched for their effectiveness in improving learning outcomes for students with and without disabilities. This section examines the research on educational applications of graphic organizers in grades K–12 and explores ways they can support UDL at both the theoretical and teacher-practice levels. A graphic organizer is a visual and graphic display that depicts the relationships between facts, terms, and/or ideas within a learning task. Graphic organizers are also sometimes referred to as knowledge maps, concept maps, story maps, cognitive organizers, advance organizers, or concept diagrams. They come in many different forms.

- A **Descriptive or Thematic Map** works well for mapping generic information, but particularly well for mapping hierarchical relationships.
- Organizing a hierarchical set of information, reflecting superordinate or subordinate elements, is made easier by constructing a **Network Tree.**
- When the information relating to a main idea or theme does not fit into a hierarchy, a **Spider Map** can help with organization.
- When information contains cause-and-effect problems and solutions, a **Problem and Solution Map** can be useful for organizing.

Descriptive or Thematic Map

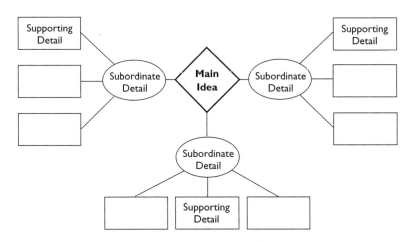

Network Tree

Spider Map

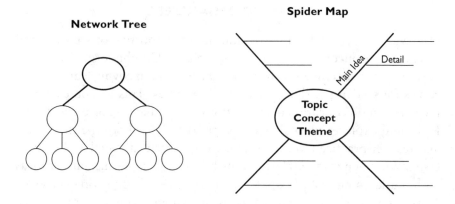

Problem and Solution Map

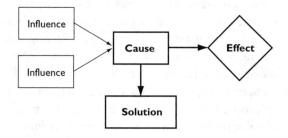

Problem-Solution Outline

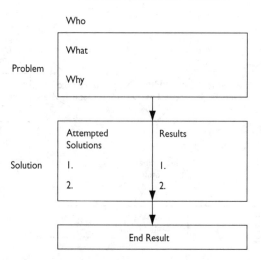

Sequential Episodic Map

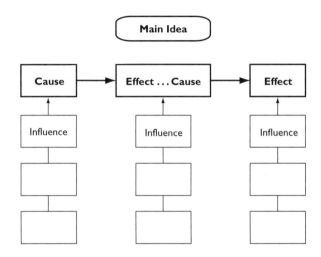

Fishbone Map

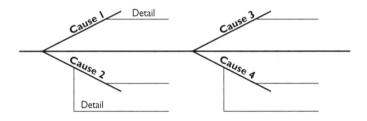

- A **Problem-Solution Outline** helps students to compare different solutions to a problem.
- A **Sequential Episodic Map** is useful for mapping cause and effect.
- When cause-effect relationships are complex and nonredundant, a **Fishbone Map** may be particularly useful.
- A **Comparative and Contrastive Map** can help students compare and contrast the features of two concepts.
- Another way to compare concepts' attributes is to construct a **Compare-Contrast Matrix**.
- A **Continuum Scale** is effective for organizing information along a dimension, such as less to more, low to high, and few to many.

Comparative and Contrastive Map

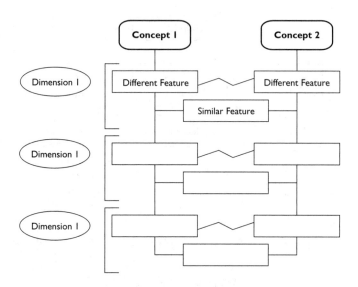

Compare-Contrast Matrix

Attribute 1		
Attribute 2		
Attribute 3		

Continuum Scale

- A **Series of Events Chain** can help students organize information according to various steps or stages, while a **Cycle Map** is useful for organizing information that is circular or cyclical, with no absolute beginning or ending.
- A **Human Interaction Outline** is effective for organizing events in terms of a chain of action and reaction (especially useful in social sciences and humanities).

Series of Events Chain   **Cycle Map**

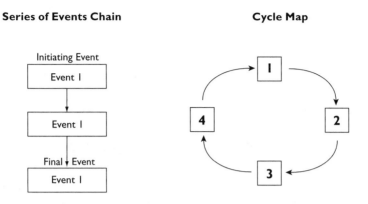

Human Interaction Outline

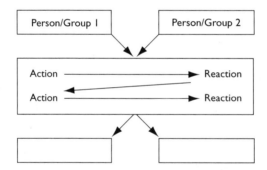

Graphic organizers have been applied across a range of curriculum subject areas. Although reading is by far the most studied application, science, social studies, language arts, and math are also represented in the research base on graphic organizers. In these subject areas, graphic organizers have been shown to have benefits that extend beyond their well-established effects on reading comprehension (Bulgren, Schumaker, & Deschler, 1988; Darch, Carnine, & Kameenui, 1986; Herl, O'Neil, Chung, & Schacter, 1999; Willerman & Mac Harg, 1991). Operations such as mapping cause and effect, note-taking, comparing and contrasting concepts, organizing problems and solutions, and relating information to main ideas or themes can be broadly beneficial.

There is solid evidence for the effectiveness of graphic organizers in facilitating learning. Ten of the 12 studies reviewed by NCAC that investigated the effects on learning of using graphic organizers reported some positive learning outcome (Strangman & Hall, 2003). Of course, a wide variety of factors may influence the effectiveness of graphic organizers for improving student learning, including grade level, point of implementation, and instructional context. A fair number of studies have included students with disabilities in their investigations of graphic organizers. Successful learning outcomes have been demonstrated for both students with learning disabilities (Anderson-Inman, Knox-Quinn, & Horney, 1996; Boyle & Weishaar, 1997; Bulgren et al., 1988; Gallego, Duran, & Scanlon, 1990; Gardill & Jitendra, 1999; Idol & Croll, 1987; Newby, Caldwell, & Recht, 1989; Sinatra, Stahl-Gemake, & Berg, 1984) and students without disabilities (Alvermann & Boothby, 1986; Bulgren et al., 1988; Darch et al., 1986; Willerman & MacHarg, 1991). Table 7 provides a basic description of these findings.

Smartly implemented, graphic organizers have the potential to have a positive impact on learning by offering teachers a means to improve all students' comprehension and vocabulary knowledge.

Graphic Organizers and Universal Design for Learning

Digital materials such as graphic organizers are an excellent resource for diversifying the curriculum in a UDL way, because they themselves are flexible. The following sections explore how graphic organizers can support individual differences in how students recognize cues and patterns, master skills, and engage with learning.

UDL Principle 1: Recognition Learning

No single teaching method can make every student an expert at recognizing patterns. But graphic organizers can help ensure that every student masters patterns in part by viewing multiple examples. For example, a teacher could facilitate students' understanding of cause and effect by developing concept maps of different examples or by using different types of maps (Fishbone Map, Sequential Episodic Map, or Problem and Solution Map) to map the same cause-and-effect information. Because graphic organizers can be saved in a digital format, these multiple examples can be stored and accumulated for future use. Students can se-

TABLE 7

Main Research Findings Regarding the Impact of Graphic Organizer Use on Students with Disabilities

Boyle & Weishaar (1997)	Students with learning disabilities	Students taught to generate cognitive organizers for use during reading and students who were taught to use expert-generated cognitive organizers during reading scored significantly higher than untaught peers on a comprehension test of literal and inferential comprehension.
Bulgren et al. (1988)	Students with learning disabilities and students without learning disabilities	When teachers used a concept-teaching routine to present concept diagrams to students, students with and without learning disabilities significantly improved performance on tests of concept acquisition and improved their note-taking.
Gallego et al. (1990)	Students with learning disabilities	Learning and rehearsing a semantic mapping procedure was associated with a significant increase in quantity and quality of in-class verbal contributions and a significant increase in the quality of students' written summaries.
Gardill & Jitendra (1999)	Students with learning disabilities, one student with neurological impairments, all experiencing difficulty with reading comprehension	Direct instruction with an advanced story-map procedure led to an improvement in students' basal comprehension scores and story grammar comprehension.
Idol & Croll (1987)	Special education students with reading comprehension problems	Training to use story-mapping procedures led to an improvement in most students' ability to answer comprehension questions.
Sinatra et al. (1984)	Students referred to a reading clinic	Students who took part in instruction with a story-mapping procedure answered significantly more comprehension questions correctly on average than students who took part in a directed reading approach.

lect the examples most effective for them. Teachers can also use graphic organizers as an alternative means to highlight the critical features of a pattern. Story grammar maps are an example.

Students vary in their ability to process different media and formats. Graphic organizers, which can incorporate not only text but also multimedia, provide an alternative to speech and linear text that may be preferable for some students. The geometric shapes used in some graphic organizers may help some students visualize patterns more easily. Making graphic organizers available increases the odds that individual students will be able to find the formats and media that are accessible and useful to them. And within the broad class of graphic organizers is a great variety of formats to choose from. Even students for whom access is not a problem will benefit from the redundancy of mixed media and formats, which can foster deeper understanding of a pattern's essential characteristics.

Another way graphic organizers can help minimize barriers to recognition learning is by supporting background knowledge. What students learn is partly a matter of what they already know. Graphic organizers can help students make connections between existing knowledge and new knowledge. They are a good complement to familiar ways of supporting background knowledge, such as linear text. And because they are digital, they can be built into reading and other material, enabling students the choice of accessing a variety of information when and as is best for them.

UDL Principle 2: Strategic Learning

Students have different strengths and weaknesses in this area, making it important to vary the instruction of skills and strategies. Graphic organizers can provide flexible models of skilled performance. Completed graphic organizers offer students an alternative to linear text-, audio-, live demonstration-, or image-based models that they may be unable to access. Access issues aside, adding graphic organizers to the usual mix of models helps to expose students to different, effective ways to do something. Students also need flexible opportunities for demonstrating skill, and the use of graphic organizers helps to diversify options, offering alternatives to traditional ways of demonstrating skill, such as written compositions. Students can put together text in a nonlinear format, organize a collection of images, or develop a multimedia display.

UDL Principle 3: Affective Learning

Students vary widely in their preferences and interests, and tools such as graphic organizers can help keep everyone engaged. Graphic organizers support multiple, flexible options for engagement in three key ways. First, they can offer students a choice of tools. The freedom to select tools based on personal interests and strengths can help maintain a good level of interest and even reengage learners. Moreover, when working with graphic organizers, students can select from different media and formats (text only, images, multimedia). Graphic organizers can also be used to provide adjustable levels of challenge during a task. Scaffolds can be flexibly accessed to ensure that each student is working at the appropriate level of difficulty. Similarly, varying the availability of scaffolds and other built-in forms of structure will increase the chances that they will find one suitable to them—with maximal or minimal structure.

Examples from Practice

Here we present examples of UDL applications of graphic organizers, one from CAST's work and one from an outside source. For the CAST example, we highlight the ways that graphic organizers are used to implement UDL teaching methods. For the outside example, we identify general UDL features in the existing lesson and highlight ways that graphic organizers could be used to reduce lingering barriers.

Example 1: The Monkey's Paw Unit[5]

This unit is a series of ten lessons around the story "Monkey's Paw" by W. W. Jacobs. The unit supports ninth- and tenth-grade English language arts courses in which students read and analyze short stories, novels, and classic literature. We focus on Lessons 2 and 4, which have the common goals of building student engagement in story reading and comprehension and developing vocabulary and the ability to analyze plot elements. Graphic organizers, in the form of plot diagrams and semantic maps, are used in several ways.

During the vocabulary development portion of Lesson 2, the teacher uses a graphic organizer in PowerPoint to organize a discussion of examples and nonexamples consistent with various word definitions. Later, students work with a printed or digital version of the story's plot diagram as they read Part 1 of the story and try to define what a story exposition means. During Lesson 4, graphic organizers are used again

TABLE 8

UDL Features of Sample Lessons

UDL Teaching Method	Supportive Graphic Organizer Feature(s)
Provide multiple examples.	During the vocabulary activity, the graphic organizer is used to present multiple examples and nonexamples to the students.
Highlight critical features.	Using the graphic organizer to contrast examples and nonexamples of words consistent with a definition is a way to highlight critical features of vocabulary. In addition, the plot diagrams help highlight key plot elements through both text and graphics.
Provide multiple media and formats.	Students have the option of working with graphic organizers in different media and formats: large presentation/display version, printed version, digital version with text and/or images. With the digital version of the graphic organizers, text-to-speech can be used.
Support background context.	The vocabulary instruction provides background knowledge so that students can comprehend the reading. In addition, students can review plot diagrams created in Lesson 2 as background for their work around plot elements in Lesson 4.
Provide flexible models of skilled performance.	The teacher provides multiple models for use of the storyplot diagram: large display, paper-pencil, and digital versions.
Provide opportunities to practice with supports.	With the digital version of the graphic organizers, text to speech can be used, as well as a spell checker. The format of the text can be altered to suit a student's visual needs. And, the type-entry mode supports students who have trouble writing by hand.
Provide ongoing, relevant feedback.	Students can use text-to-speech to play back their entries into the digital graphic organizers, providing them with a way to self-monitor.
Offer flexible opportunities for demonstrating skill.	Students have a choice of how to complete their plot diagrams. They can print their responses on a hard-copy graphic organizer or type them into a digital version.
Offer choices of content and tools.	Students have a choice of using a digital or hard-copy graphic organizer, and they can input text and/or images into the plot diagrams.
Offer adjustable levels of challenge.	Students have the opportunity to collaborate with others to complete the plot diagram, and the digital version offers supports.
Offer choices of learning context.	Students can complete the plot diagram in varying contexts: 1) large group, 2) cooperative study groups, and 3) individual students.

as the teacher reviews the exposition plot diagrams from the previous lesson and students continue to work on their plot diagrams, using them to depict other plot elements. These lessons are good examples of how graphic organizers can be used to support UDL and accommodate diverse learners. In Table 8, we detail specific ways that these lessons use graphic organizers to put UDL teaching methods into practice.

Example 2: SAS in School's "As the Tide Turns: Radio Broadcasts from the Front" [6]

One of the main objectives of this lesson plan, which is focused on building an understanding of key World War II battles, is to use a graphic organizer to plot the course of an important military turning point in the war. This lesson is consistent in a number of ways with UDL principles and teaching methods (see Table 9). Through clearly stated goals and the use of digital materials, such as the Internet, audio files, and graphic organizers, a good amount of flexibility has been injected into the lesson, helping to minimize barriers. There are additional ways to minimize barriers in this lesson using UDL teaching methods and graphic organizers.

TABLE 9

Existing UDL Elements in "As the Tide Turns:
Radio Broadcasts from the Front" Lesson Plan

UDL Teaching Method	Supportive Lesson Feature(s)
Provide multiple examples.	The teacher provides multiple Web resources for each battle.
Provide multiple media and formats.	The teacher provides suggested Web resources that offer text, images, and audio.
Provide opportunities to practice with supports.	The teacher scaffolds the research process by providing suggested Web resources.
Offer flexible opportunities for demonstrating skill.	Students have the opportunity to create a graphic organizer, write a news broadcast, or produce and record a news broadcast.
Offer choice of content and tools.	Students can choose what graphic organizer to use. Some students are permitted to choose a task to complete, and along with it the tools they can use. The lesson plan leaves open the possibility of working with a digital or hard-copy version of the graphic organizer.

:

TABLE 10

UDL Strategies for Using Graphic Organizers to Further Minimize Lesson Barriers in "As the Tide Turns: Radio Broadcasts from the Front"

Barrier	UDL Strategy
Choosing the appropriate graphic organizer for the task.	Provide background information on graphic organizers and their use (in printed and digital formats).
Writing the headings and brief explanations that go in the graphic organizer.	Offer use of speech recognition, spell-checker, and grammar-checker when using graphic organizers; link from graphic-organizer program to supports such as a thesaurus.
Organizing the headings and brief explanations to connect the different pieces of researched information.	Offer students the option of inserting images or sound clips to help organize thoughts and information before beginning to write the text. Provide links to background information that may help with the task of connecting pieces of researched information. Provide models of completed graphic organizers. Provide templates customized to the student; some will be partially filled in, some will provide tips on connecting information.
Task is too easy for some students.	Provide students who need more challenge with a list of more complex graphic organizers.
Task is boring for some students.	Offer students the option of incorporating images, audio, and video into the graphic organizer; show students how to customize the graphic organizer by using different colors and text styles.

In Table 10, we give some examples of how the UDL features of graphic organizers can be used to further improve this lesson's ability to reach all students. Please note that we are not making generalized recommendations for making this lesson more UDL, but instead are focusing on ways that graphic organizers, specifically, can help achieve this goal.

As more and more teachers begin to explore UDL in their classrooms, they will begin to augment books and lectures with new technologies. Graphic organizer software is undoubtedly a technology that can help teachers succeed at implementing UDL and developing curricula that make information and learning more accessible. Although these teachers will undoubtedly encounter challenges, models and resources continue to build—and along with them the opportunity to realize the potential of graphic organizers and UDL in the classroom.

VIRTUAL REALITY AND
COMPUTER SIMULATIONS

Many people associate virtual reality and computer simulations with science fiction, high-tech industries, and computer games; few associate these technologies with education. But virtual reality and computer simulations are potentially powerful learning technologies, offering teachers a means to concretize abstract concepts for students and provide them with opportunities to learn by doing what they might otherwise encounter only in a textbook. This section examines the research on educational uses of these technologies and explores points of intersection with Universal Design for Learning.

Computer simulations are computer-generated versions of real-world objects (e.g., a skyscraper or chemical molecules) or processes (e.g., population growth or biological decay). They may be presented in two-dimensional text-driven formats or, increasingly, three-dimensional multimedia formats.

Virtual reality is a technology that allows students to explore and manipulate computer-generated, three-dimensional environments in real time. Examples of virtual reality environments are a virtual solar system that enables users to fly through space and observe objects from any angle, a virtual science experiment that simulates the growth of microorganisms under different conditions, a virtual tour of an archeological site, and a re-creation of the Constitutional Convention of 1787.

There are two main types of virtual reality environments. Desktop virtual reality environments are presented on an ordinary computer screen and are usually explored by keyboard, mouse, wand, joystick, or touch screen. Web-based "virtual tours" are an example of a commonly available desktop virtual reality format. Total immersion virtual reality environments are presented on multiple room-size screens or through a stereoscopic head-mounted display unit. Additional specialized equipment such as a DataGlove (worn as one would a regular glove) enables the participant to interact with the virtual environment through normal body movements. Sensors on the head unit and DataGlove track the viewer's movements during exploration and provide feedback that is used to revise the display—enabling real-time, fluid interactivity.

Computer simulations and virtual reality offer students the unique opportunity to experience and explore a broad range of environments, objects, and phenomena within the walls of the classroom. Students can observe and manipulate normally inaccessible objects, variables, and processes in real time. The ability of these technologies to make what is abstract and intangible concrete and manipulable suits them to the study of natural phenomena and abstract concepts, bridging "the gap between the concrete world of nature and the abstract world of concepts and models" (Yair, Mintz, & Litvak, 2001). They are an intriguing alternative to the conventional study of science and mathematics, which requires students to develop understandings based on textual descriptions and two-dimensional representations. The concretizing of objects—atoms, molecules, and bacteria, for example—makes learning more straightforward and intuitive for students and supports a constructivist approach to learning. Students can learn by doing in addition to, for example, learning by reading. They can test theories by developing alternative realities. This greatly facilitates the mastery of difficult concepts, for example, the relation between distance, motion, and time (Yair et al., 2001).

In addition, the ability of virtual reality and computer simulations to scaffold student learning (Jiang & Potter, 1994; Kelly, 1997), potentially in an individualized way, enables them to be integrated across a range of curriculum areas. An illustration of scaffolding possibilities is a simulation program that records data and translates between notation systems for the student so that he or she can concentrate on the targeted skills of learning probability (Jiang & Potter, 1994).

These environments also help put students in control of their learning; they can revisit aspects of the environment repeatedly. The multisensory nature is also a scaffold and can be especially helpful to students who are less visual learners and those who are better at comprehending symbols than text. With virtual environments, students can encounter abstract concepts directly; without the barrier of language or symbols, computer simulations and virtual environments are highly engaging: "There is simply no other way to engage students as virtual reality can" (Sykes & Reid, 1999).

Our survey of the research literature shows that virtual reality and computer simulations are technologies that have the potential to have a positive impact on learning by offering teachers and students a means to experience abstract concepts (Strangman, Hall, & Meyer, 2003).

UDL Applications

As digital materials, virtual reality and computer simulations have flexibility that suits them to the task of diversifying a curriculum in a UDL way. In each of the following sections, we discuss some specific ways that virtual reality and computer simulations can support curriculum diversification. The three UDL principles and their associated broad teaching methods will set the context for this discussion.

UDL Principle 1: Recognition Learning

The first UDL principle recommends that we support recognition learning by providing multiple, flexible methods of presentation. No single teaching method can make every student an expert at recognizing patterns, but the right set of teaching methods can support every student's success. Virtual reality and computer simulations, as part of a diversified tool kit of classroom materials, can help curriculum designers and teachers achieve this end. They support all four UDL teaching methods for recognition learning.

One thing teachers can do to facilitate the recognition of patterns is to provide multiple examples. Text-, speech-, and image-based examples are an excellent start. The addition of computer simulations and virtual reality can help to further enrich a teacher's arsenal of examples. Even a single simulation or virtual reality environment can offer a multitude of examples within, and this increased exposure greatly expedites the learning of patterns by recognition networks.

Another route toward teaching patterns is to highlight their critical features. Virtual reality and computer simulations create some new possibilities for drawing attention to specific features, such as digitized pointers, highlighting, sound cues, and text captioning. In the case of virtual reality, features can be made to pop out, and/or digital tour guides can be programmed to point out important details. Best of all, these materials are flexible enough to permit the offering of a variety of highlighting methods, enabling each student to pick what is optimal for him or her.

Another powerful way that computer simulations and virtual reality support a UDL approach to recognition learning is by helping teachers to provide multiple media and formats. Virtual reality and computer simulations incorporate multiple media into a single presentation, offering a rich, multisensory experience of a pattern. In this manner, they go well beyond what traditional media can do. They also are able to present these patterns in a three-dimensional format. These features may help to create access to aspects of a pattern that may be difficult to communicate through traditional media, and they support students who struggle with printed text or speech.

The fourth broad UDL teaching method for recognition learning is to support background knowledge. Virtual reality and computer simulations can be mined as a tool to help students review background knowledge on a topic, priming their recognition networks for new knowledge. These digital environments not only provide a change of media for students seeking background information, but also set up a situation where students can access various pieces of background knowledge as they see fit, ensuring that every student is supported at the appropriate level. Students may select from a range of computer simulations, depending on what they want to review. Similarly, students can flexibly access background information in a virtual environment. Perhaps they might tour a virtual library, pulling off the shelves only the materials that they find useful.

UDL Principle 2: Strategic Learning

The second UDL principle asks that we support strategic learning by providing multiple, flexible methods of expression and apprenticeship. This principle and its associated teaching methods guide teachers in anticipating barriers to strategic learning and in selecting materials and practices that are flexible enough to overcome these barriers. These are tasks with which computer simulations and virtual reality are inherently compatible.

Generally, we learn well by example, but there are definitive individual differences. Different students may learn best from different examples, making it vital to provide students with multiple models of skilled performance. In a classroom short on digital materials, there are a limited number of models for students to pick from because it is simply too hard to accumulate and store them when bound by printed text and images. And even the most generous set of models in printed text and printed images is limited in what information it can provide.

In contrast, digital environments such as computer simulations and virtual reality can provide students with rich, multisensory models, and it is relatively straightforward to offer students a large number of such models to choose from. For example, a student learning to do an oral presentation could visit a virtual environment full of scientists, businessmen, poets, and politicians, and listen to a presentation by any or all of them. Computer simulations also make it easy to give students multiple models to choose from. A computer program could, for example, easily simulate multiple solutions to solving an algebra problem or to balancing the dynamics in a pond's food chain.

Of course, students also need opportunities to develop skills on their own. To be successful they need opportunities to practice with supports. Teachers need a way to simplify complex strategic patterns so that students can master individual subcomponents one by one. Computer simulations and virtual reality offer some unique means to accomplish this. Computer simulations can be presented at varying levels of complexity and are amenable to digitized supports, such as note-taking features, links to resources, and tools such as automated graphing and unit conversion. With virtual reality there are interesting possibilities, such as programming helpers, tutors, and guides into the environment, to simplify its use.

As students practice skills, it is important that teachers provide ongoing, relevant feedback. This is how students know whether they are succeeding and what tasks or skills may need continued work. Feedback provided during the course of learning is most effective (Rose & Dolan, 2000; Rose & Meyer, 2002). It enables students to incorporate feedback and make corrections while learning is still happening. Digital materials like computer simulations and virtual reality offer a relatively facile means to integrate ongoing feedback into practice and learning. Students can get immediate feedback from the program about their success. In addition, different types of feedback can be made available, helping to ensure the right fit to the student.

Without flexible opportunities for demonstrating skill, these skill-building supports would be of little use. Here, computer simulations and virtual reality offer some unique options. A student could construct a simulation to demonstrate his or her ability to apply algebra to real-life situations or to predict the outcome of a bacterial growth experiment or viral outbreak. Instead of writing a timeline of historical events, a student could demonstrate his or her ability to organize these events by navigating in proper order through a virtual historical environment.

Computer simulations and virtual reality offer opportunities to demonstrate skill without some of the usual barriers. Consider, for example, the skill of identifying the parts of a frog's respiratory system. Traditionally, a teacher might have tested this skill by having a student dissect a frog, but for a student with a physical impairment or an allergy to formaldehyde, this would be impossible. But these same students could demonstrate their skill in the context of a simulated dissection.

UDL Principle 3: Affective Learning

If students are not interested in what they are learning, efforts to support them in any of the above ways will have a much smaller return. This is why the third UDL principle recommends that we support affective learning by providing multiple, flexible options for engagement. Computer simulations and virtual reality can be important tools in ensuring that students across the board are engaging with learning.

The introduction of virtual reality and computer simulations into the classroom will greatly improve teachers' ability to offer choices of content and tools because their nature is so vastly different from those typically made available in the classroom. The nonprint, interactive, multisensory, three-dimensional, and in some cases hands-on nature of these tools can be highly engaging for students. Researchers Sykes and Reid (1999) have even said about virtual reality, "There is simply no other way to engage students as virtual reality can." These tools make certain types of content unusually accessible and enable students to work with that content in a way not normally possible. They can witness historical events and foreign cultures firsthand, manipulate objects in faraway galaxies, explore cause and effect on a shortened timescale, test complex principles of physics, and try out alternatives that might otherwise be too dangerous or difficult. Because computer simulations and virtual reality are programmed and digitized, it would be realistic for a teacher to offer students a selection of different environments and simulations with different content.

Another way to motivate students is to provide rewards. But no one kind of reward will motivate every student, so teachers are encouraged to offer a choice of rewards. Computer simulations and virtual reality can help mix things up. It is not difficult to generate recreational forms of these materials that could be offered to students as an extrinsic reward for a job well done. In terms of intrinsic rewards, these materials are also valuable in terms of their ability to build students' sense of accomplishment by providing feedback and knowledge of results.

Students also benefit when teachers offer a choice of learning context. Factors like the degree of structure or support, the speed of the work, the level and timing of feedback, and the degree of game-like elements are important to different students in different ways. With computer simulations and virtual reality, teachers can vary some of these features and offer students enough choices that they can find a personally effective learning context.

Classroom Example

CAST Model Spinner Lesson

[From Planning for All Learners (PAL) tool kit on CAST's Teaching Every Student interactive website—www.cast.org/tes]

This lesson plan from CAST highlights ways that computer simulations can be used to implement UDL teaching methods and reduce curriculum barriers. It addresses standards of the National Council of Teachers of Mathematics by teaching students the relationship between theoretical and experimental probability.

Whereas a traditional approach might use a text-based or mechanical spinner to teach students this relationship, this UDL lesson employs a computer-simulated spinner from the Shodor website. The simulated spinner is flexible. Students can create a spinner with one to twelve sectors (each a different color), vary the number of spins, and view the theoretical and experimental probabilities both numerically and graphically. This flexibility fits right in with UDL. Table 11 lists the UDL features made possible by the use of this computer simulation.

Virtual reality and computer simulations, although still new and developing technologies, have the potential to deliver great benefits in the classroom. One of their greatest areas of potential is in supporting UDL and its efforts to generate more flexible and broadly accessible curricula. Indeed, UDL and new technologies such as virtual reality and computer simulations are mutually supportive—and a worthwhile focus of attention for education researchers, teachers, and supporters of genuine education reform.

TABLE 11
UDL Features of the CAST PAL Tool Kit Model Spinner Lesson

UDL Teaching Method	Supportive Computer Simulation Feature(s)
Provide multiple examples.	Because the digital spinner can perform multiple trials in a very short time, multiple questions can be posed and answered quickly to illustrate multiple examples of the relationship between experimental and theoretical probability. In the large-group setting, students are able to view and discuss the results of multiple spinner configurations and multiple spins. Without the digital spinner, there are multiple instances of a particular event (e.g., coin flipping), but the *relationship* is only illustrated once in a very large number of trials.
Highlight critical features.	The digital format makes it possible for the teacher to highlight critical features of the spinner for the entire class using a projection plate. Students can also view a probability table and pie chart that highlight key features of the relationship between theoretical and experimental probability.
Provide multiple media and formats.	Theoretical and experimental probability are presented in multiple formats: a percentage table below the spinner and a pie chart showing the proportion of times that each sector is spun. The digital format of the spinner enables the use of text-to-speech.
Provide flexible models of skilled performance.	Because the spinner can be viewed and discussed by the whole class via a projection plate, each student can observe the teacher and their peers modeling questioning and seeking data. Or students can work together at the computer in mixed-ability groups. This means that lower achieving students can observe and participate with higher achieving students as they explore the relationships between the two types of probability.
Provide opportunities to practice with supports.	The spinner can be installed on multiple computers in school (and home), giving students ample opportunity to practice. The digital spinner offers supports, such as the ability to simplify the spinner and text-to-speech compatibility. And it scaffolds the mechanical and calculation processes so that students can focus on the true purpose of the lesson.
Provide ongoing, relevant feedback.	Unlike mechanical tools like coins and dice, the digital spinner provides immediate feedback following each spin and feedback about large numbers of spins in an instant. This feedback is germane to the learning goal, understanding the relationship of theoretical to experimental probability.
Offer choice of content and tools.	Students can make a number of choices involving the spinner configuration, the type of data displays, and the number of spins.
Offer adjustable levels of challenge.	The adjustability of the spinner makes it possible to vary the difficulty level. With one to twelve sectors, students can work with a spinner whose complexity is appropriate to their level of understanding. In the group context, the complexity can be changed as the group gains understanding.

Offer choices of learning context.	Students can work with the spinner individually or view it with the whole class via a projection plate. Students can pursue the spinner activity on one of many computers at different times during the day. The spinner activity could also be taken home and installed on students' home computers, if available, or accessed via the Web from home.

NOTES

1. This lesson is available online at CAST's Teaching Every Student website in the Planning for All Learners (PAL) tool kit (www.cast.org/teachingeverystudent).
2. More can be learned by reading the complete NCAC literature review online at http://www.cast.org/publications/ncac/ncac_backknowledgeudl.html
3. In 2004, Tom Snyder Productions/Scholastic, in cooperation with CAST, developed nine commercial Thinking Reader editions of popular middle school novels, such as *Tuck Everlasting* and *A Wrinkle in Time*, based on these prototypes.
4. http://www.infotoday.com/MMSchools/may02/cybe0502.htm
5. In the Planning for All Learners tool kit at www.cast.org/tes
6. http://www.sasinschool.com/products/pathways/

REFERENCES

Alvermann, D. E., & Boothby, P. R. (1986). Children's transfer of graphic organizer instruction. *Reading Psychology, 7*(2), 87–100.

Anderson-Inman, L., Knox-Quinn, C., & Horney, M. A. (1996). Computer-based study strategies for students with learning disabilities: Individual differences associated with adoption level. *Journal of Learning Disabilities, 29,* 461–484.

Bean, T. W. (1995). Strategies for enhancing text comprehension in middle school. *Reading and Writing Quarterly, 11,* 163–171.

Biemans, H. J. A., Deel, O. R., & Simons, P. R. (2001). Differences between successful and less successful students while working with the CONTACT-2 strategy. *Learning and Instruction, 11,* 265–282.

Biemans, H. J. A., & Simons, P. R. (1996). Contact-2: A computer-assisted instructional strategy for promoting conceptual change. *Instructional Science, 24,* 157–176.

Boyle, J. R., & Weishaar, M. (1997). The effects of expert-generated versus student-generated cognitive organizers on the reading comprehension of students with learning disabilities. *Learning Disabilities Research and Practice, 12,* 228–235.

Bulgren, J., Schumaker, J. B., & Deshler, D. D. (1988). Effectiveness of a concept teaching routine in enhancing the performance of LD students in secondary-level mainstream classes. *Learning Disability Quarterly, 11*(1), 3–17.

Carr, E., & Ogle, D. (1987). K-W-L plus: A strategy for comprehension and summarization. *Journal of Reading, 30,* 626–631.

Carr, S. C., & Thompson, B. (1996). The effects of prior knowledge and schema activation strategies on the inferential reading comprehension of children with and without learning disabilities. *Learning Disability Quarterly, 19,* 48–61.

CAST. (n.d.). *Teaching every student.* Retrieved September 3, 2003, from http://www.cast.org/teachingeverystudent/

CAST. (n.d.). *UDL toolkits: planning for all learners.* Retrieved September 3, 2003, from http://www.cast.org/teachingeverystudent/toolkits/tk_introduction.cfm?tk_id=21

Croll, V. J., Idol-Maestas, L., Heal, L., & Pearson, P. D. (1986). *Bridging the comprehension gap with pictures.* Champaign: University of Illinois at Urbana–Champaign, Center for the Study of Reading.

Dalton, B., Pisha, B., Coyne, P., Eagleton, M., & Deysher, S. (2001). *Engaging the text: Reciprocal teaching and questioning strategies in a scaffolded learning environment.* (Final report to the U.S. Office of Special Education). Peabody, MA: CAST.

Darch, C. B., Carnine, D. W., & Kameenui, E. J. (1986). The role of graphic organizers and social structure in content area instruction. *Journal of Reading Behavior, 18,* 275–295.

Davis, S. J., & Winek, J. (1989). Improving expository writing by increasing background knowledge. *Journal of Reading, 33,* 178–181.

Dochy, F. J. R. C., & Alexander, P. A. (1995). Mapping prior knowledge: A framework for discussion among researchers. *European Journal of Psychology of Education, 10,* 225–242.

Dochy, F. J. R. C., Segers, M., & Buehl, M. M. (1999). The relation between assessment practices and outcomes of studies: The case of research on prior knowlege. *Review of Educational Research, 69,* 145–186.

Dolan, R. P., & Hall T. E. (2001). Universal Design for Learning: Implications for large-scale assessment. *IDA Perspectives, 27*(4), 22–25.

Dole, J. A., Valencia, S. W., Greer, E. A., & Wardrop, J. L. (1991). Effects of two types of prereading instruction on the comprehension of narrative and expository text. *Reading Research Quarterly, 26,* 142–159.

Ellis, E. S., & Worthington, L. A. (1994). *Research synthesis on effective teaching principles and the design of quality tools for educators* (Technical Report No. 5). Eugene: University of Oregon, National Center to Improve the Tools of Educators.

Fisher, D., Frey, N., & Williams, D. (2002). Seven literacy strategies that work. *Educational Leadership, 60*(3), 70–73.

Gallego, M. A., Duran, G. Z., & Scanlon, D. J. (1990). Interactive teaching and learning: Facilitating learning disabled students' progress from novice to expert. In J. Zutell & S. McCormick (Eds.), *Literacy theory and research: Analyses from multiple paradigms: Thirty-ninth yearbook of the National Reading Conference* (pp. 311–319). Chicago: National Reading Conference.

Gardill, M. C., & Jitendra, A. K. (1999). Advanced story map instruction: Effects on the reading comprehension of students with learning disabilities. *Journal of Special Education, 33*(1), 2–17.

Graves, M. F., & Cooke, C. L. (1983). Effects of previewing difficult short stories for high school students, *Research on Reading in Secondary Schools, 6,* 38–54

Graves, M. F., Cooke, C. L., & Laberge, M. J. (1983). Effects of previewing difficult short stories on low ability junior high school students' comprehension, recall, and attitudes. *Reading Research Quarterly, 18,* 262–276.

Hansen, J., & Pearson, P. D. (1983). An instructional study: Improving the inferential comprehension of good and poor fourth-grade readers. *Journal of Educational Psychology, 75,* 821–829.

Herl, H. E., O'Neil, H. F., Jr., Chung, G. K. W. K., & Schacter, J. (1999). Reliability and validity of a computer-based knowledge mapping system to measure content understanding. *Computers in Human Behavior, 15,* 315–333.

Idol, L., & Croll, V. J. (1987). Story-mapping training as a means of improving reading comprehension. *Learning Disability Quarterly, 10,* 214–229.

Jiang, Z., & Potter, W. D. (1994). A computer microworld to introduce students to probability. *Journal of Computers in Mathematics and Science Teaching, 13,* 197–222.

Joseph, L. C. (n.d.). *Cyberbee: Building prior knowledge.* Retrieved February 24, 2004, from http://www.infotoday.com/MMSchools/may02/cybe0502.htm

Kelly, P. R. (1997). Transfer of learning from a computer simulation as compared to a laboratory activity. *Journal of Educational Technology Systems, 26,* 345–351.

King, A. (1994). Guiding knowledge construction in the classroom: Effects of teaching children how to question and how to explain. *American Educational Research Journal, 31,* 338–368.

Langer, J. A. (1984). Examining background knowledge and text comprehension. *Reading Research Quarterly, 19,* 468–481.

Long, S. A., Winograd, P. N., & Bridget, C. A. (1989). The effects of reader and text characteristics on imagery reported during and after reading. *Reading Research Quarterly, 24,* 353–372.

McKeown, M. G., Beck, I. L., Sinatra, G. M., & Loxterman, J. A. (1992). The contribution of prior knowledge and coherent text to comprehension. *Reading Research Quarterly, 27,* 78–93.

Meyer, A., & Rose, D. H. (1998). *Learning to read in the computer age.* Cambridge, MA: Brookline Books.

Newby, R. F., Caldwell, J., & Recht, D. R. (1989). Improving the reading comprehension of children with dysphonetic and dyseidetic dyslexia using story grammar. *Journal of Learning Disabilities, 22,* 373–380.

Oaksford, L., & Jones, L. (2001). *Differentiated instruction abstract.* Tallahassee, FL: Leon County Schools.

Ogle, D. M. (1986). K-W-L: A teaching model that develops active reading of expository text. *Reading Teacher, 39,* 564–570.

Palincsar, A. S., & Brown, A. L. (1986). Interactive teaching to promote independent learning from text. *Reading Teacher, 39,* 771–777.

Park, J. C. (1993). Time studies of fourth graders generating alternative solutions in a decision-making task using models and computer simulations. *Journal of Computing in Childhood Education, 4*(1), 57–76.

Peeck, J., van den Bosch, A. B., & Kreupeling, W. J. (1982). Effect of mobilizing prior knowledge on learning from text. *Journal of Educational Psychology, 74,* 771–777.

Pettig, K. L., (2000). On the road to differentiated. *Education Leadership, 8*(1), 14–18.

Pflaum, S. W., Pascarella, E. T., Auer, C., Augustyn, L., & Boswick, M. (1982). Differential effects of four comprehension-facilitating conditions on LD and normal elementary-school readers. *Learning Disability Quarterly, 5,* 106–116.

Pisha, B., & Coyne, P. (2001). Smart from the start: the promise of Universal Design for Learning. *Remedial and Special Education, 22,* 197–203.

Pressley, M., Johnson, C. J., Symons, S., McGoldrick, J. A., & Kurita, J. A. (1989). Strategies that improve children's memory and comprehension of text. *Elementary School Journal, 90*(1), 3–32.

Rose, D., & Dolan, R. P. (2000). Universal Design for Learning [Associate editor's column]. *Journal of Special Education Technology, 15*(4), 47–51.

Rose, D., & Meyer, A. (2000a). Universal design for individual differences. *Educational Leadership, 58*(3), 39–43.

Rose, D., & Meyer, A. (2000b). Universal Design for Learning [Associate editor's column]. *Journal of Special Education Technology, 15*(1), 67–70.

Rose, D., & Meyer, A. (2002). Teaching every student in the digital age: Universal Design for Learning. Alexandria, VA: ASCD.

Rose, D., Sethuraman, S., & Meo, G. (2000). Universal Design for Learning. *Journal of Special Education Technology, 15*(2), 26–60.

Rowe, D. W., & Rayford, L. (1987). Activating background knowledge in reading comprehension assessment. *Reading Research Quarterly, 22,* 160–176.

SAS in School. (n.d.). *As the tide turns: Radio broadcasts from the front.* Retrieved, September 3, 2003, from http://www.sasinschool.com/resource/pages/lesson_plan_ww2.shtml

Scanlon, D., Deshler, D. D., & Schumaker, J. B. (1996). Can a strategy be taught and learned in secondary inclusive classrooms? *Learning Disabilities Research and Practice, 11*(1), 41–57.

Schallert, D. L. (1982). The significance of knowledge: A synthesis of research related to schema theory. In W. Otto & S. White (Eds.), *Reading expository prose* (pp. 13–48). New York: Academic.

Sinatra, R. C., Stahl-Gemake, J., & Berg, D. N. (1984). Improving reading comprehension of disabled readers through semantic mapping. *the Reading Teacher, 38*(1), 22–29.

Smith, L. C., Readence, J. E., & Alvermann, D. E. (1983). *Effects of activating background knowledge on comprehension of expository prose.* Paper presented at the annual meeting of the National Reading Conference, Austin, TX.

Spires, H. A., & Donley, J. (1998). Prior knowledge activation: Inducing engagement with informational texts. *Journal of Educational Psychology, 90,* 249–260.

Stevens, K. C. (1980). The effect of background knowledge on the reading comprehension of ninth graders. *Journal of Reading Behavior, 12,* 151–154.

Stevens, K. C. (1982). Can we improve reading by teaching background information? *Journal of Reading* (January), 326–329.

Strangman, N., & Hall, T. (2003). *Graphic organizers.* Peabody, MA: National Center on Accessing the General Curriculum.

Strangman, N., Hall, T., & Meyer, A. (2003). *Differentiated instruction with UDL.* Wakefield, MA: National Center on Accessing the General Curriculum.

Sykes, W., & Reid, R. (1999). Virtual reality in schools: The ultimate educational technology. *T.H.E. Journal, 27*(7), 61–63.

Tobias, S. (1994). Interest, prior knowledge, and learning. *Review of Educational Research, 64*(1), 37–54.

Tomlinson, C. A. (2001). *How to differentiate instruction in mixed-ability classrooms* (2nd ed.). Alexandria, VA: ASCD.

Tomlinson, C. A., & Allan, S. D. (2000). *Leadership for differentiating schools and classrooms.* Alexandria, VA: ASCD.

Walraven, M., & Reitsma, P. (1993). The effect of teaching strategies for reading comprehension to poor readers and the possible surplus effect of activating prior knowledge. *National Reading Conference Yearbook, 42,* 243–250.

Willerman, M., & Mac Harg, R. A. (1991). The concept map as an advance organizer. *Journal of Research in Science Teaching, 28,* 705–712.

Yair, Y., Mintz, R., & Litvak, S. (2001). 3-D virtual reality in science education: An implication for astronomy teaching. *Journal of Computers in Science Education, 20,* 293–301.

Some of the content in this chapter was published online by The Center on Improving Outcomes for All Students K–8 (www.k8accesscenter.org) at the American Institutes for Research and by the National Center on Accessing the General Curriculum. It has been revised and edited for this volume. The implications for UDL content and lesson plan information in this chapter were developed by CAST through a subcontract agreement with The Center on Improving Outcomes for All Students K–8 at the American Institutes for Research. This work was funded by the U.S. Department of Education, Office of Special Education Programs (Cooperative Agreement #H326K02003). Other content in this report was developed pursuant to Cooperative Agreement #H324H990004 under CFDA 84.324H between CAST and the Office of Special Education Programs, U.S. Department of Education. However, the opinions expressed herein do not necessarily reflect the position or policy of the U.S. Department of Education or the Office of Special Education Programs, and no endorsement by that office should be inferred.

About the Contributors

Tracey Hall, a senior research scientist and instructional designer at CAST, specializes in assessment, curriculum-based measurement, teacher development, and curriculum development and instruction for special needs students. She directs CAST's initiative to create and evaluate technology-based, supported writing environments across content areas, and is coprincipal investigator for the federally funded Steppingstones of Technology Innovation grant, "Thinking Writer for Science: A Technology-Based Approach for Writing to Support Students with Disabilities." Once a special education teacher and public school administrator, Hall received her doctorate in special education from the University of Oregon.

Kelly Harper, after completing an NCAC research assistantship, earned her doctorate in curriculum and instruction from Boston College's Lynch School of Education. She has since been appointed assistant professor in the School of Education at St. Bonaventure University in Buffalo, New York.

Chuck Hitchcock, chief of policy and technology at CAST, oversees CAST's software development, technology innovation, and website development. He is the chief developer of many of CAST's Macintosh and Windows educational and tools software programs and a member of CAST's software development team. He was recognized as an information technology innovator by the 1999 Computerworld/Smithsonian Innovation Awards for CAST's development of Bobby, a technology to improve website accessibility. Hitchcock has extensive practical experience in special education administration, technology education, and teaching at all levels. He completed his undergraduate work in special education at Fitchburg State College and received his master's degree in educational administration and counseling from Antioch's Graduate Center.

Janna Jackson completed a research assistantship with NCAC, then went on to earn her doctorate in curriculum and instruction from Boston College's Lynch School of Education. She has been appointed an assistant professor in the Lynch School's Department of Teacher Education, Special Education, Curriculum, and Instruction.

Richard Jackson, a senior research scientist at CAST, assists in the development of CAST's universally designed technology to meet the needs of individuals with visual disabilities. He is also an associate professor and a director of projects in low-incidence disabilities at Boston College. Jackson, who is visually impaired, has earned major federal grants for training teachers of the blind and multiply disabled. Jackson brings to his work at CAST three decades of experience as a teacher, project director, researcher, and advocate in the field of education and visual disabilities. He has conducted research for the National Eye Institute and is the founder of the Association of Massachusetts Educators of Students with Vision Impairments. Jackson holds a doctorate in special education from Columbia University.

Joanne Karger is an advanced doctoral student in special education policy at the Harvard Graduate School of Education. Her research focuses on implementation of the legal requirements of the Individuals with Disabilities Education Act, including the provision of access to the general education curriculum for students with disabilities and parental rights associated with due process hearings. She has worked on a number of lawsuits involving disability and education-related issues, and has been a research associate for NCAC. She currently provides consulting services to school districts on matters pertaining to the administration of special education policies and procedures. She has a joint J.D. and master's of education from the Boston College Law School and Lynch School of Education.

Anne Meyer is a founding director of CAST and its chief officer of educational design. She has played a leading role in shaping, refining, and disseminating the research-based concepts and framework of Universal Design for Learning. Drawing on a long-term focus on the psychological aspects of learning and learning disabilities, Meyer leads CAST's design of multimedia technologies to support diverse learners. She is a coauthor (with D. H. Rose) of two books, the seminal *Teaching Every Student in the Digital Age: Universal Design for Learning* (2002) and *Learning to Read in the Computer Age* (1998), as well as numerous journal articles. With her CAST colleagues, she is an author of successful learning software programs such as Literary Place and WiggleWorks, for which CAST was awarded the Computerworld/Smithsonian Innovation Award. Meyer served as a national advisor to President Clinton's Educational Technology Panel, and in 1995 she received a gold medal from the National Association of Social Sciences for her work at CAST. A licensed clinical psychologist, Meyer earned master's and doctoral degrees from the Harvard Graduate School of Education.

David H. Rose is a founding director of CAST and its chief scientist for cognition and learning. Since helping to found CAST in 1984, Rose has played a leading role in defining and articulating the research-based concepts and framework of Universal Design for Learning. A specialist in developmental neuropsychology and the universal design of learning technologies, he also lectures at the Harvard Graduate School of Education, where he has been on the faculty for 20 years. He is principal investigator for two national centers to develop and implement the National Instructional Materials Accessibility Standard, which he helped to author. Rose is coauthor (with A. Meyer) of the seminal *Teaching Every Student in the Digital Age: Universal Design for Learning* (2002) and *Learning to Read in the Computer Age* (1998). With his CAST colleagues, he contributed to the creation of successful learning software programs such as Thinking Reader, Literary Place, and WiggleWorks, for which CAST was awarded the Computerworld/Smithsonian Innovation Award. Rose earned his doctorate at the Harvard Graduate School of Education.

Nicole Strangman is a writer and editor at CAST, where she authors and edits journal articles, reports, and book chapters, as well as contributing research services to numerous projects. Strangman brings to her work a strong background in basic scientific research; she has a doctorate in neuroscience from Brown University and special expertise in the pharmacology of chronic pain, spinal cord electrophysiology, and immunohistochemistry. She has published articles in *Proceedings of the National Academy of Science, Journal of Neurophysiology,* and other scholarly publications.

Index

Information contained in figures and tables is indicated by an italic *f* and *t* respectively.